Revised for the

How to Make
BIG
MONEY
IN
REAL ESTATE

Tyler G. Hicks

PRENTICE HALL PRESS

Library of Congress Cataloging-in-Publication Data

Hicks, Tyler Gregory.
    How to make big money in real estate / Tyler G. Hicks.
        p. cm.
    Rev. ed. of: How to make big money in real estate in the tighter, tougher
'90s market. c1992
    Includes bibliographical references and index.
    ISBN 0-7352-0116-1 (paper)
    1. Real estate business investment. I. Hick, Tyler Gregory, 1921– How to make
big money in real estate in the tighter, tougher '90s market. II. Title.
HD1382.5.H535   1999
332.63'24—dc21   99-44127
                                                 CIP

Acquisitions Editor: *Susan McDermott*
Production Editor: *Eve Mossman*
Formatting/Interior Design: *Robyn Beckerman*

© *2000 by Prentice Hall*

*All rights reserved. No part of this book may be reproduced in any form or by any means,
without permission in writing from the publisher.*

Printed in the United States of America

10 9 8 7 6 5 4 3 2 1

ISBN 0-7352-0116-1

ATTENTION: CORPORATIONS AND SCHOOLS

Prentice Hall books are available at quantity discounts with bulk purchase for educational, business, or sales promotional use. For information, please write to: Prentice Hall Special Sales, 240 Frisch Court, Paramus, New Jersey 07652. Please supply: title of book,
ISBN, quantity, how the book will be used, date needed.

PRENTICE HALL PRESS
Paramus, NJ 07652

On the World Wide Web at http://www.phdirect.com

What This Book Will Do for You

As you've no doubt heard, some parts of the real estate business are in deep trouble today. So why should *you* think of getting into this excellent business right now? For a number of very good reasons—all of which are explained in the book you're holding at this moment!

True, rougher—and tougher—times have a grip on much of real estate today. Money may be harder to get for mortgages and property improvements. But beginning wealth builders (BWBs) who call me or visit me in my New York City office are getting the money they need for their income real estate buys.

While getting a loan for real estate may take longer, money *is* available for those BWBs who look for it in the right places. And these BWBs *are* getting rich in real estate in their spare time—today. You—too—can do the same!

This book shows you how to avoid the troubled areas of real estate. For instance, office space in some areas of the country is enormously overbuilt today. Experts say it will take 10 years—in those areas—to rent all the recently finished office towers. And if you want to develop land—that is, put up houses of any kind on it—you'll have to scratch around for the money you need. But the money *IS* there, and you *CAN* get it, as I show you later in this book.

Yet, through *every* previous downturn, real estate bounced back. And property values always soared far above what they were before the downturn. Property values *will* recover again. I guarantee this for you!

Meanwhile, *you* have the greatest opportunities of the last 20 years to get rich in real estate in your spare time. Bad times have produced millions of property bargains. So long as you plan your financial future carefully—and I show you exactly how to do this in this book—*you* can acquire enormous holdings in real estate. Hundreds of letters from readers throughout the world testify to the fact that *you* can make millions in real estate, starting with little—or no—cash! So I ask *you:*

Are you stuck in the boring 9-to-5 rat race? Having trouble paying your bills on a salary that hardly ever seems to rise? Never get more than a two-week vacation every year? Your bank balance is much lower than you like? Need a second car but your budget can't handle it?

If you answer "yes" to any of these or similar questions, read on. Why? Because this book shows you how to:

- Get started in real estate on zero cash—even when you have a full-time job in another business (a job which you probably don't like, and job which you don't want to hold forever)
- Improve your borrowing power and quality of life using zero cash real estate as your solid base for greater personal prosperity and affluence
- Make a new career for yourself in just days—free of cranky bosses, pay-stopping layoffs, and future job uncertainty in the age of down-sizings and RIFs (reductions in force)
- Zoom your bank balance with tax-free no-withholding money every time you take over income-producing real estate on zero cash
- Make big money in real estate to supplement your regular salary—in good times and bad
- Prosper in real estate when values zoom, and when they fall—even while those around you who hit it big without effort during the good and easy days struggle to hang on when times get tough

Thousands of people consult me every year about their real estate business in *today's* market. They tell me what they're doing, how much money they're making, and what cash profits they expect to add to their bank account. Many write me letters showing exact income and expense figures. You'll see dozens of these actual letters in this book. Each tells you what people are doing *today* in real estate to bring in big cash dollars *every* day. And almost all these people hold another job until they build a large enough income—often more than $100,000 a year—to enable them to quit their boring 9-to-5 drudgery.

You can do the same! How? By just following the simple steps presented in this book. What's more, I'm as close to you as your telephone. If you have a real estate or money problem, just pick up your phone and call me. I'll answer on the first ring and give you specific steps you can take to:

- Raise money to buy real estate quickly and easily, anywhere, any time
- Get a seller to work with you so you can get the property you seek without a lot of hassle

- Take cash out of a property (called *mortgaging out*) so you walk away from the closing with cash money in your hand after having acquired an income-producing asset
- Build a real estate empire in properties *you* like—starting with no (or very little) cash—even though most of your time and attention may be taken up by a full-time job or small business

Not only do I see, and help, people make big money in real estate in so-called good times and bad times, I'm doing the same myself! So I'm in an ideal position to help *you* in many special ways. To do this, I also give you in this book:

- Surefire, clever tips on using borrowed money (other people's money—OPM, I call it) to build your real estate fortune even when you're struggling to keep up with payments on a car, a home, a boat, or any number of other items you like.
- Dozens of ways to make every property you buy a big source of ready cash that puts money into your pocket the instant you own real estate.
- Smart and effective ways to make thousands of dollars from foreclosure properties you can get for almost pennies.
- Wheeler-dealer ways to buy two—or more—properties a month with *no* money down to zoom your real estate wealth in just weeks.
- Offbeat financing methods that allow *you* to take over prime properties even when your bank balance is nudging zero and your boss won't give you a raise.
- Slick ways to figure your cost of money so you hold it to the minimum while getting your full tax deductibility.
- Canny ways to get time on your side so you pull the biggest dollars out of every property you like and want to own.
- Clever ways to find, buy, and make money from your favorite types of property.
- Reasons why a dollar from your real estate holdings is so valuable compared to a dollar from your salary, which is already spent before you get it. Your real estate dollar is a discretionary dollar—you can invest it, save it, use it for a vacation, put it toward a child's education, and so on. It gives you the ultimate in financial freedom!

Yes, you *can,* and *will,* make big money from real estate in good times and bad—if you follow the tips in this book.

So come along with me, good friend, and we'll make you rich in real estate. And I'll show you how—and where—you can borrow *all* the money you need for your real estate business— no matter how bad your credit rating may be.

As director and member of the board of a large lending organization, I'll show you exactly what to do to get every real estate loan approved. I'm a lender myself—approving loans every day of the week. So I give you valuable lending secrets which clue you in on what makes a lender say yes. No other real estate author I know of directs a $100-million-plus lending organization with hundreds of property loans on its books—today!

To get started, just turn to Chapter 1. Let a real estate entrepreneur and lender show you how to get rich today—right now. Good luck in your real estate wealth building.

Tyler G. Hicks

Contents

Real Estate Always Has Value—And Will Forever • Down Cycles Are Always Followed by Rising Values • Bad Times in Real Estate Give *You* Big Opportunities • Buy in Bad Times and Sell in Good Times to Get Rich • Buy to Hold and Build Your Assets—While Kicking 9-to-5 Misery • Build Your Daily Income with Positive Cash Flow Properties • Real Estate Can Make *You* Rich in Good Times and Bad Times • Your Formula for Assured Success and Affluence in Real Estate Today • Success Strategies for Building Your Real Estate Wealth in Good Times and Bad Times • Important Pointers to Keep in Mind

You Start Faster When Using Zero Cash • Use Your Job's Borrowing Power • Harder Work *Does* Pay Off • You Can Control More Real Estate with Zero Cash • Doing Zero Cash Deals Gives You Great Negotiating Skills • How to Start Using the Zero Cash

Approach • Decide What Types of Properties You Want to Own • Link Your Life's Goals and Objectives to Property Types • Start Looking for Suitable Properties • Begin Your Riches Notebook • Make Offers on Suitable Properties • Take Over Your First Income Property • Success Strategies for Building Your Real Estate Wealth in Good Times and Bad Times • Important Pointers to Keep in Mind

Dollars Per Hour • Six Magic Tips for Getting More from Each
Hour • Get—and Stay—Free of Tenant Demands • Grow Rich in
Your Spare Time • Keep Your Paperwork Simple • Four Key
Rules for Getting Rich in Your Spare Time • Make Lower Prices
Your Path to Wealth • Success Strategies for Building Your Real
Estate Wealth in Good Times and Bad Times • Important Pointers
to Keep in Mind

Start with Very Little—or No—Money of Your Own • Borrowing
is Expected in Real Estate • You *Can* Borrow the Money for *Any*
Real Estate You Like • Make Every Application a Work of Art •
Keep Your Job When First Applying for Loans • How to Line Up
Lenders for Your Real Estate Deals • How to Have Every Loan
Application Approved • Use the Knowledge-Is-Power Approach •
Ten Key Rules for Getting Every Real Estate Loan Approved •
Getting Real Estate Loans for Varied Projects • Success Strategies
for Building Your Real Estate Wealth in Good Times and Bad
Times • Important Pointers to Keep in Mind

Real Estate Is a Free-Time Business • Get Your Time Priorities
Straight—At the Start • Build Your Real Estate Assets to Achieve
Your Income Goal • Tax Strategies to Build Your Real Estate
Profits • Use Property Swaps to Build Wealth • Six Key Steps for
Keeping Taxes Low • Know the Joy of Being Your Own Person •
Success Strategies for Building Your Real Estate Wealth in Good
Times and Bad Times • Important Pointers to Keep in Mind

Real Estate Can Make *You* Rich— In Good Times and Bad Times

"Times are tough in real estate" is a remark you're likely to hear again and again these days. Or "Money is tighter than it used to be." But *don't believe* everything you hear!

True, times *are* rougher and tougher for some real estate operators. For example, office space in some areas is way overbuilt, with a 10-year supply on hand. But moderate-rent multifamily residential real estate (the typical apartment house) is in short supply. Never has the demand been greater than it is today for such units. People are scrambling to rent neat, well-maintained apartments in decent neighborhoods. So things are not so bleak in every segment of the real estate market today.

Further, real estate is the best business for you—if you want to rid yourself of the 9-to-5 grind while you make money and have fun! "How can anyone say this?" you ask.

I can say it because daily I talk to, work with, or advise dozens of real estate wealth builders who're making money in these tougher times. And most are doing this while holding a job, running another business, or caring for a family. *All* are making money—daily. *All* have a *positive cash flow* (more money coming in than going out) on *every* property. And the real estate properties I personally deal with all do as well.

So I speak from daily firing-line experience, plus that of thousands of other, active money-making wealth builders. And *you* can do the same. Why? Because I showed—and am showing—many of these people how to get rich in real estate in good times and bad times. Now I want to show *you* the same!

1

REAL ESTATE ALWAYS HAS VALUE—
AND WILL FOREVER

Buy a car, a boat, an airplane, a TV, a computer, and it will, in general, go down in value as time passes. But buy a piece of real estate, and it will, almost always, go up in value as time passes. So the money you put into the real estate goes *up* in value as time passes. Let's see how this characteristic of real estate can put money into *your* pocket.

- You buy a piece of real estate for $300,000.
- Prices of property rise—on average—5 percent a year in the area.
- So the first year you own the property, its value rises by $(0.05) \times$ $300,000 = $15,000. And at the end of the first year your property is worth $300,000 + $15,000 = $315,000.
- In the second year your property rises in value by $(0.05) \times $315,000$ = $15,750. So at the end of the second year your property is worth $315,000 + $15,750 = $330,750.
- This increase in value can go on year after year—while *you* collect income from the property *every* month.
- So *you* benefit in *two* ways—your asset (the property) is becoming *more* valuable while you're collecting money from it!
- Meanwhile, there are certain tax advantages you'll have which can shelter most—or all—of your positive cash flow from the ravages of the tax code. Remember: There's *no* payroll withholding on your real estate income! What you earn, you get. (More about this later.)

Few people recognize early enough in their lives the value that almost all real estate truly has—and will continue to have forever. But since you're reading this book, I think of you as a friend of mine. So, good friend, I want to show *you* why real estate always has value—and always will. The main reasons are:

- Land areas are limited—you can't manufacture land at a low price.
- Buildings of all types go up in value as time passes—if properly maintained.
- The price of building materials is almost constantly rising in all parts of the world.
- The price of labor to construct a building is also almost always rising.

- Taken together, these factors create lasting value in nearly every piece of real estate.
- *You* can cash in on this value in your spare time and create a significant fortune for yourself and your loved ones just by following the ideas in this book.

So don't listen to the doomers and gloomers who predict the demise of real estate. Tain't so! Real estate *always* has value—and will forever. And *you* can latch onto lots of this value to give you the freedom and choice in your life that you'll never have slaving for someone else!

DOWN CYCLES ARE ALWAYS FOLLOWED BY RISING VALUES

Real estate ownership is a *business*. Some beginners—I call them beginning wealth builders (BWBs)—overlook this important aspect of real estate. As a business, real estate can—and does—have its ups and downs. But my experience with real estate shows that:

- Real estate cycles are seldom as damaging to people as some other business cycles.
- Some types of real estate—residential—are almost immune to the ups and downs of the business cycle because people always need a place to live.
- A wise choice of deals can insulate you from some of the wild gyrations of values like those that occur in the stock market every few years.
- Real estate *always* comes back. When values recover after a downturn, they often "go through the roof"—giving *you* enormous profits from every deal.
- Even in "bad" years real estate rises in value. A "bad year" is one in which values rise only 3 percent as compared to 5 percent or 10 percent in earlier years.

So you can rely on real estate to come back and zoom ahead. It's as sure as day follows night. And if you invest wisely, you can be certain that *your* wealth will grow steadily and surely. Can you ask anything more of a business?

BAD TIMES IN REAL ESTATE GIVE
YOU BIG OPPORTUNITIES

Readers of my books and newsletters write me, call on the phone, fax me, access my Internet website, and come to my Manhattan office for lunch. Many of these readers are like yourself—ambitious, hardworking people on a puny salary looking for safe ways to create wealth for themselves without risking loss of their main source of income. Thousands of these reader friends report great success in their real estate deals—in both good times *and* bad times.

Many of these friends say they do better in bad times than in good times. Why is this? Because in bad times:

- Property prices are lower.
- Sellers are much more anxious to make favorable deals.
- It's a "buyer's market"—that is, sellers will chase after you to get you to take over their property, often for zero cash.

So don't let bad times frighten you. Instead, use the know-how you get in this book to take over properties on *your* terms. Just be sure to know what type of property you're looking for, and what financial goals you have. With these requirements in mind, you can make bad times the best of times in your real estate fortune building!

BUY IN BAD TIMES AND SELL IN
GOOD TIMES TO GET RICH

In bad times you're king when you're the buyer. In good times you're still a desired person because there are usually more buyers than sellers! When you buy in bad times, you pay lowest dollar for a property. When you sell in good times, you get top dollar—making your profit large.

Two readers who wrote me recently tell of a deal that well illustrates what I mean. They say:

> *In July my partner (a first-time investor) and I took ownership in a very profitable single-family dwelling. This was my third deal in four months with no money down. My partner found the house, and acting as a consultant, I structured the trans-action to net us $3,000 each at closing. The terms and con-*

ditions of this transaction gave us a rented house before clos-
ing, a positive cash flow, and lifetime control to profit when
we no longer own the property by inserting the clause con-
tract to survive deed. In addition, the seller took back a fully
assumable second deed of trust with no payments for 7
months, no early payoff penalty, and we have the first option
to buy or sell the second deed of trust. Again, thanks for your
books and creative financial thinking in real estate.

(Note: A *second deed of trust** is much like a *second mortgage,* which is a
second loan you get on a property. The first loan, or *first mortgage,* is usually a long-term loan running anywhere from 15 to 40 years with interest
and principal repaid monthly. Second mortgages, or second trust deeds, are
usually short-term instruments, 3 years to 5 years at the longest.)

When times are bad everyone runs scared. Your daily rat race
becomes more unbearable. That's the time to get out and:

- Look over what's available in local income real estate that fits your
  interests.
- Get prices from sellers, brokers, and real estate agents handling
  properties *you* like.
- Ask for the income and expense statement on each property that
  interests you.
- Study the income figures. See if they make sense in terms of rents in
  your area. See if any other sources of income listed (such as garage
  rentals, washing machine and dryer income, etc.) are realistic for
  your area.
- Review the expense statement very carefully! Why? Because an anxious seller will shave expenses to make the property look more profitable. Look hard at fuel and maintenance costs. It is these two costs
  which permit big "adjustments" to make the building look more
  profitable. Don't be fooled by very low fuel or maintenance costs!

Recognize—here and now—that taking the first step toward *your*
real estate fortune will be frightening. You'll get worried as to what may
happen. All sorts of bad outcomes may flash across your mind. But don't
panic! Why? Because:

---

*A trust deed (also called deed of trust) is much like a mortgage but it allows for faster sale of
a property in the event the borrower fails to pay the money due.

In my years in real estate I've never seen any BWB go broke, go bankrupt, or lose money if he or she used a sensible approach to buying and selling real estate. Further, in the worst of times, only about 1 percent of real estate loans go bad. This compares with 6 percent or more of business loans that go bad in tough times. Real estate is one of the safest businesses you can enter!

Knowing that you will be scared helps you forge ahead. Being able to handle fear makes you a better businessperson. Meanwhile, of course, the fear makes you more alert and helps you avoid mistakes. How can you let fear hold you back when you see real-life results like these:

- A property bought at $74,500 brought an offer of $800,000 10 years later.
- Land bought at $95 an acre sold for $3,000 an acre 4 years after the purchase.
- A $45,000 house bought for zero cash down sold for $80,000 just a few months later.

Buy in bad times and sell in good times. Do this while you're working and you'll never become a "puppy"—poor urban professional! What's more, you'll be able to shed the office or plant daily drudgery once you get a few profitable properties putting money into your bank every day of the week! Then you can write me, as this reader did, saying:

> *Just a note to let you know that, based on my few telephone calls to you, being a steady subscriber to your International Wealth Success, and following your advice, my net worth is $3.5 million.*

But if you're still worried about taking your first step toward building your own money machine on zero cash, I have this offer for you:

> As a reader of any of my money books and a subscriber to my monthly newsletter, International Wealth Success,* you are free to call me at my office from 8 A.M. to 10 P.M. New York time and I'll answer any business question you may have on starting, or expanding, your real estate fortune building. And—if you wish—I'll gladly

---

* The BWBs monthly newsletter of great wealth chances for you. To subscribe, send $24 for 12 issues to IWS, Inc., P.O. Box 186, Merrick, NY 11566.0186.

analyze any business statements supplied to you by a seller. Also, if you need any "hand holding" to overcome your fears, I'll be glad to provide that!

Buy in bad times and sell in good times and you're almost certain to get rich. The world's best business won't do you wrong!

BUY TO HOLD AND BUILD YOUR ASSETS— WHILE KICKING 9-TO-5 MISERY

How are riches measured? In many ways. But the one universal measure is assets. And what are assets? They are things of value. Such as:

- Land
- Buildings
- Air rights (space above a property)
- Cash, bank accounts
- Stocks, bonds

To get rich and rid yourself of salaried slavery, you *must* build up your assets! And the easiest assets to build are those represented by real estate of some kind—land, buildings, air rights, and so on.

Why are real estate assets the easiest to build? For a number of good reasons, but mainly because:

- Real estate is a borrowed money business.
- You can take over and control valuable assets without using any of your own money.
- Well-financed income-producing real estate taken over on borrowed money will pay for itself, giving you a valuable asset on zero cash.
- Once you hold some real estate, you can use it as collateral to borrow more money to take over more income-producing real estate.

When you buy any asset, it is immediately shown on your *balance sheet.* Your balance sheet is a listing, in the form of a table, Exhibit 1—1, showing what you own and what you owe, that is, your *assets* (what you own) and your *liabilities* (what you owe).

As a jobholder you will have few assets. Most jobholders who don't own their own home have only a few assets—a car, a TV, some furniture, and, perhaps, a little cash. But once you start buying real estate—even if it's only your first home—the asset appears on your balance sheet. And it's your balance sheet to which lenders will look when you show up to borrow money for any use. So you should aim at showing a strong balance sheet because it will make your life a lot easier and much more enjoyable!

Let's say you buy a small home and a 10-unit income property within 1 month. Your balance sheet *before* you bought these two properties looked like that shown in Exhibit 1–1a. After you buy the properties your balance sheet immediately improves to that shown in Exhibit 1–1b.

Exhibit 1–1a

BALANCE SHEET
(BEFORE YOU BUY ANY REAL ESTATE)

Assets (What You Own)		Liabilities (What You Owe)	
Cash	$ 850	Credit card accounts	$1,200
Furniture	1,250	Auto loans	15,000
Autos (2)	28,300	Department store bills	1,100
Hi-fi equipment	900		
Total assets	$31,300	Total liabilities	$17,300

Net worth = Total assets − Total owed = $31,300 − $17,300 = $14,000

If you came to me for a loan (I'm president of one, and director of another, for a total of *two* active real estate lending organizations), I'd have a hard time giving you a loan with Exhibit 1–1a balance sheet. But with the Exhibit 1–1b I'd beg you to borrow from us!

Why? Because with the the Exhibit 1–1b balance sheet *you* show strength, even though you're in debt. You've got *assets!* With the Exhibit 1–1a balance sheet, you're just another wage slave living in a rented apartment. You have no real future, unless you take it on yourself to do something to build your assets.

Now if you *hold* these two properties and they rise in value the 5 percent a year we mentioned earlier, let's see what your balance sheet looks like two years later. Exhibit 1–2 shows your new balance sheet, after you've held these two assets (the home and the 10-unit income property) for 2 years. Your net worth (the difference between your assets and liabilities) has gone *up*. And, of course, you will probably have bought other properties during this time, making *your* balance sheet even stronger!

Exhibit 1–1b

BALANCE SHEET
(AFTER YOU BUY SOME REAL ESTATE)

Assets		Liabilities	
Cash	$ 850	Credit card accounts	$ 1,200
Furniture	1,250	Auto loans	15,000
Autos (2)	28,300	Department store bills	1,100
Hi-fi equipment	900	Home down payment	20,000
New home		Home mortgage loan	80,000
($100,000		Income property down	
purchase price)	100,000	payment loan	60,000
10-unit income		Income property	
property		mortgage loan	240,000
($300,000			
purchase price)	300,000		
Total assets	$431,300	Total liabilities	$417,300

Net worth = $431,300 – $417,300 = $14,000

It's clear that if you continue buying good real estate assets and hold onto them, your net worth will rise. And this increase in your assets and net worth will allow you to kick the 9-to-5 grind right out the door, as one reader recently wrote:

> *In my travels I met and befriended a fellow real estate investor. He is much farther along in his investing career than I am. He's been at it for over 5 years and has 72 properties valued at over $6 million and shows a net worth of nearly $2 million. He is obviously doing something right.*

You, too, can build a net worth in the $2 million and more range by buying your real estate assets smartly and holding them as they rise in value. And if you buy *only* properties with a positive cash flow after *all* costs, including loan payoff, you'll have a free ride to your wealth and freedom! So buy and hold—it makes millionaires.

Exhibit 1–2

BALANCE SHEET*
(2 YEARS LATER, WITH NO NEW REAL ESTATE BUYS)

Assets		Liabilities	
Cash	$ 1,850	Credit card accounts $	1,400
Furniture	1,450	Auto loans	32,000
Autos (2, 1 new)	32,500	Department store bills	1,600
Home	110,250	Home down payment loan	18,000
10-unit income property	330,750	Home Mortgage	79,000
		Income property down payment loan	58,000
		Income property mortgage	238,000
Total assets	$476,800	Total owed	$418,000

Net worth = $476,800 – $418,000 = $58,800

*This balance sheet is based on the assumption that during the 2 years you bought a new auto, some new furniture, ran up some credit card bills, and spent some more money in department stores. You did not buy any more real estate. (In another situation you would probably have bought more income-producing property.) Your home rose in value 5 percent a year, as did your 10-unit income property. At the same time you've paid down the mortgage on your home and on the income property. Note that your net worth has risen by some $44,800 while you are getting income from your rental property!

If this $2 million jump in real estate assets in about 5 years seems big, you're welcome to visit my New York office to examine every one of the letters quoted in this book. All I ask is that you give me a few days' notice so I can get the letters out of the safe deposit box in which we store them. These readers are getting rich in real estate today while working in their spare time. And they're slowly distancing themselves from nasty bosses who threaten layoffs daily. Just to reinforce the millions concept, here's an excerpt from another recent letter:

> *Over the last 4 years, with the help of several of your books, my wife and I have bought 18 properties with none of our own money down. Now we have an accepted offer on a $3.6 million complex.*

BUILD YOUR DAILY INCOME WITH POSITIVE CASH FLOW PROPERTIES

Real estate *is* a business! And the sooner BWBs understand this, the earlier will their bank accounts begin to grow. Why?

Because the objective of every *business* is to earn a profit for its owners. As the owner of a real estate business, the only way you can earn a daily profit from your properties is to have a *positive cash flow.* This means you bring in—every month—more money than you spend on your property. Without a positive cash flow, you *lose* money on a property.

True, you can hold a property and wait for it to rise in value. And you *can* do this while you have a *negative cash flow,* that is, while you're paying money out of other income to keep the property going. Some people do this very successfully. But all my experience shows that it's wrong for BWBs to accept a negative cash flow when they're just starting in the real estate business. Why?

Because a negative cash flow property can lead to problems like the following:

- Slow depletion of your bank account
- Buildup of your debts over time
- Disgust with a "cash-eater" property
- Disenchantment with real estate

So go for positive cash flow properties. They pay the bills *every* month and *add* to your bank account. So your cash on hand (I call it COH) *rises* rather than falls, as for this reader:

> *I am a motivated BWB who entered the income-producing real estate market in the past few months. I presently own a duplex and a triplex which I bought with other people's money (OPM) and have had a positive cash flow from day 1. Your books and IWS Newsletter were instrumental in giving me the courage and information I needed to get started.*

With a positive cash flow, *all* your costs are paid for by the income from the property. These costs include fuel, electricity, insurance, maintenance, taxes, and mortgages. And after paying *all* these costs, you still have money in fist (MIF), which you can:

- Deposit in your business savings account
- Use to repair or improve your building
- Invest in other buildings or land
- Spend on a much needed vacation for yourself and family
- Put to any other use you choose

Getting a positive cash flow from your properties needn't take years. Knowing *what* to do, and *how* to do it is important. Like this BWB who writes:

> *Thank you for your publications. I subscribed to the IWS Newsletter in November and bought my first income property with no money down the same month. I got an investor's loan from a local S&L and the seller paid all closing costs and took back a second mortgage for the balance of the purchase price. This duplex gives me about $100 per month profit after the two mortgage payments and all expenses. Not bad for no cash investment of my own. Now this same property owner wants to sell four other properties under the same terms. I'm on my way to building my wealth in real estate.*

Now I can just hear some people saying, "What's $100? I spend more than that when I take my wife out to dinner!" Could be. But that $100 per month positive cash flow is the *start*. Ten such properties will give you $1,000 per month. And 100 properties like this will put $10,000 a month into your bank. Your wife could have a lot of dinners on that income. Or a wife who's a real estate BWB could take her husband to a few fancy meals with that level of monthly income!

Meanwhile, of course, the properties generating your positive cash flow every day are rising in value while you sleep! So not only do you have spendable money in fist (MIF, again), you also have an asset that's going *up* in value—second by second. And a strong positive cash flow can allow you to tell your boss that you've better things to do than working for him or her.

REAL ESTATE CAN MAKE *YOU* RICH
IN GOOD TIMES AND BAD TIMES

When you hear of people going belly up in real estate, it's usually a large firm that went against common sense and:

- Overbuilt properties during sagging demand
- Specialized in office buildings or shopping centers
- Thought they could outsmart the market and force properties on people

Seldom will you see owners of residential properties in trouble. Why? Because owners of apartment houses, garden apartments, townhouses, and the like know that:

- People always need a place to live.
- A home is the last item a family will give up in bad times.
- Today one spouse can earn enough to pay the rent for almost any sensible apartment.

To make money in real estate in good times and bad times, you just need to use your head now and then. You don't need a university degree. Most of the successful real estate operators I know (and I know thousands) never saw the inside of a college. Many left high school because they wanted to make money.

One good friend of mine who owns thousands of square feet of storage buildings left high school in his second year. Yet today he's so successful that he owns one of the biggest yachts on the East Coast of the United States. He started with everything against him: no education, *no job, no* rich parents. But once he started buying (and later building) storage warehouses using OPM, his wealth began to build. Today he has a home with an indoor swimming pool, racquet ball court, gym, and so on. Plenty of college graduates look at him and mumble to themselves: "How did I go wrong?"

Bad times in real estate—of which there are very few—offer you great bargains which will grow into cash-laden jewels. Take the two highest-priced real estate areas in the United States—California and Connecticut. These two states are separated by some 3,000 miles of land. Yet prices of real estate in the two states are high, high, high!

But a recent auction of condominiums in Connecticut shows the bargains you can get during real estate lulls. Here are a few of the *actual* prices BWBs paid (in borrowed money, of course) to take over prime condos in a renovated historic mill:

- A 2-bedroom, 2-bath condo priced at $121,900 sold at auction for just $48,000—$73,900 less than list price.
- A 1-bedroom condo priced at $107,000 sold for just $26,000—$8 1,000 less than list price.
- A 3-bedroom, 3-bath condo sold for $84,000, a saving of $111,000 on its list price of $195,000.

Yet, I guarantee you that in a few years, each of these units will:

- Rise in value to equal—and exceed—its list price
- Bring rental income to the buyer that is steady and dependable— every month
- Repay its cost out of rental income while giving each buyer a positive cash flow, month after month

Was there much competition for these condos? *No!* Only about 100 people attended the auction at which 43 units were offered. And the seller even had financing ready for the buyers. What's more, these condos are in the high-priced state of Connecticut. This is how real estate bought in "bad" times can make you rich in good times!

Other key facts about this deal are:

- Condos *can* be rented to anyone without the approval of a board of directors, as in a co-op. (If you buy to rent, do *not* invest in cooperative apartment units. The co-op board can seriously restrict your rental activities.)
- Renting a condo in the area where these are located is easier than renting a home in the same area because home rentals are much higher in price when fuel and water costs are added to the rent, as they must be by the renter.
- Ready-made financing was available to the buyers of these condos. And since the financing was arranged by the seller, the requirements to qualify for the long-term (30-year) mortgage loan were eased. This made it much easier for someone with less than perfect credit, or with a number of other outstanding loans, to qualify.

With a steady job (which you may hate intensely), you should not have any trouble qualifying for real estate loans in bad times. Sellers will welcome you with open arms. And lenders will be glad to make you a fast loan because you're a gainfully employed applicant.

With such bargains available with ready financing behind them, *you* need only one other ingredient to zoom your income and pluck you out of the ranks of the wage slaves. That ingredient? It's a four-letter word spelled

TIME

All you need do is wait for real estate values to rise as time passes. And I guarantee you, good friend, that values *will* rise! How can I say this? Just look at real estate history and you'll quickly see that:

- Well-located properties have always risen in value with the passage of time.

- Inflation increases the price of land, materials, and labor. These increases force up the price of well-located and properly maintained real estate everywhere. And *your* real estate *will* be among those whose price rises! Can you ask for anything better?

Now let's travel about 3,000 miles west to another high-value real estate area—California. We'll see that time, good value, and so-called bad times can really help a BWB, instead of hurting him or her. Here are the facts:

- A BWB sold a house for $133,000 to a buyer, making money on the deal after having held the home for a short time while renting it out for a positive cash flow.

- The buyer lost his job and couldn't continue to make payments on the mortgage; this was 2 years after buying the house from the BWB.

- Nearly 6 months passed without any mortgage payments from the buyer. So the BWB decided to foreclose (take back) on the house and sell it in the open market to recover the money he was owed. But market conditions were—everyone said—"bad" for sales. Yet the BWB decided to listen to his own judgment and feelings and put the house up for sale.

- No sooner was the house put up for sale by the BWB than it sold—for $174,000! The original buyer still owed $132,000 on the mortgage.

- So the BWB benefited from the passage of time (2.5 years), good value (the house is in an excellent area), and his own analysis of so called "bad" times. He made money on the deal!

All my life I've listened to people carry on about how tough it is to make a buck in various businesses. Yet I've gone on making money— in good times and bad—just as thousands of my readers have. And *you* can, too!

YOUR FORMULA FOR ASSURED SUCCESS AND AFFLUENCE IN REAL ESTATE TODAY

You can rid yourself of time clocks, salary reviews, performance evaluations, and all the other rigmarole of job life by getting into real estate *now!* You and your family *can* live better, *can* take more vacations, *can* get the car, house, boat, or airplane of your dreams. How? By using the simple tips I give you in this book. Here are the elements of *your* formula for outstanding success in real estate today:

Get Your Financing Lined Up Early

As some of you who've read one or more of my earlier books know, I'm the president of one real estate lending organization and director of another. We make all kinds of real estate loans, like:

- Long-term mortgage loans (15 to 30 years)—usually called the *first mortgage*
- Shorter-term *home equity loans* (15 years, or less) (which are really *second mortgages)*
- Refinance loans (*refi* in lending slang), in which an existing mortgage (or mortgages) is paid of f and a new one substituted that goes for a longer *term* (the number of years over which the loan is to be repaid), which reduces the amount of the monthly payment the borrower must make
- Home down payment loans, which allow a borrower to take over an income property with no cash of his or her own
- Property improvement loans to fix up an existing property to make it both more livable and more salable

- Bridge loans, which enable a borrower to buy one new property while in the process of selling another property which they own but for which the paperwork and other procedures in the sale are not yet finished

Many millions of dollars have been loaned to borrowers for these real estate purposes, plus other similar uses. And do you know what?

The number of times we've had to foreclose on a real estate loan is so small—less than 1 percent—that they are the best types of loans we make. So we're happy with real estate loans and our borrowers are delighted as well. We're so pleased with these loans that I'm constantly urging our management staff to find more real estate borrowers. Every month at our board of directors' meeting I plead with each director to find more borrowers for us. Why? Because we make more money from our real estate loans than from any other type of loan. We need more of them!

Our newsletter company, IWS, Inc., also encourages loan applications from readers who are two-year—or longer—subscribers to our *International Wealth Success* newsletter. These loans* can range from $5,000 to $500,000 with flexible repayment terms for up to 7 years. Information on this newsletter, which I've been publishing for more than 34 years, is given at the back of this book. It's another handy place to apply for real estate down payment loans.

To get your financing lined up early, take these easy steps:

1. *Decide how much money you'll need to get started.* Do this by checking the down payment amounts given in ads for local income properties. While you may not be able to get the exact amount from such ads, you will be able to decide if you need $5,000, $10,000, $20,000, and so on. This is enough to get you started.

2. *Contact suitable lenders (those that do make real estate loans) and ask for their lending guidelines.* Do this by calling, faxing, or writing each lender. You will be supplied the lender's guidelines (amounts, term, purpose, rates, and so on) free of charge. Keep all the data you get in a neat file so it's handy when you need it. There's no point in wasting time running around for scraps of paper you may have misplaced and can't find when you need them.

3. *Know what type of loan or loans you'll need.* Most BWBs I meet need a down payment loan and a long-term mortgage loan to take

---

* Are made *only* where permitted by state statute.

over an income property they want. While many of "my" BWBs (those who get my newsletter and read my books to learn which methods to use) often report getting zero cash real estate (more about this later), it's always wise to have down payment money lined up in advance. Do this by following step 2.

4. *Plan on using any type of loan for your down payment that will get you started.* Thus, many BWBs use personal signature loans, credit card lines of credit, and similar loans for their down payment. With a clear idea of where your funds will be coming from, you can start looking for your ideal properties free of any worry about financing. When you have money freedom, you can wheel and deal with greater force and better results. To me, negotiating the deal for good real estate is fun!

If *you* have trouble getting real estate financing lined up early, I'll be glad to help you if you're a 2-year, or longer, subscriber to my newsletter. We've helped many readers find money and have never asked for, accepted, or charged a fee of any kind for finding the money.

Or you might want to use a financial broker, or become one yourself, to find the financing you seek. Then you may be able to write me, as one reader recently did, saying:

> *I've been a subscriber to International Wealth Success for 2 years and feel I have truly benefited from it. This past month I have been able to negotiate and close three real estate loans, making a 5 percent commission on each. These loans have been made to a licensed general contractor who buys properties with the intention of reselling them as soon as he has repaired and refurbished them. Now I would like to negotiate and close loans on a full-time basis (I've been doing it part time until now).*

Lining up money in advance can make your real estate life a lot easier. So start doing it now!

Buy When Prices Are Low

Real estate values run in cycles. While the length of such cycles varies, they will often be 5 to 6 years in duration. By this I mean that real estate prices will rise for 5 or 6 years and then begin to fall. But they almost never fall to the level they were before the rise began.

So if you buy when prices are falling (called a "buyer's market"), you're almost certain to get one or more bargains for your money. What's more, when you buy during a price decline:

1. *Zero cash deals,* where you do not put in any of your own money, are much easier to work out.

2. *Sellers will take back paper,* that is, accept a mortgage from you (a promise to pay money over a period of time) in place of a cash down payment. This is called a *purchase money mortgage* and can be for the entire amount of cash down needed or for part of it. (You can even get into the business of *cashing out* purchase money mortgages. We'll tell you more about this later in the book.)

3. *You can get the asking price reduced* much more easily when you're in a buyer's market. Sellers want to get out. You can help them get out—at a price that's a bargain for you!

4. *It's easier to find* the gemstones of real estate, namely, high-quality assets in superb locations when prices are declining. These gemstones will almost always rise in value as time passes—increasing your wealth while you sleep. Be sure to look for a return of at least 15 percent on the cash you put into such properties. Of course, if you put down zero cash, your return is infinite—that is, beyond measurement.

5. *Internet listing of desirable properties increase.* Now you can use the Internet efficiently to search for attractive income properties. Various Internet sites show exterior photos, floor plans, interior views, and key financial data for each building they feature. These websites allow you to review—quickly—many properties in a short time. Yes, the computer is helping us in real estate! And it can save you time and money when you're searching for good properties to buy.

Get Positive Cash Flow Every Time

Never buy a negative cash flow property—one in which you'll have to shell out money every month to keep it from going into foreclosure. You're much better off with no property! While you may be anxious to get started, a negative cash flow property is *not* the way to take your first step in real estate.

There *are* positive cash flow properties in every section of the country, and the world. But you *must* work to find them. Do this by looking—every day you have the time. And do *not* give up! You *will* find the property you seek.

Here are a few good rules of thumb for positive cash flow properties that you may want to apply to the properties *you* like:

1. They must bring in at least 30 percent more cash each month than you pay for interest on your mortgage(s), real estate taxes, insurance, and operating expenses (maintenance, labor, electricity, and so on). With such a cash flow you'll easily be able to pay your mortgage expenses and still have a nice wad of MIF at the end of each month.

2. The lower the *gross rent multiplier* (GRM), the easier it is for you to get a positive cash flow. Typical GRMs run from 3 to 12. This means that the price of the property (and the amount of money you'll have to borrow) will run between 3 times and 12 times the annual rental income. For a building with a $25,000 annual rental income, the price will range from 3 × $25,000 = $75,000 to 12 × $25,000 = $300,000. So look for the lowest GRM because it will give you a higher positive cash flow!

3. Work positive cash flow from both ends, that is (a) reduce your costs, which will free up cash for MIF, and (b) raise rents where you can, which will increase the cash coming into you every month. In this business of real estate, *cash is king!*

4. Today's rents for well-located property in large cities can range from $2,000 (or more) per month for a 1-bedroom apartment to as high as $10,000 per month for a 3-bedroom apartment. With such rents, it is easier to obtain a positive cash flow from even the most expensive buildings.

Hold Your Properties for a Rise in Value

There's no better investment in this world than one that gives *you* a positive cash flow *every* day while its value rises *every* day! You're being paid to hold an asset that gets more valuable every day you own it. Compare this to a car, a boat, a TV, computer, or fax machine. They all go *down* in value as time passes—unless they're unique. So, to profit, follow this proven rule: *Hold for rise in value!*

Real estate goes *up* in value while you sleep! Some years the rise in value will take your breath away—10 percent, 20 percent, and so on. Other years, which some ill-informed people call "bad," the value of your real estate will rise "only" 5 percent! Give me five years at 5 percent a year and I'll make *you* rich in your spare time!

Take this recent letter from a BWB who sees the sense to holding real estate for a rise in value:

> *As a BWB following your expert instructions, I just closed on my first income-producing property. The house is a 5-bedroom Victorian single-family dwelling in surprisingly good condition. The seller agreed to hold a second mortgage for $1 1,000 (including interest) and $24,000 was financed through a mortgage company, thus giving me 100 percent financing! The house is currently rented, and the rent covers both the first and second mortgages. I am planning to renovate the house, which could bring the price to $80,000. I'm already working on a similar deal on another house— can't stop now!*

This letter brings out all the important points I want to get across to you in this book, namely:

- Use other people's money to buy your real estate.
- Never buy unless you have a positive cash flow after *all* expenses associated with the property.
- Hold your property for a rise in value. (If you want to sell after the value rises, that's *your* decision. I'm happy that I put you into a position where you *can* make a profit, if you wish!)

Even if you think that I push you too hard, good friend, to follow the guidelines, don't get annoyed. Why? Because these ideas *do* work. I've seen them work thousands of times—everywhere. And they *will* work for you—if you just apply these guidelines to properties in your area of the world! If you do, you'll be ready for the next step—borrowing more money. Let's see how *you* can increase your cash assets using OPM.

Use Your Assets to Borrow More Money

Real estate—as we saw earlier—is an asset. And a valuable one, too. So you can use the real estate you take over with OPM to borrow more money to invest in more real estate, if you want to increase your holdings!

To guide your borrowing you should set up a series of investment and income goals for yourself. Thus, you might have goals like these:

- Own five income buildings by the end of this year.

- Receive an income of $25,000 per year from the five buildings, after paying *all* expenses and mortgages.

- Borrow against these buildings enough to take over ownership of three more buildings next year.

Once you own a few properties, your financial statement will improve enormously, as we saw earlier. Lenders will welcome you with open arms because you have assets! You're a person of substance who's looked up to by everyone.

Don't borrow until you have a specific property in mind. But you can line up your loans in advance. Lenders admire a forward thinker who knows what he or she want to do in the future. Delay taking any loan until you close on the property. Even though interest is provable and tax deductible to you as a businessperson in real estate, there's no sense in wasting money on interest until you're ready to move ahead!

To use the real estate you already own as collateral for a new loan, follow the tips given later in this book. You'll quickly get the money you need for the new properties you want to buy to increase your income.

Invest Your Borrowed Money in More Real Estate

If real estate is the way to a fortune for you, stick to it! Don't use the money you borrow on your existing properties to go into another business. Why? Because, for the BWB, there's *no* business really as good as real estate! I've seen people waste their real estate profits on franchises of various kinds, small businesses for their spouse, and so on.

Invest your borrowed money in more real estate until you reach the income and asset levels you set in your goals. Then, and only then, should you start thinking of using real estate—generated funds for other businesses. Thus, a reader writes:

I have been a subscriber of your newsletter for about 1 year and have learned a great deal from it and from your books. I started a successful business and all is going well. I am a dealer for a log home company and have sold six homes in the last five months. I am planning to expand my business.

Your real estate is one of your most valuable assets. Use it to build more wealth and you'll easily escape 9-to-5 bondage while giving yourself and your loved ones a much better life.

To show you how much I believe in the value of real estate assets, I'm ready to help you finance any down payment you might need for good, solid income property. Why? Because:

- I consider you a friend because you read my books.
- Two-year subscribers to our newsletter (see the back of this book) are entitled to apply to my firm, IWS, Inc., for a loan* for any active business use. And real estate is, as you'll recall, a business!
- While we do have lending guidelines and rules, they are, I believe, much more liberal than conventional lenders' loan requirements.
- Backing up a belief with potential cash on the barrel-head is, I believe, a mighty strong way to convince people of one's faith in a procedure, such as the one I give you in this book!

SUCCESS STRATEGIES FOR BUILDING YOUR REAL ESTATE WEALTH IN GOOD TIMES AND BAD TIMES

1. Get low-interest-rate real estate loans in bad times. Insist on a fixed rate of interest. This enables you to lock in a low interest cost because—in general—interest rates are lower in bad times than in good times. The result? Your mortgage costs are lower and you earn a higher profit on the property. Use the Internet to search for the lowest interest rate and the longest term for your real estate loan. Remember this at all times: When times are bad, lenders reduce their interest rate on mortgage loans. Why? Because lenders want to encourage borrowers to apply for loans, even though times are bad. Lenders usually earn more on loans than on

---

*Where permissible by state statute.

any other business they may be in. So lenders are anxious to put out more loans. Help them out by getting fixed low-interest-rate long-term mortgage loans for your income real estate properties. Result? You'll have more money in your bank at the end of every month. So be a hero to lenders! Borrow from them in bad times when almost no one else is even thinking of borrowing to build their real estate wealth.

2. Sell appreciated properties in good times. Why? You'll get a higher price for the property and your profit on the appreciation will be larger. Try to sell at the peak of good times so you take the maximum cash out of the property. Keep good records during the life of your property so you can legitimately deduct the cost of all improvements from the gain you have on the sale. Thus, if you sell a property for $150,000 more than you paid for it four years earlier, but you made $50,000 worth of improvements to it during that time, your average annual profit on the sale will be ($150,000 - $50,000)/4 years = $25,000 per year. You add this to the annual profit you earned from rental income during the four years you owned the property. Taken together, your average income can be enormous! So pay attention to the trend in property values during good times by reading good real estate magazines and newsletters. Don't let riches opportunities pass you by!

3. Buy high-potential-appreciation properties in bad times. Real estate is an intensely cyclical business. What goes down always comes back up. When good times return—as they will—you can sell high-potential-appreciation properties at a large profit to yourself. So don't let the doomers-and-gloomers of bad times discourage you. See clearly what can happen when good times return—invest when prices are down and sell when prices return to a higher level. You'll be rich before you know it! True, it takes courage to go against the tide of public opinion in bad times. But every real estate downturn has been followed by an upturn. You can count on that. So if you buy high-potential-appreciation properties for little money in bad times you're almost guaranteed to sell at a profit in good times. Use your head; listen to your inner voice and do what you think will make you money. Why? Because it will!

4. Work sharp, advantageous deals in bad times to get the properties you seek at the lowest price with the longest mortgage terms possible at the lowest fixed interest rate. Never be afraid to be a "bottom-fisher"— a buyer who searches for the lowest price possible. The most the seller can say is "No." And the seller may say "Yes." If the answer is "Yes" you can have a really profitable deal at an unbelievably low price! Remember that "bad times" can be good times for you. Why? Because you work shrewd deals with people who want to run away from their real estate because they're scared. Just remember that real estate will always come back. Base your investment decisions on this truth and you'll seldom go wrong!

IMPORTANT POINTERS TO KEEP IN MIND

- Real estate is the *best* business for you—if you want to rid yourself of the 9-to-5 grind.
- Real estate always has *value*—and always will.
- Down cycles in real estate are always followed by rising values.
- "Bad" times in real estate give you *big* opportunities.
- Buy in "bad" times and get rich by selling in good times.
- Assets on your balance sheet can build your net worth, making your life much easier and more enjoyable.
- Daily income can be yours with positive cash flow properties.
- When bargain real estate is available in "bad" times, all you need to zoom your income and build wealth is *time* for your properties to rise in value.
- To make it big in any real estate deal, get your financing lined up early—it makes deals go faster, and easier.
- Buy when prices are low—you'll always be able to sell at a higher price later.
- Get positive cash flow every time. Then you'll never have any problem with the real estate you buy because it will pay for itself while it rises in value.
- Aim for at least 30 percent more cash each month than you pay for all expenses, including mortgage interest, but not including your principal payment on the mortgage(s).
- Hold your properties for a rise in value so you make a profit on your eventual sale of your holdings. Then your real estate will make money for you two ways: the monthly positive cash flow which you bank and (2) the profit you make on the sale of your property in the future.

- Use OPM—other people's money—to take over the properties that bring you the income you seek.

- Invest the money you borrow on your existing properties to take over other income-producing real estate assets.

- Remember: You always have a friend in your author—day and night. I'll even consider helping you finance good, solid properties if you're a 2-year, or longer, subscriber to my newsletter.

- Real estate is a tax-favored investment that hardly ever fails and is the growth business of the future—for *you*!

Starting, and Getting Rich, On Zero Cash Real Estate

2

Doomers and gloomers will tell you things are so bad now that zero cash—where you put *no* money down on income real estate—can't work today. They're wrong! Today some sellers are so desperate to get out of a property that they'll "give it away" to you for *no* cash of your own up front! This chapter shows *you* how—despite meaner and leaner times— you can get rich on no-down-payment real estate.

Why do I say zero cash (no money down) is the way to go? For a number of very good reasons:

- You start faster—you don't have to wait years to save up the money to invest.

- Your present job gives *you* borrowing power! And real estate is, as we said earlier, a borrowed money business. As a result, your real estate business has a greater chance of success.

- Very few established real estate projects fail, especially if they're in areas where people like to live or where industries want to be located. Even in the worst of times people must live somewhere. *You* can get rich providing this *somewhere* with clean, well-maintained, reasonably priced housing.

- You can control *more* real estate for less. This means your daily positive cash flow will be higher, giving you greater freedom from the 9-to-5 yoke.

- Doing zero cash deals gives *you* enormous negotiating skills. These will come in handy during your entire real estate career, which will be long and profitable, with my help!

27

Let's take a quick look at each of these reasons and see how they apply to you. We'll show you how zero cash can put big bucks into *your* pocket!

YOU START FASTER WHEN USING ZERO CASH

Most BWBs have trouble finding the down payment for the income property they want to buy. So they often say to themselves:

I'll start saving from my regular income, and when I get enough for a down payment, I'll buy my first income property. Then I'll save for another down payment and buy my second property.

This sounds good—and it may work. But for most BWBs, it doesn't work. Why? Because:

- Something always seems to come up to wipe out the down-payment nest egg, like
- You (or your spouse) decide you need a new, faster computer to access the Internet for real estate and personal use.
  - The car breaks down and you need a new one.
  - Someone in the family becomes ill and needs help.
- Your spouse wants wall-to-wall carpeting from the most expensive shop in town and says: "Why shouldn't we get it. After all, we *do* have the money!" (The "money" is your income real estate nest egg.)

The result of all this is to delay your first purchase of real estate that will make money for you. What to do?

Your answer is clear. And it doesn't cost a dime to put it into action, if you exclude a few local phone calls and a few postage stamps. You can:

- Use borrowed money for the down payment for your first few income properties.
- Shorten the time it takes for you to get your first positive cash flow income from real estate.

Readers of my real estate books regularly get started fast on zero cash. Here's a recent letter from such a reader:

> *Less than two weeks ago, I closed on my second investment property, 45 days after closing on my first investment property for zero cash. Using 100 percent-plus financing enabled me to cash out nearly $5,000 at closing with no money down. In addition, I received favorable financing from the seller. Within a year I aim to have $3,000 per month positive cash flow from rental properties.*

(Note: In "cashing out" this reader walked away from the closing with $5,000 in his pocket *plus* full ownership of the income property—all on *zero cash* of his own!)

So to start faster, use zero cash, that is, borrowed money. It can cut years off your startup time!

USE YOUR JOB'S BORROWING POWER

You now have a job of some kind. If you've been on it a year or more, *you* have borrowing power! This means you can borrow the money you need for the down payment on an income property of some kind.

Keep some easy facts in mind when you're thinking about income real estate. These facts are:

- Getting a long-term mortgage loan (15 to 40 years) on well-located property is easy. Lenders are happy to loan on such real estate.
- The big roadblock for BWBs is getting the down payment loan for the income property they want to buy.
- Your job can give you the borrowing power to get one or more down payment loans for the property you seek.
- When you hear of zero cash or 100 percent financing of real estate, you will almost always have two loans on the property. The first loan—called the *long-term mortgage*—is easy to get because the property is the collateral and lenders like to loan on good properties. The second loan—called the *down payment*—is a personal loan based on your income and job history. Getting such a second loan gives you zero cash financing of income real estate.

So your job—even though you may hate it—does give you the way out! How? By the borrowing power it gives you. As one reader writes:

By using your methods I bought a house for $17,000, even though it was appraised at $27,000. We only put in $600 worth of materials, using borrowed money.

HARDER WORK DOES PAY OFF

When you borrow money with the sincere intention of repaying it, you *do* work harder. Why? Because you want to repay your loan and get rid of those burdensome monthly payments.

This "working harder" approach is good for you and your business! Why? Because your business (real estate) has a greater chance of success when you work harder. So the money you borrow not only gives you the funds you need to take over an income property. It also acts as a stimulant to improve your cash flow and profit.

Remember this: Zero cash or 100 percent financing is rarely done with just one loan. Lenders are reluctant to loan 100 percent on a property. So you'll need at least two loans on every property, as shown later in this book. Knowing this in advance, you can prepare yourself to have the fun of working to pay off the loan(s) that give *you* a positive cash flow *every* month!

Some people ridicule hard work. But in real estate hard work *does* pay off! I see it every day of the week with readers who *are* making big money while building a fortune in real estate.

YOU CAN CONTROL MORE
REAL ESTATE WITH ZERO CASH

The name of the game in real estate is *positive cash flow!* With positive cash flow *you* can get free of slavelike work for a ruthless boss. But to build significant positive cash flow, you *must* have enough properties to reach the income level you seek.

Using other people's money (OPM) allows you to control more property, giving you a higher income. If you wait around to save up enough money to get the number of properties you seek, you may be too old to care! So go the zero cash route to your real estate wealth and you'll build fast wealth.

To show you how hard work and controlling more real estate can help you build the positive cash flow you seek, here's a recent letter from a reader who writes:

Just purchased a 3-bedroom house with attached garage at 50 percent of appraised value and cashed out $5,100 at closing. This was my fourth straight zero cash no-dollars-down deal (in less than 6 months). Terms and conditions of the contract are excellent. I negotiated 0 percent owner financing and the first option to buy or sell the fully assumable, no-qualifying second deed of trust with no payments for 4 months.

Just a few notes about this letter: (1) "Cashed out $5,100" means that this reader walked out of the closing with $5,100 in his pocket that he got for buying this income property! He was paid, you might say, to take over an asset that will make him money every month! Could you ask for more?

(2) "This was my fourth . . . ." shows that *you* can control more with zero cash. (3) "I negotiated 0 percent owner financing . . ." shows that you *can* get money at *low* interest rates. And in this connection, I must tell you how disbelief can harm a BWB.

Our company, IWS, Inc.,* makes loans to BWBs for *active* business purposes. We do *not* lend for personal uses like buying clothing, a primary residence, or a recreational-use car. But we *do* lend for almost any type of business activity including, of course, real estate.

In making these loans our normal interest rate for years was 6 percent. But so many BWBs with limited business experience said, "Six percent? That's impossible! *Nobody* lends at 6 percent. I never heard of such a low rate!"

So we raised the rate to 12 percent and nobody says things like this anymore. Yet these same BWBs fooled only themselves. Why? Because you can get loans at as little as 3 percent from certain state development companies. Other state development companies today make *0 percent* loans to firms that will increase the number of jobs in the area in which they operate. And you saw that the reader above got a C percent loan from the seller. (All letters quoted here—remember—are available for free inspection by anyone.)

---

* Where permitted by state statute.

Disbelief just because someone never heard of a lending practice prevents such BWBs from making it big. I sympathize with them—every day! (And, by the way, we still *do* make 6 percent loans for "business emergencies," that is, where a going business has problems and needs funds to solve them. The 6 percent rate for these loans has not generated any of the foregoing comments!)

So don't be too quick to shoot down something *you* disbelieve because you never heard of it. You could be wrong, as my teenage son likes to remind me. And being wrong could cost *you* money! Low-interest-rate money can give *you* the control you need to build your real estate fortune faster!

DOING ZERO CASH DEALS GIVES YOU GREAT NEGOTIATING SKILLS

Real estate is a *negotiation* business. Why? Because, in real estate, you should follow the Hicks Rules of Buying Success, namely:

1. *Never pay the asking price.* No one selling a property expects the buyer to pay the asking price.
2. *Recognize that every asking price is inflated above what the seller really seeks.* This allows room for negotiation.
3. *Negotiate or suffer.* Get concessions from the seller. Remember, there are usually more sellers than buyers!

Sure, you may be embarrassed by negotiating. But why pay a higher price for a property when—with a little give and take—you can get it for 10 percent less? Further, once you get into negotiating, you'll find it's fun—and profitable.

What's more, as your real estate career advances, you'll buy larger and larger properties. When you get into the big leagues, you'll have to negotiate. So everything you learn with your smaller, starter properties will help you work sharper deals on your bigger income holdings.

When a person or firm decides to sell an income property (or any other type of property), he or she almost always "packs" the asking price with an amount that can be reduced to please the buyer. If you're afraid to negotiate, you'll pay this pack amount, and the seller will think you're a real amateur. Don't let this happen to you! Typical pack percentages you'll meet in today's real estate market are shown in Exhibit 2–1.

Exhibit 2–1

TYPICAL "PACK" ALLOWANCES FOR INCOME PROPERTIES*

Asking Price	Price Seller Will Accept	Pack Percent
$ 250,000	$ 225,000	10
500,000	450,000	10
1,000,000	850,000	15
2,000,000	1,700,000	15
3,000,000	2,700,000	10
4,000,000	3,700,000	7.5
5,000,000	4,600,000	8
10,000,000	9,000,000	10

*The price a seller will accept, and hence the pack percentage, will vary with the property, its location, and the degree of need a seller has to make a deal. you can negotiate larger discounts when the seller is under pressure to unload the property.

Never be afraid to negotiate! You can make as much money negotiating as you can from operating a property for one year. Recognize this and your real estate future is secure. Ignore negotiating and you'll pay a heavy price!

HOW TO START USING THE ZERO CASH APPROACH

Get started on zero cash and you'll never give up this approach! Why? Because it has the many advantages we listed for *you*. What's more, you can get started using zero cash today! There's no waiting period. And I'm a firm believer that the best time to get started building your wealth is right now—today!

Here are the easy steps you'll take to start using the zero cash approach to building real estate wealth:

1. Decide on the types of properties you want to own.
2. Prepare a chart to link your goals and objectives in life with the types of properties you want to own.
3. Start looking for "your" properties locally.

4. Begin a "riches notebook" to keep a record of your search and the results you're getting.

5. Make offers on suitable properties that meet your goals and objectives.

6. Take over your first income property.

Let's take a close look at each of these steps so you can see exactly what to do. And, remember, if you have any questions or need financing help, call or write me, if you're a 2-year, or longer, subscriber to my newsletter. I'm here to help in every way I can all those readers needing assistance.

DECIDE WHAT TYPES OF PROPERTIES YOU WANT TO OWN

There are many different types of real estate *you* can own. Not all real estate will "turn you on." Why is this? Because:

- Some people don't enjoy dealing with tenants; they want to conduct their rental business by mail.
- Other BWBs enjoy meeting, and dealing with, tenants. "Being there" is half the fun of making money, for them.
- Some real estate in your area might require lots of fixing up before it will give you the income you seek. Such work may, or may not, appeal to you.

To decide what types of properties you want to own, do some self-analysis. On a piece of paper separate from this book, enter answers to the following questions:

	Yes	No
1. Do I enjoy working closely (face to face) with people?	_____	_____
2. Would I rather be at a distance from my tenants?	_____	_____
3. Would tenant problems such as those met in multifamily buildings (apartment houses) "bug" me to the point where I would give up the business?	_____	_____

	Yes	No

4. Could I find happiness running industrial
   or factory buildings in my area?   _____   _____

5. Are shopping centers and strip malls
   attractive to me, knowing that they do
   involve lots of negotiations with tenants?   _____   _____

6. Should I consider only raw land to be held
   until it rises in value, giving me *no* tenant
   problems or negotiations?   _____   _____

Answering these questions quickly tells you if you're a "people person" or a loner. If you're a loner, that is, if you don't want to deal with too many people, you should consider owning factories or industrial, commercial, or warehouse buildings. Why? Because you will usually deal with fewer people in such structures.

The ultimate no-people real estate is raw land. But raw land investments have certain factors which may make them unattractive. The main factor that's unappealing to most BWBs is that raw land gives you *no* monthly income unless you can rent your raw land out. Most land outside a city or town can't be rented. So you have a monthly cash drain for mortgage and real estate tax payments.

All this points to a fact of real estate life every BWB must recognize before starting out:

- All real estate *does* involve some person-to-person dealing. So if you want to derive the many benefits from investing in real estate, you should learn to deal with other people, even though it may not be appealing to you right now.
- Success—as is often said—does have a price! But in real estate the price is really very low
- What's more, you'll eventually learn to enjoy dealing with people in real estate because your rewards will be large!

As an aid in helping you pick the types of property you'd like to own, we give you a guide in Exhibit 2–2. You can use it as is, or you can take it and make any changes you wish. The main purpose of this guide is to help you decide what types of properties you'd like to own—by using this guide in the privacy of your own office or room, without anyone telling you what to do! The guide is shown in Exhibit 2–2.

Exhibit 2–2

BWB'S GUIDE FOR DECIDING TYPE OF PROPERTY TO OWN

Type of Property	*Desirable Features for BWBs*	*Undesirable Features for Some BWBs*
Multifamily dwellings (apartment houses)	Income is steady; rents can be collected by mail; value usually rises with time.	Tenant dealings necessary; repair costs can be high.
Industrial/ commercial/ factory/warehouse buildings	Rental income can be large when building is fully occupied; there's little competition when buying these buildings because few BWBs know about them; fewer are interested in them.	Rental income can rise and fall with the economy; your business depends on your tenants' business.
Shopping centers/ strip malls	Income can be high when you share in the gross receipts of tenants; land value can increase quickly.	Buying can be difficult because of high cost; zero cash deals are hard to work out; tenant negotiations can be complex.
Raw land	Land can often be obtained for as little as $1 down; land in good areas can rise in value quickly.	Raw land rarely gives you a positive cash flow; taxes can be a burden when there's no income from the land.

LINK YOUR LIFE'S GOALS AND OBJECTIVES TO PROPERTY TYPES

Why do you want to make money in real estate? Most people have a ready answer to this question. Typical reasons for wanting to make money in real estate are:

- To get away from my pain-in-the-neck boss and the silly office politics I have to put up with
- To get a regular monthly income over and above my paltry salary so I can do the things I dream of doing for myself and family
- To own something that will fill my bank account with money while what I own continues to grow in value over time
- To build my assets (what I own) without putting up any of my own money

You can link these—and other reasons for owning property—to the types of properties considered in Exhibit 2–2. To do this, prepare a list of your life goals and objectives in the form shown in Exhibit 2–3. Then list the types of properties you might want to own across the top of the exhibit, as shown. Where each type of property crosses your goal or objective, enter those features of the property that might help you achieve your goal in life. Or, if there are negative aspects to a type of property, enter these so you see the whole picture.

Looking over Exhibit 2–3, you can see that multifamily buildings such as apartment houses are probably best for most BWBs. Your own life goals study will probably be different. But do it *now*—it will help you to start building *your* wealth in real estate today!

Once you do your goals study you're ready to start looking for the type(s) of property that will help you achieve your goals. Let's get started doing that right now for *you!*

START LOOKING FOR SUITABLE PROPERTIES

You now know what type of real estate property *you* want to own. Once you know this you're ready to start looking for zero cash properties that will give you the financial freedom and power you seek.

Exhibit 2–3

HOW TO RELATE YOUR LIFE GOALS TO TYPES OF REAL ESTATE

Types of Real Estate I Like

Goals/ Objectives	Multifamily Buildings (Apartment Houses)	Industrial or Commercial Buildings/ Factories/ Warehouses	Shopping Centers/ Strip Malls	Raw Land To Hold or Develop
Regular monthly cash income from my own business	Good income in my area	Can give high income, if there are any in my area	Income good, but purchase price can be very high	No income and not much hope for raw land in my area
Growth in value of my real estate investment	Brokers report 5 percent rise in value per year	Slow rise in value; not too many buildings to choose from	Big down payment possibly needed; slow value growth	Land-value growth very slow in my area
Build my assets without investing any of my cash	Not too many zero cash deals in my area	Zero cash deals hard to find for these properties	Very few zero cash deals around for these properties in my area	Plenty of zero cash deals for raw land are in my area

At the start, your greatest chances for finding properties that will help you achieve your goals, are those in your local area. Why? Because local properties:

- Can be seen sooner at low, or *no,* cost to you
- Are often easier to finance because lenders in the area know, and trust, the properties
- Have a value which is easier to ascertain from people "who speak your language"
- Are easier to negotiate for price reductions and other valuable concessions
- Can be easily traced from construction to the present time

The one hurdle you might meet in dealing locally is that there might not be any properties of the type you're seeking. If this happens, you must then start looking elsewhere. Or you can change the type of property you're seeking to a type that is available locally.

To find local properties to meet your investment goals, look in the following places:

- Local newspapers under the heading "Real Estate for Sale." You may find other headings under this general category, such as "Apartment Houses for Sale," "Factories for Sale," "Shopping Centers for Sale," and so on. Look under the heading for the type of property you seek.
- Local magazines—both real estate and business—carrying classified ads for real estate.
- Local apartment owners' association publications and bulletin boards listing properties available from members of the association. (In some areas the name of the organization may be different but the purposes will be the same.)
- Local real estate brokers' listings. Such listings can give you an enormous amount of useful information for no more than a local phone call or short visit to a brokers' office.

If you make an all-out "run" on these sources of information, you'll soon begin to accumulate what seems like tons of paper. To get through this paper and make the right decisions, you must be organized. That's why I suggest you get control of your information. Here's how.

BEGIN YOUR RICHES NOTEBOOK

When you start looking for zero cash income properties, you'll be fed an enormous amount of numbers information. You'll get numbers on:

- Gross income of the property
- Vacancy rate—a percentage
- Other income—from laundry machines, garages, and so on
- Monthly expenses for maintenance
- Real estate taxes
- Mortgage payment expenses, including interest
- Miscellaneous items

You can't possibly keep all these numbers in mind for each property you consider. So I suggest you start your own riches notebook. It will help you get rich in real estate faster in good times and tough times.

What should you put in your riches notebook? You should have the money numbers shown for *each* property. Since paper is cheap, I suggest that you have at least one page per property. Then you'll be able to see at a glance the key data about each property. Exhibit 2–4 shows a typical page from the riches notebook of a successful BWB.

If you're concentrating on properties in one area, as I suggest, you can also have a general section for that area in your riches notebook covering topics such as:

- Typical asking price for each type of property in terms of dollars per rental unit, dollars per square foot, and so on
- Real estate taxes in terms of dollars per square foot, dollars per dollar of income, dollars per $1,000 of assessed valuation
- Usual down payment requested, if any
- Average age of properties offered
- Maintenance cost as a percentage of property income

If you're interested in investing in raw land because you believe it has great potential in your area, many of these numbers won't be needed. So just ignore them.

When you find a property that turns you on because its income and expenses are such that you can make money from it, do a simple Deal Potential Study, as in Exhibit 2–5. In this, you:

1. Put down, in writing, why you want to buy the property. While this may seem like a chore, it *will* clarify your thinking and bring out any negatives in the deal.

2. Give your estimate of whether a zero cash deal is possible with the seller.

3. List how you'll negotiate the deal. State what you'll give up to get the price and down payment arrangements *you* want. Again, having it all in writing before you start to deal will put *you* in a powerful position to get what *you* want because you know what you want!

4. Insert the dollar offers you'll make to the seller, based on what the property will do for your financial future.

5. Allow space to enter information on how the seller reacts to your various offers.

6. Have a final space for entering the outcome of each deal. This will help you learn which approaches to a seller get the results *you* want, namely the property you seek at the price you're willing to pay with an acceptable down payment, which is preferably zero.

Now I know that all of this may seem like extra work. But it really isn't! How can I say that? Well, when you're attempting to buy income real estate of some kind, you mentally go through all the steps listed. It's my finding—based on hundreds of *successful* deals—that writing down your deal strategies really helps every BWB. Further, the time it takes to jot down your strategies is minimal, just a few minutes, at the most.

MAKE OFFERS ON SUITABLE PROPERTIES

Once you finish studying a few potential deals you're ready to make offers on suitable properties. But before you go out and make any offers, you *must* take certain steps to safeguard yourself and your income. These steps are:

1. Seek the advice of an experienced, competent real estate attorney.

2. Be certain the property has a positive cash flow *after* all expenses are paid.

3. Negotiate a zero cash down deal—or as close to zero cash as you can.

Exhibit 2-4

TYPICAL PAGE OF A BWB'S RICHES NOTEBOOK

Date: _May 18_

Name of Property: _10- Family Apartment House_

Address: _128 Echo Place_

Asking Price: **$195,000**   Down Payment Requested: **$35,000**

Annual Income   Miscellaneous
  from Rentals: **$66,000**   Income: **$10,200**

Annual Expenses: _R.E. Taxes_ $13,200
                 Trash   600
                 Water   720
                 Electric   960
                 Ads & Tele   480
                 Insurance   2,400
                 Maint. & Clng. 2,400
                 Salaries   6,000
                 Comm & Legal   3,000
                 Other   3,000

Seller's Name and Address: _John Jones_
128 Echo Place

Seller's Telephone No.: _456-4321_

My Written Opinion of This Property: _Good; high current income; fair price for income level; rents can easily be raised._

Rating (0 to 10, with 0 = don't buy, 10 = the best buy ever for me): _8_

Exhibit 2–5

DEAL POTENTIAL STUDY

Date: *May 20*

Property Name: 10-*Family Apartment House*

Property Address: *128 Echo Place* Tel. No.: *123-4567*

Seller's Name: *John Jones* Tel. No.: *456-4321*

My Rating of This Property (from riches notebook): *Good*

Why I Want to Buy This Property: *High current income; good price for the income level; rents can easily be raised in a few months.*

Outstanding Features of This Property: *Good structural condition; top location — near shopping and transportation.*

Potential for Zero Cash Deal: *Fair to good.*

Negotiation Steps:	Buyer	Seller Reaction
1. Price I'll Offer	$160,000	*May not accept*
2. Down Payment I'll Offer	$20,000	*May accept*
3. Give-ups to Get Results I Want	*Higher offer larger down*	*Delighted* *Delighted*
4. Increases I'll Accept to Get Results I Want	$10,000 *(on price)* $5,000 *(on down)*	*Pleased* *So-so*

Deal Outcome: *I bought this property at $165,000 with $21,000 down. It's better than I thought it would be.*

What I Learned While Working on This Potential Deal: *You can negotiate almost any deal — with almost any seller!*

4. Be ready to snap up properties where an owner is under pressure to sell.

5. Make certain that there are flexible rent rules in the area so you have the right to raise rents, if necessary.

Let's take a quick look at each of these steps to see how you can apply it in your wealth building activities. You'll make money much faster by starting right!

Use a Competent Real Estate Attorney

When you buy any kind of real estate you're in an area that's full of laws, rules, and guidelines. You're the *businessperson* in the deal. You analyze the deal's potential with your study, Exhibit 2–5. But you *must* have guidance about the *legal aspects* of the deal because a mistake could mess up the business features.

You can find a competent real estate attorney by calling your local bar association (listed in your telephone book) and asking for several names. Contact each attorney and decide which one you'd like to work with. When you contact an attorney, don't be afraid to ask such questions as:

- Do you do many real estate deals?
- Are you a specialist in any type of property (residential, commercial, industrial, and so on)?
- How many real estate closings did you do last year?
- What are your normal fees for a person like myself who wants to buy income real estate?
- Do you have contacts in real estate who can help me build my holdings?
- Will you protect me from making silly mistakes when I come across a lucrative property?

In my own real estate deals I work with two highly competent real estate attorneys. Both these professionals have taught me much about safe ways to make money from real estate. Their fees have always been moderate. In every purchase and sale they more than earned their fees. The same will happen to *you*—if you work with a competent real estate attorney. Instead of *costing* money, these professionals will *make* money for you!

Buy *Only* Positive Cash Flow Properties

You *must* come out with money in fist (MIF) *after* you pay *all* expenses for your income property, *including* paying off the mortgage, called *mortgage amortization* when paid on a monthly principal and interest (P&I) basis. Why do I say this?

Because when you're building wealth to make yourself independent of a slavelike daily grind, you must:

- Bring *in* money from your business activities to build your cash reserves
- Avoid, at all costs, having to pay out money to support your business
- Make every business self-supporting, including paying *you* a salary for your work

People say: "I can't find any *profitable* properties. I've looked and looked, but there aren't any around. What can I do?" My standard response is "Look some more. There *are* such properties available!"

Almost every day of the week I get letters from readers telling me about the high-income-producing properties they bought. Letters like

> *I am a somewhat successful investor who started out a year and a half ago. I now own four buildings with 8 units worth about $140,000 with a $35,000 per year gross rental income. Net income is about $6,500. I bought all with little or no money down.*

This reader followed all my ideas, namely, positive cash flow income from zero cash properties. You, too, can do the same!

Dependable cash income is, of course, of prime importance from a profit standpoint. You can't get rich if you have to pay out money to "carry" a property. And accepting anything less than a known cash income (where you wind up with money you can spend or deposit in your bank every month) can cause you to become depressed. Why? Because with a negative cash flow property:

- You feel saddled with debt.
- Paying the property expenses takes money from other of your life's activities.
- You become so discouraged you give up your real estate efforts and resign yourself to job slavery forever.

So seek reliable money generating properties at *all* times! You'll never regret this approach because it will always put money into your pocket.

Work Out Zero Cash Deals with the Seller

If you're like most BWBs who call or visit me, you have plenty of ambition but little cash. Not to worry. You can overcome your cash shortage! How? By taking over positive cash flow real estate on zero cash.

When I say *zero cash,* I mean that you do not take any money out of your bank to buy a property. Instead, you *borrow* all the money you need and use the income from the property to repay the loans you use to buy the asset. And even after you pay *all* expenses, including the loans used to get the property, you still have money to put into the bank! Readers of mine do this every day. Like this one who writes:

> After completing your book How to Borrow Your Way to Real Estate Riches, *I went looking for my first deal. I located a recently rehabbed legal 2-family building whose income would service an 80 percent mortgage. Since I did not have the remaining 20 percent, I remembered the suggestion in your book to use your credit card. I did this for part of the down payment and convinced the seller to carry back a second mortgage at eleven percent interest for 3 years. Thus, I bought this property by financing the entire deal with other people's money. Currently the property is generating a $400-per-month positive cash flow for me. Using the ideas from your book I was able to borrow the full purchase price and end up with $400 per month income! Thanks, Ty; your ideas are great.*

This interesting letter brings out all the points on zero cash that I want you to keep in mind. These points are:

- The BWB who's really sincere about getting rich will use every idea he or she can to get needed funds.
- It may take a little selling to get the seller to do what's needed (in this case a second mortgage) so you can take over the property for zero cash.
- Never be afraid to ask the seller to make concessions to you! As a buyer, you're in the driver's seat.

- Always know what your loans will cost you. Then check to see that the cash flow from the property will allow you to repay *all* loans and still have cash in hand.

Few real estate deals are simple and direct. You'll almost always have to do some wheeling and dealing. But this is the fun part of real estate. And when times are tough it's much easier for you to get what *you* want out of any real estate deal! Start—now—to work only on deals that will make you rich while giving you a positive cash flow *every* month.

Snap Up Properties from Owners Under Pressure

Today people will often use poor judgment in their business lives. So you'll find some sellers who are under strong pressure to sell. This is *your* opportunity to get the property you seek at a bargain price.

To find pressured sellers, you must develop some simple character analysis skills. To do this:

1. *Listen carefully to what people say.* A quavering voice, a sweaty brow, or a quick looking around the room while talking to you can often indicate external pressures.

2. *Try to draw out the seller to determine what is pressuring the person.* You'll often become a "father confessor" type, whether you're a man or woman! The seller will "unload" his or her troubles on you. Listen carefully and start plotting your strategies.

3. *Never feel guilty about using the seller's external pressures to get a better deal for yourself.* Why? Because by buying the property, you're helping the seller out of his or her difficulties. You're setting up a win-win situation for both yourself and the seller. You *both* win!

4. *Negotiate strongly to get zero cash deals from every seller.* A seller under pressure will often be willing to do a zero cash deal just to get the property off his or her hands. So you can help the seller from having to be burdened with the property while you "pick up" an ideal cash machine which puts dollars into your pocket *every* month—without having to put up one penny in cash!

Negotiating is work. But it's work that can put millions into *your* bank account in just a few years. And it will often be much more pleasant than that snarling boss who wants everything yesterday!

Check the Rent Laws in Your Investment Area

Most BWBs start with residential income properties as their source of real estate income. You may be interested in other types of properties. If so, fine. We'll be giving you more information on them as we go along in this book.

But if residential properties are your bag, then you *must* check the rent control laws in the area in which you plan to own properties. Why? Because rent control laws can:

- Limit your profits
- Prevent you from making property improvements
- Cause endless litigation
- Turn fun into misery in business

Now don't get scared! Most cities and states have *no* rent control laws. So there's really nothing to worry about. But some areas *do* have rent control laws. You should be aware of them.

As a new owner of a residential property you will often have advantages over the seller. These advantages might include:

- The right to raise rents on vacated apartments
- The right to raise rents on renovated apartments
- The right to new considerations when you want to raise rents

The best way to learn what your rights are is to work with a competent real estate attorney who knows the rent control law in your area. Listen to what the attorney advises. And *do* what the attorney recommends! Why pay for good advice and then not follow it?

When dealing with laws written for the public, keep several facts in mind at all times:

- Every law has "a way out"—that is, a loophole allowing exceptions to the requirements.
- Read the rent control law yourself, even if you have the world's best attorney. Since you're dealing with *your* money, you will often spot loopholes that the attorney overlooked. Call these to the attorney's attention.

- It's completely legal, and ethical, to read the law and search for ways in which you can make rent increases within the framework of the law.

You *must* have good legal advice in your real estate activities. But you also *must* look out for your own interests. My experience with real estate attorneys keeps me constantly on the alert to new developments in the law so I can gently "remind" the attorney of the most recent changes in the law. This has paid off for me several times when the attorney was not aware of the latest changes in the law.

You're now ready to take your first big step in real estate—if you've found a property that meets the standards we've suggested. So let's take that first step!

TAKE OVER YOUR FIRST INCOME PROPERTY

To start, you'll be scared! I've never met a BWB—myself included—who wasn't scared when taking over his or her first income property. Why do BWBs get frightened by this first step? For a number of reasons:

- You realize that what's ahead is unknown. So you begin to fear the future and what it might—or might not—hold for you and your business.

- You're spending a large sum of money—in some cases more than you've ever spent in your life before. Just the thought of that much money can be frightening.

- As a BWB you're taking on a large debt—again, perhaps the biggest debt of your life, to date. Again, you wonder: How will I be able to pay this huge debt off?

- Your life is changing—from that of a salaried flunky to that of an entrepreneur. Any change can be scary. So you react like most of the rest of us!

But don't worry! You *will* be safe. And the deal *will* work out to your advantage—if you follow the tips I give you. So don't be frightened by worry over the deal. A little worry gets your adrenaline moving so you become more alert and watch for little problems that may pop up.

To take over your first property, follow these simple steps in the sequence I suggest:

1. Review the numbers of the property—income, expenses, mortgage payments, and so on. Do this several times, allowing a few days between each review so you come to the numbers with a fresh view each time.

2. Have your attorney review the numbers and the legal aspects of the purchase. Listen to what the attorney advises. Don't ignore good advice!

3. Make your offer to the seller. Do this through your attorney so any "earnest money" or binder (a small deposit on the property showing your good faith in the deal) is refundable if the deal doesn't go through. Why lose even $100 when—with careful planning—it will be returned to you—completely legally.

4. Negotiate the price, if necessary. Your riches notebook gives you the data you need to negotiate the deal because it shows what you're willing to pay for the property.

5. Keep in mind at all times that when you buy income real estate you're actually buying an *income stream* produced by an asset that will—in general—rise in value as time passes. The source of this income stream is the real estate you're buying.

6. Keep in close touch with the lenders you want to handle your funding. Let them know how the deal is progressing. Communication is often the best weapon you have in getting a lender to give you the funds you need for a real estate deal. Rushing into a lender at the last minute and demanding a quick loan is *not* the way to get financing for any kind of real estate! Give the lender time to analyze your project, and you'll be almost certain to get the funds you need!

7. Take your time with the paperwork. On every real estate deal you'll have lots of papers to sign. Don't rush the signings. Have your attorney explain each document to you *before* you sign it. Then you'll get a much better understanding of what you're doing. Further, you'll be better prepared for your next real estate deal!

8. Be calm at all times during the closing (when the ownership of the property is transferred from the seller to you). Sometimes emotions will run high when a seller realizes that the moment of parting with

a favorite property has arrived. Keep your cool—you want the deal to go through and not be stalled by more discussions and negotiations. At the closing the seller will deliver the deed to the property to you. Also, some closing costs will be paid by both the seller and the buyer (you). Your attorney will outline the probable costs to you before closing and will provide you with a *closing statement* summarizing these costs.

9. Recognize—here and now—that you'll be a bit nervous at the closing. We all are! But remember this: Buying a good piece of real estate is never a mistake. You can't go wrong. The property *will* rise in value while giving you a positive cash flow—if you follow the various guidelines in this book. What's more, you'll be less nervous at your second closing. By the time you reach your tenth closing you will, I guarantee, be relaxed and ready to do business with any seller.

10. Learn to live with your first property once it's yours. Take time to become familiar with all aspects of your property—its income, expenses, the way to do business with it, and so on. Allow at least three months for this learning period. Then you'll be ready to go on to your next property in a relaxed and confident manner. There's no point in being uptight about your financial future. You should have some fun in business, too!

Your real estate road to financial freedom can be smooth and hassle free if you plan right. Real estate is a long-term investment that can make you a millionaire in your spare time. As one reader writes:

> *Twenty-eight years after reading my first Ty Hicks "How to Buy Real Estate" book, I own (free and clear) properties worth more than $6 million, all thanks to my favorite author, Ty Hicks.*

The writer of this letter is a highly successful financial planner who invests in real estate in his spare time. On many of his properties he has refinanced them over and over, taking tax-free cash out of them. *You* can develop *your* real estate investments on a part-time basis while spending your "prime" time doing something else that interests you. So many people do this that I'm sure you can, too!

SUCCESS STRATEGIES FOR BUILDING
YOUR REAL ESTATE WEALTH IN GOOD TIMES
AND BAD TIMES

1. Prepare a list of ways to do zero cash deals in your area. zero cash deals vary from one area to another. Thus, in the country you'll do zero cash deals differently from in the city. So if you're operating in a city, prepare your zero cash deals list for city-type properties—which are usually multi-unit structures. In the country you'll often buy single-unit properties, some of which may have extensive land holdings attached to them. Having your zero cash deals list handy can allow you to concentrate on the details of each deal. With such a focus you can swing better deals, giving your seller benefits he/she never expected. And you—of course—benefit from a zero-down deal. Items to include in your zero cash deal are: (a) Seller take-back of a mortgage for the down payment on the property you want to buy; (b) Seller taking out a loan for the down payment with you assuming responsibility for full repayment of the loan; (c) Using your credit-card lines of credit to get down-payment money; (d) Using a wraparound mortgage to take over the property you want. As the famous slogan says—Be Prepared! Your zero cash takeover list will keep you prepared!

2. Build up your credit-card lines of credit. You can use the money in your credit-card line(s) of credit quickly and easily (a) without telling anyone what you plan to use the money for; (b) without having to have your loan application studied by a loan committee; (c) without a long delay in getting your money—funds in a line of credit are available immediately, on demand; (d) without having to prepare, and present, a business plan for your project. Aim for at least $5,000 in each line of credit. Why? Because with five such lines you have access to $25,000 immediately; ten such lines will give you $50,000 instantly. Both these sums are good amounts for the down payment for your first or second. Once you have a few properties you can get more credit cards, with more lines of credit to expand the amount of cash available to you. And if you want to improve your credit, as for our *45 Ways to Better Credit* when you subscribe to my newsletter. See the back of this book for details on subscribing to my newsletter.

3. Get access to personal loans by forming relationships with banks and credit unions. Knowing a banker and credit union loan officer can do wonders for your zero cash deals. How? By giving you quick, easy access to personal loans which you can use for the down payment on properties you want to buy. Today personal loans go as high as $35,000 per loan. One such loan could be enough for you to buy the property you seek. And by combining two or more such loans you could have enough for the down payment on a major property which can give you an income in the range of $100,000 per year. To establish a relationship with a bank or credit union, take these easy steps: (a) Look under "Banks" and "Credit Unions" in your *Yellow Pages* to locate such lenders locally. (b) Call and ask for their free information on personal loans. (c) Review the material you receive to see if you can qualify for a personal loan. (d) Fill out the application they send you, typing it throughout, except for your signature. (e) Visit the lender with your application and ask the loan officer to review it, after telling him/her that you're not applying for a loan at this time. Instead, you're just asking for an opinion as to whether the application would be accepted as presented. (f) Listen to what you're told about your application. Make any changes needed. (g) When you need your loan, go back to the same loan officer and present your fine-tuned application. Your chances of being accepted are high. Do this with at least six lenders so you increase your chance of getting the loan(s) you need!

4. *Search out sources of zero- or low-down-payment properties* of the type you want to own. Look—in your area—for (a) bank-owned properties—called REQ (Real Estate Owned). Banks will often allow you to take over such properties for zero down, even paying your closing costs. Contact the bank mortgage department for lists of REQ properties. (b) Call your local Sheriffs Department for lists of tax-sale properties available. Some of these might be available to you for zero cash down. Ask for their free list of tax-sales; they'll send it to you on a regular basis. Review it for possible zero cash deals. (c) Contact the Federal Government— many agencies, such as the Internal Revenue Service, the Federal Housing Administration, the Veteran's Administration—may have some zero cash tax-sale properties available. Again, ask to be put on their free mailing list. (d) Surf the Internet for properties available at bargain prices. You may find properties in your local area for sale that no one else knows about. Keep looking—soon you'll become an expert on zero cash properties and you'll have so many that you won't know which to pick first! If you're puzzled, call me and I'll try to help you. See the last line of the last chapter in this book for my business telephone and fax numbers.

IMPORTANT POINTERS TO KEEP IN MIND

- Follow the zero cash route in real estate today because it has built-in success factors for you.

- Control more real estate without putting up a penny of your own by applying the zero cash method outlined in this book.

- Work hard—which is really fun—it *does* pay off in real estate investing because you get better results, sooner.

- One hundred percent financing—also called zero cash—almost always requires two, or more, loans. It is seldom done with just one loan.

- The name of the game in real estate today is positive cash flow. Never buy real estate with a negative cash flow unless you're sure you can make it positive in a short time.

- Don't be too quick to scoff at a financial offer that has rates you never heard of before. There are plenty of low-interest-rate offers available to you.

- Improve your negotiating skills with zero cash deals, and your real estate future will be rosy *and* profitable.

- Never pay the asking price for real estate! You can almost always get a significant amount knocked off the asking price by just a small amount of negotiation. Why pay the asking price when almost every seller expects you to knock down the price?

- Link your life goals to property types. Buy only that type of property which will help you achieve your lifetime goals. You will be more successful when you see your real estate contributing to the goals of you and your loved ones.

- Look locally at the start when seeking suitable real estate. Local properties are easier to buy and pose fewer problems for real estate BWBs.

- Start a riches notebook to keep track of your real estate plans and deals. Such a notebook can be a valuable record for your future planning in building your wealth.

- Make an offer as soon as you find a suitable property. Remember, never pay the asking price!

- Follow these safe rules when buying any income property:
  - Use a competent real estate attorney.
  - Buy only positive cash flow properties.
  - Work out a zero cash deal with the seller.
  - Snap up properties from owners under pressure.
  - Check rent laws in your investment area.
- Be calm and efficient when taking over your first income property, with your attorney at your side. Never panic. We're all a little nervous when taking over our first income property.
- Careful planning of your real estate tactics will keep your road to wealth in real estate smooth and clear.

Build Your Wealth with a Powerful Real Estate Tool—Foreclosures

Foreclosures—where a lender or a government agency takes back a property on which money is owed and unpaid—can be bargains in bad times for BWBs like yourself. And in gloomy conditions there are plenty of bargain-priced foreclosure properties easily available to you at low prices for little cash.

Properties go into foreclosure because:

- People buy more expensive homes than they can really afford.
- Developers fail to analyze the market for their property correctly.
- Investors think the gravy-train times of recent years are still with us, overlooking the tough and tighter attitudes of today's bank lenders.

Even big-time real estate investors can get "nicked" by foreclosures when they ignore the grim realities of today's real estate market. But BWBs like yourself can make a fortune from foreclosures—if you look beyond today's dark clouds to the sunny profits behind them!

BWBs who *do* look ahead, I find, have good ideas on how they will build a fortune in their chosen field—real estate. But most lack a big bundle of cash to use as a down payment on a profitable income property. So when they come to me for advice I suggest that they:

- Get started with income property that requires little down payment cash—such as a foreclosure
- Operate a number of such properties to build a strong cash flow so as to

- Position yourself so you have the cash flow to make payments on future loans you will take out to buy conventional (nonforeclosure) income properties
- Allow yourself to acquire as many properties as you need to give you the monthly income you seek for your financial independence

One of the most powerful ways for you to get the cash income which will free you from 9-to-5 grief is to buy *real estate foreclosure properties.* Let's see how you can get rich with foreclosures.

WHY FORECLOSURES ARE SO POWERFUL FOR YOU

A foreclosed property is one which a lender has taken back because the person who borrowed to take over the property is not making the payments on the loan. Or the property may have been taken over by a taxing authority, such as a town, county, or state for failure to pay real estate taxes. And if income taxes have not been paid, the property might have been taken over by the Internal Revenue Service or a state income tax bureau.

Many of these properties are then offered to the public at sharply reduced prices. Why? Because the lender or other organization that foreclosed the property just wants the money owed to it. No lender or taxing authority wants to own and operate real estate. They just want the monthly payment, or tax repayment, due them. So they'll often sell real estate to you at a token of its real value. Foreclosures are powerful for *you* because:

- You get big value for small dollars.
- You can *quickly* build a sizable holding of valuable properties.
- You can often get started for just $100, or so.
- You will have wide availability of choice properties, allowing you to pick and choose those properties that will be best for your financial future.

A foreclosure can be a money machine for you which you take over for a fraction of its real value. And with the U.S. Department of Housing and Urban Development (HUD) offering thousands of good properties in hundreds of different locations, you have an array of income opportunities seldom seen before anywhere. With foreclosures you can make big money in both strong and sluggish real estate markets.

When a lender owns a foreclosed property, it is often referred to as an REO—real estate owned (which the lender really does not want to own). Real estate BWBs can really do well with REOs and foreclosed properties from the FDIC, the Internal Revenue Service (IRS), the Federal Housing Administration (FHA), and Housing and Urban Development (HUD) as did these BWBs who closed deals recently:

- A duplex bought from a government agency for $4,040 was sold 10 days later to an investor who paid $11,000, giving a profit of nearly $7,000.

- Another investor bought a badly abused home in a good location and did nothing to it except allow it to fall apart some more. Five years after buying the house he sold the land for three times what he paid for the house and the land!

- A new investor bought some 32 single-family homes from a government agency for $30,000. That's less than $1,000 per home. Such homes can easily be resold for many times their under-$1,000 price. Or they can be rented at an enormous monthly profit because the loan payment on the house will be less than $20 per month!

With such bargains you really can't go wrong if you buy wisely. And this chapter shows you exactly how to choose foreclosed properties that could put *you* into the millionaire class in just a few years. Why slave at a daily grind when—with some wise planning—you can be free of the yoke of working for someone else? Let's get *you* started on one of the best investments you can make, which can give you:

- Tax-favored income—often completely free of all income taxes
- Control of valuable assets, often with no down payment of any kind
- Yields of more than 20 percent on the small sums you invest in foreclosure properties
- Steady after-tax cash income that grows as you expand your property holdings while investing just minute amounts of money

- Cheap financing for the funds you need, getting money at low interest rates
- Acquisition of valuable properties at anywhere from 10 percent to 50 percent of their current market value
- Distressed property takeovers at below-market offers that can—and will—make you rich

WHERE TO FIND FORECLOSURE PROPERTIES TO BUY

There are a number of sources of foreclosure properties you can buy. In terms of general sources, you have:

1. The local taxing authority—this can be your city, county, or state
2. Banks in your area; under this term you will include similar lenders, namely, credit unions, savings and loan associations, and mortgage bankers
3. Federal government departments, including the Internal Revenue Service, Federal Housing Administration, Small Business Administration (SBA), General Services Administration (GSA), and so on
4. Bankruptcy courts handling the three types of bankruptcies: Chapter 7, Chapter 11, and Chapter 13

To work with any of these groups you must know what steps to take. Here's how to get started with each source.

Local Taxing Authority

When a home owner doesn't pay his or her real estate taxes, the local tax authority will come looking for the money. The same is true, of course, of commercial and multifamily income properties.

Who does the looking? This can vary from state to state. But most states have a tax collector's office responsible for collecting real estate taxes. You can find the name and address of the office in your state by looking in the back of your telephone book in the blue other-color pages under state and county offices. Once you have the name and telephone number of the office in charge:

1. Call the tax collector and ask for information on how they dispose of properties on which the real estate taxes are delinquent, that is, not paid.

2. Get full information on how, where, and when such properties are offered for sale. Be sure to get data on the payment requirements, that is, how you must make a deposit on a property you want to buy. Some states require cash; others seek a certified check. But no matter what is required, arranging payment is easy because the amount you'll have to lay out is usually small.

Most tax-delinquent properties are sold at an auction with voice bids. You attend the auction—which is fun—and call out your bid when a property you want is offered for sale. The smallest bid you're allowed at most auctions is the sum of tax due plus interest on tax due plus penalty, if any. Thus, if $2,000 in taxes were due for 1 year, and the interest on delinquent taxes is 10 percent, and there is a penalty of 50 percent of the tax due, your lowest bid would be $2,000 tax due + (0.1 × $2,000 interest for 1 year) + (0.5 × $2,000 penalty) = $2,000 + $200 + $1,000 = $3,200.

You can, of course, bid more, if you think the property is worth the higher bid. But you are *not* allowed to bid less. Why? Because the taxing authority wants to get its money out of the property.

Attending several property auctions can be a "college education" in foreclosures. Why? Because:

- You'll meet people who are just starting—like yourself. And you'll also meet people who've been doing it for years. They'll teach you plenty—if you just keep your mouth shut and listen!

- Seeing what bids are made on various properties will quickly show you the value levels investors attach to certain areas, types of construction, and so on. Knowing this will help you make better future bids that win the property you seek.

- You will quickly get a "feel" for going prices in the area and the upside potential for you when you take over a foreclosure property you plan to "flip," that is, resell to another investor soon after you buy it.

Be sure to check the *equity of redemption law* for your state. This is the time period during which the former owner of a foreclosed property can reclaim the property by paying the back taxes, interest, penalties, and legal fees. Many states will not allow auction of a foreclosed property unless the redemption period has expired. But to be sure, you *must* get exact information from the state or taxing authority. Your attorney can be a great help to you in explaining the law in your area.

In some states you will find real estate and personal property auctioned at a *sheriff's* sale. The same general guidelines apply, as for tax authority sales. Again, look in your local telephone book for the phone number of the sheriff in your area. Call, and get their free data on sheriff sales.

Some sheriff sales are made because a person has obtained a judgment against the property owner. The holder of the judgment is demanding that the property be sold to pay off the judgment. Attend a few sheriff sales and you'll learn a lot about both real property and human nature!

Real Estate Lenders in Your Area

Banks despise REO properties. Why? Because they're very expensive and cost the banks big bucks. That's why banks and other real estate lenders are so anxious to sell REOs at auction or on a one-to-one basis.

But if you call your local bank and ask for the Mortgage Department, you may be told that they don't have any REO properties. Why is this? Because many banks are ashamed to admit they made "bad" real estate loans. How can you get around this denial?

The best way to learn what REO properties a bank or other lender has is to:

- Be persistent in your questioning. Don't take "no" for an answer!
- Ask to speak to top-level people in the Mortgage Department. The top honcho may be a lot franker with you than an underpaid clerk who just follows the party line and feels more powerful because he or she can deny you the right to useful information.
- Get the lender to send you a list of its REO properties. Such a list can give you valuable insights into the types and locations of properties funded by this lender.

You'll often bid on a lender REO in private. That is, you won't go to a public auction. Why? Because the lender doesn't want it broadcast all over town that it's trying to unload REO properties.

As some of my readers know, I'm director of a large real estate lender. Less than 1 percent of our real estate loans are in trouble. This is only about one-fourth of the national average. So we're in great shape with our real estate loan portfolio, which approaches some $100 million.

Yet when we foreclose on a property, we do it very quietly. And then we sell off the property quickly—and quietly. Why? Because we prefer not to bandy about that we have a problem loan or two.

And our board of directors is constantly shouting at me "We gotta get more money out in real estate loans! When are *you* going to come up with more good borrowers? If you don't get more money into the hands of real estate buyers you may not be reelected director next year!"

So you see, a nonperforming loan now and then doesn't scare professional lenders. As I often say to the board, "People who cross streets will be hit by cars. Likewise, lenders who make loans will have an occasional default. But this won't stop us from making more loans!" Why? Because a lender makes more money from interest on loans than from any other source of income. So why cut off your main source of income when less than 1 percent of your decisions go bad?

To get a list of banks, S&Ls, credit unions, mortgage companies, and other lenders in your area, consult your local Yellow Pages. Then give them a ring. You'll find that you're really welcome, if you want to take their REO properties off their hands.

Federal Government Departments

The federal government can be an important source of foreclosures for you. To get the phone numbers of local offices of the departments and administrations listed earlier, consult your local phone book. (If you live in a remote area, you'll have to look in a large-city phone book.)

You can easily get lists of property for sale by calling the government department or administration and asking to be put on their mailing list. You'll be sent—free of charge—regular mailings of property that's offered. Along with the list will be instructions on how to bid for the property you seek. Some bids must be sealed, that is, enclosed in an envelope that's sealed from anyone except the group that opens the bid. That way, you don't know what the other person bid, and the bidders don't know what *you* bid. The highest bid usually wins the property.

A number of state and Federal government departments and agencies now run listings of their services and foreclosure offerings on the Internet. So if you have a computer, or can get to your local public library to use one, you can easily go online and access these listings. Many of these listings will help you build your real estate wealth using borrowed money for buying foreclosures.

Procedures will vary somewhat with each department or administration. Here are brief highlights of each so you'll know how to start:

- *Internal Revenue Service:* Can seize and sell properties when income taxes have not been paid. You can get on the *free* mailing list by writing or calling IRS offices near you. When you buy an IRS-seized property you are helping the country because the money goes to pay back taxes.

- *Federal Housing Administration:* Foreclosed properties—from single-family homes to multiunit buildings containing hundreds of apartments—are available through FHA sales. Some sales are for people who plan to live in the property they buy, primarily single-family homes. Other sales are for investors—people like yourself who are buying for income. You can get on both free mailing lists by calling or writing your local FHA office.

- *Small Business Administration:* Sells both real estate and business equipment at auction to interested buyers. Typically you'll be required to put down 25 percent of your offering price in cash or certified check. But prices can be low, so the amount you'll have to bring with you can be small. Free lists—again—are available for the asking.

- *General Services Administration:* Sells many types of property—real, personal, surplus, and so on. Offerings range from tiny buildings to hundreds of acres of land. Get on the free listing to receive notices of upcoming sales of seized and surplus properties.

- *Veterans Administration:* Mostly sells single-family homes. Prices can be extremely low—sometimes just $25! Get on the free listing to get in on the gold available here.

Bankruptcy Courts

Courts hold bankruptcy sales of real estate owned by both individuals and companies. To learn what properties are being offered in your area, write the clerk of the court (listed in your local phone book). Ask for the free listing. You'll be sent a list of trustees holding property for bankruptcy sale. Along with the list will be a schedule of upcoming bankruptcy sales.

A PIECE OF SOUND PREPURCHASE ADVICE

Attend a few sales to get a feel for the procedures. Talk to people there. They'll give you lots of valuable information on how to win at one of these sales. When you see a property you like, bid on it. You may get a jewel for just a few dollars!

HOW TO DECIDE IF YOU WANT TO BID ON A FORECLOSURE

You can control your financial life with just a little thinking and a few notes on a piece of paper! Some people call this *planning,* which it is. But I find that many BWBs are turned off by the word "planning." So I just call it deciding what to bid. That way, BWBs go ahead and do what's best for their financial future. If I can get you to do that, my job is done!

To decide if you want to bid on a property, you must:

- Know what type(s) of property you want to invest in—single-family, multifamily, vacant land, and so on
- Have a dollar amount you can handle comfortably, based on your present financial situation
- Decide how much work you can do (or have done) on a property after you take it over

To get answers to these questions, you should use a small *offer notebook* in which you make notes to yourself that answer these questions. Why? Because without such answers, you really can't bid intelligently on any foreclosure.

How should you decide what type(s) of properties are best for *you?* Here are a few guidelines that will help you, based on my dealing with thousands of BWBs throughout the world:

- *Residential properties* are usually the best starter types if you enjoy meeting and dealing with people. While it's true you *can* stay in the background and collect your rents by mail, the most successful BWBs meet, and mingle with, their tenants. This way they get to know what housing problems the tenants have. Then the BWB takes action to solve the problem(s) to create a happy and satisfied tenant.

- *Industrial properties* like factories and warehouses don't require that you deal with as many people as residential properties. But industrial properties require previous management experience if they are to be run profitably. So I suggest that you delay taking over such properties until after you've had some experience with other types of properties.

- *Commercial properties* such as office buildings, stores, shopping centers, and the like, are good—if you start small. And today there are plenty of opportunities to start small because there are thousands of desirable properties for sale through state and Federal government agencies. To get free listings of these properties, just call, fax, or write the agency which interests you and ask to be put on their free mailing list. You will also find listings of many government agencies on the Internet on the agency's website. Again, start small with commercial properties and you won't go wrong! For, as they say, "Small is beautiful."

- *Vacant land* can be obtained for almost mere pennies! Some government land sells for as little as $1 per acre. But the land has *no* improvements. That is, there are *no* streets, *no* sewers, *no* electric service, and so on. So unless you have a specific buyer, or user, for such land, stay away from it at the start! Later, when you have more experience, you can start to invest in vacant land.

Now that you have rough guidelines on the *type* of property you might bid on, let's look at how much money you can invest. But first let me "paint a picture of you" so you understand where I'm coming from, good friend. I see you as:

> A hardworking person who has held several jobs during your career; today you're at a crossroad in your life. You enjoy working. But you don't enjoy the paltry wages you're earning. So you're looking around for another source of income which will eventually allow you to quit your boring, dead-end job. You'll build your business to the point where you're financially free to enjoy your hobbies, take vacations when you want, and, above all, not have to answer to a capricious boss. Last, you've saved a few dollars from your paycheck to invest in real estate. But you'd really like to hang onto that money and start on zero cash.

Now your actual picture may be a little different from the above. But, in the main, it will fit. Given this picture, how much can—or should—you invest? Here's my answer:

- *Invest as little as possible in your foreclosure real estate.* This means you should look for the lowest-priced foreclosures in your area. How can you do this? Get printed results of foreclosures in your area and look them over. See what the average price is for the foreclosures sold. Some may go for as little as $100. If this amount represents the most you can invest now, plan on looking for offerings of this type in future sales. With a price averaging, say, $1,000, and with that amount in your kitty, look for offerings of that kind. Keep in mind your goal of investing as little as possible at all times.

- *Look beyond your buying price to the amount of money you'll have to lay out to fix up the property.* Some foreclosures are in beautiful condition and you won't have to do much to offer them for sale at a big profit. Or you can offer the property for rent without doing any interior or exterior work. If a small amount of painting is needed, you can have the tenant do it—just supply the materials. Most new tenants are willing to take on this task because it gives them a nicer home with little effort.

Exhibit 3–1

OFFERING GUIDELINES*

Cash on Hand $ __2,150.00__   Date: __May 1__

Money Needed for Emergencies $__2,500.00__

Annual Savings for Last 3 Years $__800.00__

Future Probable Savings for Next 5 Years

    Year 1 $__900.00__

    Year 2 $__1,000.00__

    Year 3 $__1,500.00__

    Year 4 $__1,800.00__

    Year 5 $__2,000.00__

Amount I'm Willing to Invest in Properties Annually $__1,500.00__

*Almost everyone has a money "comfort zone." This is an amount of money in a savings account, certificate of deposit, money market fund, or other form of "safe" investment which gives a person a feeling of being able to cope with almost any kind of financial problem. Be sure you know your comfort zone and have enough money on hand to feel that you're solidly in that zone.

- *Control your offers using your "offering guidelines" sheet* (Exhibit 3–1, in your offer notebook). Then you won't be carried away by a beautiful property on which you make an emotional offer far beyond your financial capability. You *can,* as we said earlier, take charge of your financial future. And the best way to do this is to control the amount of money you invest in foreclosure properties.

- *Look for bargain properties everywhere.* In some inner-city areas you'll see foreclosures for an *upset price,* or minimum bid price of $25. I'm sure you can afford such an investment because it's a relatively small amount for a property you can either sell or rent out. Again, of course, you *must* be alert to any work that must be done *after* you buy the property. A good friend of mine, Cliff Leonard, who has an excellent course on foreclosure procedures, described in the appendix to this book, uses the evaluation sheet in Exhibit 3–2 to predict the profit he'll earn on a foreclosure property which he has earlier studied in his property information sheet in Exhibit 3–3. You can use such forms to be certain that bargain properties don't have a big back-end cost for renovations and other updates.

USE YOUR SUCCESS FORMULA
TO PICK THE RIGHT DEALS

You now have a wealth of data about local foreclosures and about yourself which you accumulated using the tips just given. You're ready to mine the golden lode of the world of foreclosures. Your success formula should give these key numbers for every property you'll consider:

- *Price:* Pick a price level beyond which you will not go, based on your offering guidelines in Exhibit 3–1. You *must* control your investments so you have a secure future. You'll often hear stories of how people broke the rules and made millions. But, as a BWB, you must follow the rules until you've built a strong feel for properties you can easily sell quickly or rent at high levels in just days. I want you to succeed, and I'm here to help you do so. The best guarantee of success for you is to plan and carefully follow what has worked for thousands of other BWBs buying foreclosures in their spare time! Follow the rules I gave you at the start and I guarantee you won't go wrong. I'm so sure of this that I'm willing to offer you financing sources for your good projects, if you're a 2-year, or longer, subscriber to my newsletter, described in the appendix.

- *Income:* You *must* get an income from your foreclosure properties. If you don't, there's no point in buying them! Your income can be either in the form of *rent* from units you lease to tenants or in the form of *profit* you derive from the sale of units you take over in foreclosure actions. Either way, you *must* come away from each deal with MIF that you can spend for yourself and loved ones, invest in other properties, or save for the future. Real estate, as we said earlier, is a *business.* As such, it must give you an income. If it doesn't, get into another business!

- *Expenses:* Every property you deal with that's in foreclosure will have expenses associated with it. Exhibit 3–2 shows you the typical expenses you might encounter with a foreclosure property. It's rare that any property will have all these expenses. But most will have some of these expenses. So you must be ready to pay them. And the way you get ready is to

  - Know how much you can afford to spend on your investments, Exhibit 3–1

  - Analyze—in advance—your probable expenses, using Exhibit 3–2. While this may seem like work, it really is *fun,* especially when you go to the bank to deposit your income or profits checks!

- *Cash flow:* You *must* have a positive cash flow from every rental property you own, no matter how you bought it. People sometimes think that if they get a property for a low price, it doesn't need a positive cash flow to make money for them. Not so! You *must* have a positive cash flow for *every* property—even if it costs you only $25 to take over. Why? Because a negative cash flow property can drain your resources, leading to financial ruin. So avoid such properties like the plague. It's better to take longer to find the right positive cash flow property than to jump into an investment that gives you nothing but grief. So don't be fooled by a low purchase price—you still *must* have a positive cash flow from every property!

Exhibit 3-2

EVALUATION SHEET

Property Address *123 Main St.*

Approx. Value (As Is) $ *60,000*

Retail Value Repaired $ *95,000*

Size of Lot *75'* × *100'* # Bedrooms *3* # Bathrooms *2*

Cost to Resell:

Cost to Resell:		Acquisition Cost:	
Cleanup Cost	$ *250*	Cost to Acquire Deed $ *2,000*	
Commission	*5,700*	Cost to Bring Current *4,000*	
Title Insurance	*175*	(One lump sum paid to agent of mortgage company)	
Legal Cost	*750*	Title Insurance	*175*
Repair Cost	*2,075*	Transfer Fee	*1,500*
Escrow Fees	*200*	Documentary Stamps	*150*
Pro-Rata Insurance	*350*	Insurance (fire, etc.)	*600*
Pro-Rata Taxes	*850*	Junior Mortgages	*18,000*
Termite Work or Bond	*100*	(Cost to bring current or pay off)	
Points If FHA or VA	*0*	Junior Mortgages	*0*
Miscellaneous	*500*	Encumbrances or Liens	*400*

Total Cost to Resell $ *10,950* Total Cost to Acquire $ *26,825*

Total Cost to Sell $ *10,950* + Total Cost to Acquire $ *26,825* + All

Outstanding Loans $ *37,150* – Sales Price = $ *20,075* Your Net Profit

Possible Cost:

Paint Exterior	$ *200*	Landscape	*100*	Screens	*100*
Paint Interior	*250*	Fencing	*0*	Sewers	*0*
Termite	*100*	Windows	*200*	Heating	*100*
Floor Covering	*100*	Roof	*100*	Miscel.	*100*
Yard Work	*0*	Plumbing	*200*	Wallpaper	*0*
Kitchen Work	*225*	A/C	*0*		
Electrical	*300*	Hardware	*0*		

Exhibit 3–3

PROPERTY INFORMATION SHEET

Case # _123_ Date _5-21_

Foreclosure _yes_ Delinquent Taxes _____ Levy _____ Other _____

Attorney & Phone _T. Jones_ ^{vs} _123-4567_

Address of Property _123 Main St._

Legal _____

Address of Owner _123 Main St._ Phone # _432-7654_

Mortgage Company _ABC Mtg._ Phone # _____

Mortgage Amount _$37,150_

Interest Rate _8.5_ % Origination Date _1-85_

Type of Mortgage:

Conventional _yes_ FHA _____ VA _____ Wrap _____ Other _____

Prepayment Penalty _none._ Amount _____

Monthly Payment $ _310_ Mortgage Balance _$37,150_

Homestead Exemption Yes _____ No _✓_

Assessed Value $ _12,000_ RE# _____

* *

Taxes-Encumbrances-Judgments-Federal Tax Liens-Problems

	Name	Recorded	Date	$ Amount Due
1.	J. Smith	Yes	1-98	400.00
2.				
3.				
4.				
5.				

Cost to Bring Current $ _400.00 + 150.33 interest._

Positive Features of Property _Good location; near shopping and transportation._

Negative Features _needs repairs; electrical system must be inspected._

Let's take a look at some real-life examples of BWBs who're using the foreclosure route to financial freedom that allows them to kiss their last boss goodbye:

A BWB in the Northeast found a building having an MAI (Member, Appraisal Institute) appraisal of $1.2 million. (Such appraisals are highly respected everywhere and are the basis of many real estate sales.) But the building was on the verge of foreclosure and the owner wanted out. This BWB saw an opportunity to take over a beautiful building for zero dollars down. The one requirement was that the building be renovated to make it more suitable for renting. The BWB figured that once he had control of the building he could use it as collateral for a property improvement loan. So he took over the building from the seller for zero cash down with a promise to pay the seller income from the rentals for a period of time. Then he used the building to serve as collateral for a $70,000 improvement loan. Today he's sitting pretty with a strong positive cash flow from the building, including payments to the seller. He's building his wealth with the most powerful real estate tool—the foreclosure (in this case a near-foreclosure!).

Another BWB, in the Midwest, has his own business selling popcorn franchises. But, as a profitable sideline, he buys and fixes up foreclosure properties which he then sells at a big profit. Not being handy with tools, this BWB subcontracts the fix-up work to local firms that do it in their spare time or when they're not busy with their regular work. This fill-in work is done at a much lower cost than regular rehab work because it's extra income for the subcontractors. Renting the property out is not a goal of this BWB. All he wants to do is sell the property at a profit. And his experience shows that "Even in bad times, I've been able to sell every property when I had it fixed up and priced a bit lower than anything else in the area. By taking the property over at foreclosure, my cost is so low that I can easily beat local prices and still make a bundle on every sale. The key to making money when real estate sales are slow is competitive pricing!"

NEW LENDING METHODS MAKE
YOUR LIFE EASIER

Today lenders are so anxious to put money into the hands of real estate borrowers that they developed the "125% loan." With this type of loan they'll lend you 125% of the equity you have in a property. Thus, if you have a property worth $250,000 with $100,000 equity in it, they'll lend you $1.25 \times \$100,000 = \$125,000$, using the property as collateral. This is a much larger loan than the traditional "75% loan" which would give you only $75,000 on your $100,000 equity.

You can use the money you get from your 125% loan to bid on the best foreclosures in your area, or anywhere else. Having the money to bid on good foreclosures puts you in the driver's seat!

MAKING THE BID PROCESS WORK FOR YOU

Except in private foreclosures, as in the case of the first BWB, you'll have to *bid* on properties you want to buy. Foreclosure bids are made:

- In public, where you call out your offer, or
- In secrecy, with a sealed bid in an envelope

At the start you're better off attending public auctions where you hear and see other offers for various properties. Each auction will be a learning experience for you because:

- You'll see how other bidders value properties.
- You'll talk to other bidders and get useful information about properties and the procedures used.
- You'll get to know the auction staff; this can be helpful when you make bids for yourself.

Sealed bids can be traps for a beginner. Why? Because you may—in your desire to get started quickly—bid much too *high*. Sure, you may "win" the bid. But you may be paying two, three, or four times what an experienced foreclosure operator would pay.

To learn how to make safe sealed bids, take these easy steps:

1. Watch for sealed-bid offers.
2. Check each offer out and write down what you believe is a fair price for the property.
3. Compare your price with the actual winning price when it's published by the foreclosure authority (public auctions conducted by government organizations are required by law to publish the winning bid amount).

Now let's get you to the public auction of your choice in a condition that will guarantee you a winning outcome. Here are your steps to
success.

Be Prepared

You can't go to a public foreclosure auction without certain supplies.
These are:

- A copy of the auction announcement. This will be sent to you free
  of charge when you ask for it. It will also be sent free once you're
  on the list of interested persons maintained by the foreclosure
  authority.

- Your "offer notebook" in which you can record the prices and other
  details of the sales that take place.

- A pen, a watch, and some cash.

For the first few auctions you attend, just go as a watcher. Why?
Because that way you'll learn a lot without having to put up any money at
all. Then when you're ready to start bidding you'll be an "old hand" at the
methods and procedures. Coming prepared will give you the jump on others who rush in and expect to close a deal in just minutes. Sensible buys
are *not* made this way!

Let's see some of the ways in which you can prepare yourself to win
at any auction, based on the auction data supplied to you:

Auction Data Supplied	Your Readying Action
Absolute auction of 30-unit rental building	Do you want to own the building being offered?
Financing available for qualified buyers	What are the qualifications? Do you qualify?
Certified check or money order for 10 percent of offering price required	Do you know what you'll offer? Do you have 10 percent of your offer in the required form?
No reasonable offered refused	Have you decided on your "reasonable" offer and know its exact amount?

Auction Data Supplied	Your Readying Action
Minimum bid of $ _____ considered	Do you know how much your maximum bid will be? Does it match the minimum bid considered?
Buyer will assume the mortgage debt on the property at the time of the sale	Do you know the amount of the mortgage debt? Is this amount suitable for you, based on your other numbers for the property?
Balance of payment must be made within 2 weeks of the purchase	Can you make the balance of the payment within 2 weeks?
Contact John/Jane for more information on this property	Have you obtained as much data as you can before you bid?

Watch your local papers for auction notices. Read each carefully. This will prepare you better for what you'll need to win at auctions in *your* area!

Arrive on Time

Every auction is started at a specific time. Arrive *before* the stated time. Why? Because then you can:

- Look over the attendees and "size them up" to see if they offer strong competition

- Get a good seat where you can see all the action

- Fill out, and sign, any forms that might be requested of you

- Examine photos, maps, drawings, and documents that may be offered to help you make your buying decision

- Look over the people who'll control the auction so you get a good idea of how helpful they might be

When you arrive and find that you're the only person at the auction, you'll know that your chances of winning are great. If you arrive and the auction room is jammed, you know you're probably in for some competition. But don't despair!

Wait until a property you want is offered and make your bid. If you're on time, you *always* have a chance of winning!

Have Any Needed Funds with You

At most auctions you'll be required to pay something to secure your bid. This may be as low as $10, or $25, or $100. But don't go to any auction expecting to "walk away" with "your property without leaving some money—even just a small amount—in the auctioneer's hands. After all, the auctioneer has to eat, too!

For larger amounts of money, say, more than $500, bring a certified check. You can always bid *less* than the amount of the check. If you win, then the excess will be applied against the purchase price, if it's larger. If the purchase price is smaller, the auctioneer will refund the excess to you after the amount of the check is collected.

Never worry about the honesty of auctioneers! Their work is closely controlled by local legal authorities. So you'll find that any money due is promptly, and fully, repaid to you.

Set Bid Limits for Each Property

Your offer notebook tells you the maximum bid you can afford for a property. Do *not* exceed this bid! Why? Because exceeding your calculated bid for a property can:

- Throw your plans into disarray
- Lead to future financial problems
- Prevent you from getting other good properties

For example, let's say you decide to bid *no* more than $5,000 on a 15-unit apartment house being auctioned in your area. You have, we'll say, another $4,000 you know you can borrow to use to make needed repairs.

But the bidding gets hot and goes to $6,000. You're limited—by your own calculations—to $5,000. Should you go to, say $6,100, to beat the other bidder? If you do, that bidder might go to $6,500. Then where will you be? You might be tempted to offer $7,000.

The result? You're out of control! Before you know it you may "win" the bid at $10,000. But you have only $9,000 available—$5,000 for the bid and $4,000 for repairs. You might not be able to come up with the additional $1,000 needed for the $10,000 bid.

So set your bid limits, based on your analysis of the income and expenses of each property. Why do I say this? Because, if you "lose" a property to a higher bidder, you'll almost always find that:

- Another equal, or better, property will come onto the market sooner or later.
- You will build your fortune in real estate if you control your actions and plan each move.
- "Shooting from the hip" may sound romantic, but it really won't allow you to build a solid future in today's competitive real estate world.

You may think that planning your foreclosure future is difficult. But it really isn't! Once you work through a few offerings based on income and expenses, you'll find that it's both easy and fun. And attending some auctions will teach you that the person in control of his or her bids can really win at the foreclosure game!

Be Sure to Have Your Financing Lined Up

You *will* need some money to take over a foreclosure property. It may be as low as $10, but you will need that. Where only small amounts of money are needed, say, $250, or less, I consider this to be "zero cash." Why do I say this?

Because if you really can get a good property for $250 or less, I'll be glad to lend you the money to get it. So you *will* have the property for zero cash, that is, *no* money out of your own pocket.

For larger amounts, say, $5,000 and up, you should have financing available *before* you go to the auction. How can you line up the financing? Here are a few suggestions:

- Look to the line of credit on your credit cards. Many offer as much as a $10,000 line of credit. You can tap this to pay for your foreclosure purchase.
- Get a personal loan for an acceptable purpose—education, vacation, debt consolidation, and so on. Use some of the money for the stated purpose; apply the balance to your foreclosure purpose.

- Obtain a home or property improvement loan on real estate you own now, and use some of the funds to improve your new property after you get it; apply the balance to the purchase price.
- Borrow against other assets you may own—stocks, bonds, certificates of deposit, and so on. Use the money to buy the foreclosures you seek.

Hundreds of people use these sources of funds almost every day of the year to take over a property they seek. The properties they buy

- Increase the person's assets, giving them greater future borrowing power
- Raise the person's cash income to free them from a paycheck they hate
- Provide a promising future that will give them independence and freedom in a business of their own

You, too, can have these same benefits—if you line up your financing in advance. In some states the sheriff's office has foreclosure sales every Monday of the year. With so many offerings available, *you* have plenty of time to line up your financing so you get the properties *you* want!

Have Written Plans for Every Property

You will look over each property you buy in foreclosure *before* you bid on it. Why? Because by looking over a property, that is, inspecting it, before purchase you can determine:

- What repairs, if any, are needed
- How long it will take you to get the property ready for resale
- Who your potential buyers will be
- Which price level you will place the property in

You can use a form, like that in Exhibit 3–2, to get at your probable make-ready costs quickly and easily. While this step may seem like a chore, it really isn't. Why? Because it helps *you* plan your financial future. And, as we said earlier, a planned financial future is a successful one.

Some foreclosure properties are sold on an "as is, where is" basis. When you buy such a property, you take on all its benefits and problems, if any. Other foreclosure properties— particularly those sold by banks— will be guaranteed to be in livable condition. Such properties will give you fewer problems. But no matter which type of property you buy, you *must* have a brief written plan for each. Then there's less chance of running into headaches after you take the property over!

Where repairs are needed for a property, get precise estimates of the cost of the work from a contractor. Since this may delay your first purchase, I suggest that you:

- Buy properties in good to excellent condition when you first enter the foreclosure market.
- Get at least a year of experience with your foreclosures *before* you start to buy "fixer-uppers.
- Associate yourself with an interested and competent general contractor who will give you quick and reliable estimates of the cost of fixing up a property for resale.

By concentrating on good properties at the start you will be able to get the income you seek sooner. What's more, you'll have fewer problems. So you'll be more strongly motivated to go on building your wealth. And that, after all, is *my* job—to motivate you to get rich for *your* benefit!

WHAT TO DO AFTER YOU WIN A BID

You're now the proud owner of your first foreclosure property. What to do? *Follow your plan!*

When you bought property you knew you'd either rent the property out or sell it at a profit. So your first steps are:

1. List the property for rent, or for sale, depending on your original plan; use a rental agent or real estate broker.
2. Keep a careful eye on progress. Don't let your plans drift—get results. And the sooner the better!
3. Consider switching rental agents or real estate brokers if the ones you're using don't get you the results you seek in the time frame you set.

A good friend of mine is building a "horizontal apartment house" comprised of a number of (70 to be exact) foreclosure single-family homes (SFH). Here's a brief summary of a recent conversation we had about how he handles his foreclosures immediately after he acquires them:

> *I, of course, know what rent I'll charge for each SFH I take over. As soon as I have possession of the foreclosure I list it with a rental agent. Since I've worked with this agent for years, she knows exactly how I want the property listed. Once she has the listing, I have high school kids place 3" × 5" cards on the free bulletin boards in local supermarkets, drugstores, and similar locations, advertising the house for rent. These cards back up the rental agent's work. Using this method I rent a SFH in less than one week—at the price I want to charge!*

Be Ready for Unforeseen Problems

There's *no* perfect business! And foreclosures can have their problems. But let me say this:

- Of all the business problems I've seen, foreclosure problems seem to be the simplest and easiest to fix.
- Few foreclosure buildings will give you serious problems—if you check out the property *before* you bid on it.
- Know what you're getting into and your "problems" will be minimal.

But the occasional unforeseen problem may pop up. By being ready for it, you can solve it fast. Another friend who ran into an unexpected problem had it solved for him because he was ready for it. Here's how:

> Before bidding on a foreclosure property, this BWB, named Ken, had it inspected by a local property inspection service. Costing only $250 for the inspection, Ken felt secure because the service guaranteed to repair—free of charge—any defects found within one year of the purchase of the property. Three months after buying and renting the property, Ken was informed by the tenant that there was a roof leak in the house. Checking, Ken found that a number of slates on the roof were defective. They were so hidden from view that both Ken and the inspection service overlooked them before the house was purchased.

Ken called the inspection service. After looking at the slates, the inspection service replaced them free of charge, saving Ken some $1,200 in repair bills.

So the whole key to being unpleasantly surprised is to be ready for the unforeseen. Plan your purchases after you've carefully inspected each. Then you won't be taken by surprise when a minor problem pops up.

What would you do if you bought a foreclosure with the intention of selling quickly but the market for such a building is temporarily depressed? This might happen. Another good friend says:

When I buy a single-family home to resell, I always check the rental market first. Then, if sales are slow, I can rent the home for a few months until the sales of these units pick up. So the home doesn't cost me anything while I'm holding it. In fact, I usually make money on the rental. So I'm always ready for the unforeseen problem!

Don't Let Small Setbacks Get You Down

Every business has small setbacks that can drive a person nuts. Not so with foreclosures. The setbacks—if any—are small—and few. But you should recognize that you may have a few small problems like:

- Tenant checks that bounce
- Repairs caused by tenant neglect or vandalism
- Occasional equipment failures in the middle of the night
- Tenants who try to beat you out of a rent payment

None of these setbacks is the end of the world. You can overcome all of them with some simple planning. And if you're ready for such setbacks, you'll handle them as routine occurrences that aren't worth getting excited over. The foreclosure business has so few problems that a minor setback should *not* ruin your day!

Get ready and you'll be Mr. or Ms. Calm. Knowing you may have a setback here or there is half the battle. The other half is just a little common sense! If you ever have a question about handling a unique setback in a foreclosure, just give me a ring—day or night—and I'll try to give you the right answer. I'm here to help *you* get rich in real estate!

Use an Automatic Payment Plan for Your Financing

You'll have a long-term mortgage loan (15 to 40 years) on any property you take over at a foreclosure sale. The best way to pay off this mortgage is, in my opinion, to have it on an automatic plan where:

- You don't have to write a payment check every month.
- You don't have a thick book of coupons which can get you discouraged.
- Your monthly income automatically pays the mortgage, allowing you to have a clear mind for other deals.

To set up an automatic payment plan, do business with a local frontline bank. Such a bank can:

1. Receive your monthly rent payments from your tenant(s)
2. Credit these payments to your account (called *direct deposit* in banking lingo)
3. Automatically deduct your monthly mortgage payment from your rent deposits without you having to do anything once the account is set up

Not only do you have greater freedom from your business with this plan, you also establish a closer relationship with your bank. This will come in handy in the future when you're looking for more funds to do new deals.

An important aspect of the automatic payment plan that's sometimes overlooked is this:

> Having a property pay for itself gives you self-confidence. You then have more courage to go out and look for additional deals which can give you greater income. One success builds on another—to your long-term benefit!

So make a visit to your local large commercial bank. If you're in a small town that doesn't have such a bank, look in a nearby large-city Yellow Pages for commercial banks. Contact one or more by phone, telling them:

1. You want to set up a business checking account for your real estate activities.
2. You want to use direct deposit for your income checks from tenants.
3. You want an automatic payment plan for repaying your mortgage, be it to your bank or another bank.

Any modern, business-seeking commercial bank will be happy to work with you. If the bank is unwilling to work with you for accounts like these, thank the person and go on to the next bank! There are plenty of good banks looking for new business. Ben F., a good friend who specializes in foreclosure purchases and rentals told me recently:

> *Having a friendly bank on your side makes every foreclosure deal easier. Why? Because you know—in advance—that the financial aspects of your deal are set up beforehand. So you don't have to run around looking for a banking partner when you have lots of other thoughts on your mind!*

Keep Accurate and Precise Income and Expense Records

Real estate, remember, is a business! You *must* approach all your deals with this thought in mind. All deals need good income and expense records. Without such records you have chaos.

Use a simple form for your income and expense record. You can start with a form like that in Exhibit 3–4. Or you can devise your own form on computer, if you prefer. The key is to keep accurate and precise income and expense records at all times. While you can use hand-entry records, a personal computer—either a laptop or desk top model—will save you lots of time and prevent accounting difficulties. Why? Because without such records you can run into all kinds of problems—from paying bills to reporting your tax liability, if any. Here's a recent letter from a reader that shows how the keeping of accurate records helps you summarize your advances each year:

> *This was my first year of real estate investing and a very profitable one, thanks to your books, courses, and newsletters. From March to November, 1 acquired eight houses and one building lot, all valued at $350,000, with only $650 down. At the same time, I mortgaged out $27,000 of tax-free money. Including my personal home, my real estate assets total $400,000, my net worth is $150,000, and the investment property gives me a $500 per month positive cash flow. In addition to these acquisitions, I originated and closed $145,000 in first mortgages. Thanks for your creative ideas and financial genius.*

Exhibit 3–4

TYPICAL MONTHLY INCOME AND EXPENSE RECORD SHEET

Income:

Rents	$ 5,500.00
Laundry machines	200.00
Telephone(s)	150.00
Other services (Cleaning Apts.)	400.00
Interest on rent security deposits	100.00
Total monthly income	$ 6,350.00

Expenses:

Real estate taxes	$ 1,100.00
Trash removal	50.00
Water	60.00
Electric	80.00
Advertising	10.00
Telephone	30.00
Insurance—fire, liability, structural	200.00
Auto and travel	100.00
Cleaning materials	50.00
Maintenance materials	150.00
Salaries—maintenance, cleaning, supervision	500.00
Rental commissions	150.00
Legal fees	100.00
Accounting fees	100.00
Mortgage(s) principal and interest	2,060.00
Other expenses miscellaneous	250.00
Total monthly expenses	4,990.00

Net monthly cash flow = Total monthly income
– Total monthly expenses = $ 1,360.00

I'm sure this reader will go on to greater wealth in his own real estate investments. You—too—can do much the same by seeking out foreclosures in your area. A number of the properties this reader bought were near-foreclosures. In just 8 months he increased his financial statement by $350,000! And walked away with some $27,000 *cash* in his fist. Can you ask for any better deal?

If you have trouble making up a form for your real estate income and expenses, consider using IRS Schedule E, Exhibit 3–5, as a guide. Since you'll probably have to use Schedule E when reporting your real estate income, you'll be saving time by keeping your records on this form. Don't be afraid of record keeping. After a while, it's fun. Why? Because you'll really enjoy watching the money pile up—usually tax free!

Various real estate computer programs allow you to keep your records in a Schedule E format. This saves you time and allows easier preparation of tax data. And your real estate will be more profitable when you keep accurate income and expense records.

SUCCESS STRATEGIES FOR BUILDING YOUR REAL ESTATE WEALTH IN GOOD TIMES AND BAD TIMES

1. Find out who offers foreclosure properties in your investment area. Contact each of the following: (a) Banks offering real estate loans—they will usually have foreclosures they want to put in the hands of ambitious people such as yourself; (b) Your County Clerk's office where they usually have foreclosure properties listed for sale; (c) Federal Government offices—IRS, FHA, VA—that have foreclosure properties you can acquire at low cost. Get all the free information from these organizations that you can. They'll be glad to put you on their mailing list, plus they'll supply you with a packet of their current data. Study what you receive—it could give you a quick "college education" in the foreclosure situation in your investment area. Since there is a wide range of quality of foreclosure properties, you must develop a sense for the good vs. the bad. Do this by visiting a number of foreclosure properties offered to you. Make notes about each in your Riches Notebook (see Chapter 2). Be completely frank with your notes because they're for only your eyes—no one else's. If a property is in awful condition, make a note of that. If a property is in superb condition, note that also. You'll soon know the good from the bad!

Exhibit 3–5

SCHEDULE E (Form 1040) Department of the Treasury Internal Revenue Service (O)	**Supplemental Income and Loss** (From rents, royalties, partnerships, estates, trusts, REMICs, etc.) ▶ Attach to Form 1040 or Form 1041. ▶ See Instructions for Schedule E (Form 1040).	OMB No. 1545-0074 Attachment Sequence No. 13

Name(s) shown on return | | Your social security number

Part I | **Income or Loss From Rentals and Royalties** Note: *Report farm rental income or loss from* **Form 4835** *on page 2, line 39.*

1 Show the kind and location of each **rental property**:

  A ....

  B ....

  C

		Yes	No
2 For each rental property listed on line 1, did you or your family use it for personal purposes for more than the greater of 14 days or 10% of the total days rented at fair rental value during the tax year? (See Instructions.)	A		
	B		
	C		

Rental and Royalty Income:		Properties			D Totals
		A	B	C	(Add columns A, B, and C)
3 Rents received	3				3
4 Royalties received	4				4
Rental and Royalty Expenses:					
5 Advertising	5				
6 Auto and travel	6				
7 Cleaning and maintenance	7				
8 Commissions	8				
9 Insurance	9				
10 Legal and other professional fees	10				
11 Mortgage interest paid to banks, etc. (see Instructions)	11				11
12 Other interest	12				
13 Repairs	13				
14 Supplies	14				
15 Taxes	15				
16 Utilities	16				
17 Wages and salaries	17				
18 Other (list) ▶	18				
19 Add lines 5 through 18	19				19
20 Depreciation expense or depletion (see Instructions)	20				20
21 Total expenses. Add lines 19 and 20	21				
22 Income or (loss) from rental or royalty properties. Subtract line 21 from line 3 (rents) or line 4 (royalties). If the result is a (loss), see Instructions to find out if you must file **Form 6198**	22				
23 Deductible rental loss. **Caution:** *Your rental loss on line 22 may be limited. See Instructions to find out if you must file* **Form 8582**	23	(	)(	)(	)
24 **Income.** Add rental and royalty income from line 22. Enter the total income here					24
25 **Losses.** Add royalty losses from line 22 and rental losses from line 23. Enter the total losses here					25 ( )
26 Total rental and royalty income or (loss). Combine amounts on lines 24 and 25. Enter the result here. If Parts II, III, IV, and line 39 on page 2 do not apply to you, enter the amount from line 26 on Form 1040, line 18. Otherwise, include the amount from line 26 in the total on line 40 on page 2.					26

For Paperwork Reduction Act Notice, see Form 1040 Instructions.   Schedule E (Form 1040)

Exhibit 3–5 (Continued)

Schedule E (Form 1040)   Attachment Sequence No. **13**   Page **2**

Name(s) shown on return. (Do not enter name and social security number if shown on other side.)   Your social security number

Note: *If you report amounts from farming or fishing on Schedule E, you must include your gross income from those activities on line 41 below.*

Part II — Income or Loss From Partnerships and S Corporations

If you report a loss from an at-risk activity, you MUST check either column (e) or (f) of line 27 to describe your investment in the activity. See Instructions. If you check column (f), you must attach **Form 6198.**

27	(a) Name	(b) Enter P for partnership; S for S corporation	(c) Check if foreign partnership	(d) Employer identification number	(e) All is at risk	(f) Some is not at risk
A						
B						
C						
D						
E						

	Passive Income and Loss		Nonpassive Income and Loss		
	(g) Passive loss allowed (Attach **Form 8582** if required)	(h) Passive income from **Schedule K–1**	(i) Nonpassive loss from **Schedule K–1**	(j) Section 179 expense deduction from **Form 4562**	(k) Nonpassive income from **Schedule K–1**
A					
B					
C					
D					
E					
28a Totals					
b Totals					

29 Add amounts in columns (h) and (k) of line 28a. Enter the total income here **29**

30 Add amounts in columns (g), (i), and (j) of line 28b. Enter the total here . . . . **30** ( )

31 Total partnership and S corporation income or (loss). Combine amounts on lines 29 and 30. Enter the result here and include in the total on line 40 below **31**

Part III — Income or Loss From Estates and Trusts

32	(a) Name	(b) Employer identification number
A		
B		
C		

	Passive Income and Loss		Nonpassive Income and Loss	
	(c) Passive deduction or loss allowed (Attach **Form 8582** if required)	(d) Passive income from **Schedule K–1**	(e) Deduction or loss from **Schedule K–1**	(f) Other income from **Schedule K–1**
A				
B				
C				
33a Totals				
b Totals				

34 Add amounts in columns (d) and (f) of line 33a. Enter the total income here **34**

35 Add amounts in columns (c) and (e) of line 33b. Enter the total here . . . . **35** ( )

36 Total estate and trust income or (loss). Combine amounts on lines 34 and 35. Enter the result here and include in the total on line 40 below **36**

Part IV — Income or Loss From Real Estate Mortgage Investment Conduits (REMICs)—Residual Holder

37	(a) Name	(b) Employer identification number	(c) Excess inclusion from Schedules Q, line 2c (see Instructions)	(d) Taxable income (net loss) from Schedules Q, line 1b	(e) Income from Schedules Q, line 3b

38 Combine amounts in columns (d) and (e) only. Enter the result here and include in the total on line 40 below. **38**

Part V — Summary

39 Net farm rental income or (loss) from **Form 4835.** (Also complete line 41 below.) **39**

40 TOTAL income or (loss). Combine amounts on lines 26, 31, 36, 38, and 39. Enter the result here and on Form 1040, line 18 . . . . ▶ **40**

41 **Reconciliation of Farming and Fishing Income:** Enter your gross farming and fishing income reported in Parts II and III, and on line 39 (see Instructions) **41**

*U.S. Government Printing Office: — 265-193

2. Work with foreclosure sellers who will pay all closing costs for you while providing the needed legal counsel free. Banks often offer to pay all your closing costs while having their attorney act as your counsel. You can trust such an offer because the bank does not want the property back. Instead, the bank wants to see you successfully operating the property and making your mortgage payment on time, once a month. If you're nervous about the bank's attorney representing you, hire your own attorney to check the work done by the bank's counsel. In general, your attorney will approve the bank attorney's work. And the fee your attorney charges you will also—in general—be small—say $100 to $300 because no new original work is being done. Taking over foreclosures from banks can get you started in real estate on almost zero cash. Check with your local bank and see the "gold" that awaits you in foreclosure!

3. Learn bidding techniques before you make an actual bid for a property. You will have to bid on foreclosures offered at County Clerk sales and Federal Government (IRS, FHA, VA, etc.) sales because their rules require public open bidding. In making a bid you will usually be competing against others who also want to buy the foreclosed property that appeals to you. Since open bidding is based on raising the price of the offered item to the highest level possible, you must be careful not to overbid by getting caught up in the give and take of the process. So the best way to learn bidding techniques is to (a) check out several properties that appeal to you; (b) write out the price you would offer on each of the properties; (c) attend the auction and mentally pretend you're bidding on each of the properties you like; (d) observe what price each property sells at and compare this price with the one you chose; (e) do this several times and keep track of how close your imagined "bid" price is to the actual selling price. Once you feel comfortable with your bidding estimates, go and make a real bid! You'll be nervous, I know. But you'll soon grow more confident—and more wealthy!

4. Flip your foreclosure properties to make fast money without owning the property too long. You can—of course—hold onto foreclosures and rent them out. But many times you're better off flipping foreclosures—that is, selling them for the highest price you can get, shortly after you buy the foreclosure. Why is this? Because many foreclosures will require repairs and cosmetic work before they are suitable as rentals. If you want to do this work, fine. But many BWBs prefer to flip their foreclosures and walk away with cash in their pocket within days, or weeks, after they get them. Flipping usually costs much less, saves time, and brings a faster recovery of the down payment you are required to make on almost all foreclosures today.

IMPORTANT POINTERS TO KEEP IN MIND

- Use foreclosures as your road to wealth, starting with little or no cash—the zero cash way to wealth!
- Get big value for little, or no, dollars when you invest in desirable foreclosures.
- Build up your wealth fast with foreclosures.
- A wide choice of good properties is available with well-chosen foreclosures.
- Tax-favored income can be yours with foreclosures.
- You have many sources of foreclosures—banks, local tax authorities, the federal government, bankruptcy courts, and so on.
- Get to know auction procedures and you'll win with foreclosures!
- Use an offer notebook or a portable computer to keep track of properties that interest you.
- Remember—with foreclosures you can make big money in both active and sluggish real estate markets.
- To make it big in foreclosures, invest as little as possible, look beyond your buying price, control your offers, and look for bargain properties everywhere.
- Use your success formula—price, income, expenses, and cash flow—to guide you to great wealth with foreclosures.
- Make the bid process work for *you* in foreclosures.
- To win at foreclosure auctions, be prepared, arrive on time, have any needed funds with you, set bid limits for each property, be sure to have your financing lined up, have written plans for each property, be ready for unforeseen problems, use an automatic payment plan for your financing, keep accurate and precise income and expense records.

Mortgaging Out— Getting Big Money Every Time You Buy

Read your local newspapers and the message that comes through is that things are tough all over for real estate. But this message does *not* agree with what BWBs who use my methods tell me. "Sure," they say, "loans *are* tougher to get than they were a few years ago. In a down market you have to be a 'guerrilla borrower.'"

"But," these same BWBs say, "money *is* available from lenders. You just have to look longer and harder in these gut-wrenching times in real estate." And hundreds of letters and phone calls from readers tell basically the same story—they *are* getting the loans they need for real estate when they set their minds to finding needed funds.

So forget all the negatives you're hearing. There *are* ways to get the money you need to make your real estate dreams come true!

You can take over income property and get paid for doing so! Sound crazy? It really isn't. Plenty of people do—every day of the week somewhere in the real estate world. And you can do the same. This chapter shows you exactly how to walk away from a closing (where a property is transferred from the seller to you) with money in your hand, after paying *all* costs.

If you mention mortgaging out to your friends some of them may react heatedly, saying "That's impossible! *I* never heard of anyone doing that. It can't be."

My advice to you is to continue your friendship but cease mentioning anything about mortgaging out. Why? Because such people don't know what they're talking about. Yet they'll try to fill your mind with senseless negatives. They can only reduce your drive to success. So keep these people as friends. But stick to safe topics—like the weather!

WHAT IS MORTGAGING OUT?

Let's define our terms clearly so you know exactly what to expect from mortgaging out. Also called a *windfall,* mortgaging out is a real estate transaction in which you receive excess money when you take title to a property. The excess money is tax free at the time you receive it because the money comes from a loan. Present tax law does not tax loan proceeds.

To put this definition into brick and mortar terms, let's look at some real-life examples of mortgaging out.

A reader bought a $300,000 office building by assuming (taking over the liability of paying the monthly charges on the loan for the remaining months in the loan without any changes in the terms of the loan) the mortgage loan on the building. The amount of the mortgage loan that the reader assumed was $275,000. Prior to taking title to the building, this reader got approval for a $55,000 property improvement loan for the building once he took title to it. With the price of the building at $300,000 and an existing mortgage of $275,000, the reader had to pay the seller $25,000 on closing. He arranged to have the property improvement loan close the same day as the purchase. Thus, he mortgaged out with $55,000 − $25,000 = $30,000. Much of the $30,000 will be used to improve the building for its present tenants.

Another reader bought an apartment house and mortgaged out in a different way. The buyer and seller agreed on a selling price of $500,000, which was also the appraised value of the property. A mortgage lender agreed to lend 80 percent of the appraised value, or $0.80 \times \$500,000 = \$400,000$ on the property. So all the buyer had to do to take over this income property was to come up with $100,000 for the down payment (= $500,000 − $400,000). After searching for the down payment money, the buyer became discouraged because he couldn't find the money. So, at the last minute, he called the seller and said "I'll have to pull out of the deal because I can't afford to pay the $500,000, with the $100,000 down payment for this building." The seller was shocked because she was determined to sell the property so she could move to a warmer part of the country. "Well, what price would make you go through with the deal?" she asked the buyer. "I'd buy it for $365,000," the buyer said. 'What about $375,000?" the seller asked. "Good, I'll take it," replied the buyer. With a $400,000 loan already approved, the deal went through and the buyer walked away with $400,000 − $375,000 = $25,000. So he mortgaged out with $25,000.

In our last chapter, remember the reader who said: "I acquired eight houses and one building lot . . . . At the same time, I mortgaged out $27,000 of tax-free money.

What these real-life examples show is that mortgaging out is a free-form activity. That is, mortgaging out can depend on many factors such as:

- Motivation of the seller
- Ability of the property to support other loans
- Negotiating ability of the buyer
- Availability of second mortgage loans in the area
- Attitudes of lenders toward home equity loans on local property
- Credit rating of the buyer
- Existing assumable mortgage on the property

Please recognize—here and now—that there is *no* standard mortgaging out deal. Each deal varies. But if you know the general ideas behind mortgaging out, you can easily put plenty of deals together. Let's take a closer look at what makes a potential mortgaging out deal for you.

USE YOUR MORTGAGING OUT FORMULA

While the steps may vary from deal to deal, most mortgaging out situations have certain characteristics, such as:

- High appraised value for the property
- Reduced asking price because of external circumstances
- Lower selling price produced by skillful negotiation
- Ability to get two or more loans for a property
- Possibility of other "combined" types of financing
- Your ability to repay all loans you take out

As you deal in your local area in hard times, you'll find other characteristics of mortgaging out deals unique to your location. Just add these to the list. But no matter what type of property you're interested in, you'll find that the entire key to mortgaging out is getting two (or more) loans for more than you need to buy the property.

Consider this example:

Price you pay for a property	$100,000
Long-term mortgage, 75 percent loan-to-value ratio (LW)	75,000
Cash down payment	25,000
Seller purchase money mortgage	20,000
Personal loan for property improvement	10,000
Cash to you (before closing costs)	5,000

These loans, in general, will use the property as the collateral. For example:

> One of our newsletter readers wanted to buy condo apartments in the Virginia Beach area to rent out for income. He came to my firm, IWS, Inc., and asked if he could borrow the down payment for two condos. The amount he needed for the down payment was $10,000, $5,000 on each of the two condos. But he needed, he said, some "breathing room." So he applied for a $16,000 loan, pledging the excess value of the condos to us as collateral. He was able to do this because he was paying $60,000 for condos appraised at $78,000 each. We agreed and made the $16,000 loan for 3 years. So this reader subscriber mortgaged out with $6,000. He sold one of the condos a year later for $92,000 and immediately repaid his loan in full. Note that what he bought gave him the collateral to get the loan enabling him to mortgage out!

Now let's look at how *you* can apply your mortgaging out formula to deals you like. Using this formula, you can walk away from a closing with thousands of dollars in your pocket.

High Appraised Value for the Property

If you deal with property having a high appraised value, you have a better chance of mortgaging out when you buy it. Why is this? For a number of important reasons:

1. With a high appraised value, there is greater room for you to negotiate a suitable price that will permit you to mortgage out.

2. Sellers are more strongly motivated to sell properties having a high appraisal because their original investment will usually have risen

more than with other types of property. So these sellers have a definite urge to convert their rise in value to cash. You can help them do this by buying the property with a long-term mortgage.

3. Lenders are more likely to work with you when they're dealing with properties having a high appraisal.

Why? Because it's much easier to get financing on such properties, even in today's dream-crunching economy. Lenders feel safer with high-appraisal properties. So they'll lend faster on them.

For example, in a recent real-life situation, a couple bought a home for $2-million. Fourteen months later they sold this home for $3.2-million, within two days of putting it on the market, and after spending almost nothing on improvements. Figuring 30 days per month, they earned $1,200,000 profit/420 days = $2,857 a day while living in the house! Since the house is in an extremely desirable high-appraisal area, lenders were happy to loan on the property the same day it went on the market. With financing available the house sold in just two days!

Is it necessary for you to get an appraisal on every property you like? No, you do *not* have to get an appraisal on every property. What you can do is work with a recent appraisal the seller had made. Even if the appraisal is two years old, it will still give you a good idea of the real value of the property.

The whole key here is to save *you* money by using an available appraisal while you're deciding if you want to buy a property. You really can get an enormous amount of information from a recent appraisal. So use one whenever you can!

Look for a Reduced Asking Price

A motivated seller is a person who seeks to sell his or her property because of external circumstances. Such circumstances might be:

- Pending divorce
- Death in the family
- Desire to move to another climate
- Loss of job or business
- Local conditions which stimulate a move—such as a transfer or move of the owner's (or spouse's) employer

When any of these conditions prevails, you have a great opportunity of getting the asking price reduced. If the property has a high appraisal value at the start, as we recommended, and you can get its price reduced, the scene is set for mortgaging out.

While it may seem unfair to take advantage of external circumstances such as any of those listed, you should not look at the situation from this view. Why? Because you are really helping the seller by taking over the property quickly. The seller, after all, wants to get rid of the property for any of several reasons. So you become the seller's "white knight."

In hard times you will often come across properties which are for sale because the seller lost his or her job. When this occurs, the seller usually looks around for another job for several months. During this time his or her cash reserves are dwindling. When it finally appears that the seller cannot find a new job in the local area, the usual action taken is to put the seller's home up for sale.

When you offer to buy the home you—in effect—are giving the seller immediate cash. This cash will enable the seller to move to another area where he or she might be able to find a suitable job. So you become the "good guy" for the seller. That is because without your purchase of the house, the seller might have to go into foreclosure.

Negotiate a Lower Selling Price

The more time you spend in real estate, the better will your negotiating skills become. Why is this? There are a number of important reasons:

- Few real estate deals go through at the asking price.
- Almost every seller expects to have the price negotiated downward.
- Reducing the price allows you to mortgage out; every seller is in a negotiating mood when the sale of his or her property is delayed by hard times.

Never be afraid to negotiate! You are *expected* to negotiate. If you don't negotiate people will think that you're a beginner and they will try to take advantage of you. Further, negotiating will give you greater confidence in yourself while helping you save money.

The easiest way to start negotiating is to refuse to pay the asking price for any property. When you refuse, the seller will say, "If you don't want to pay the asking price, what price *do* you want to pay?"

This is an ideal opening for you to tell the seller what price you feel would be acceptable for the property. You will, of course, have made entries in your offering notebook giving the price which you feel you can afford to pay for the property. But when you quote the price you would be willing to pay, you should always reduce it so you can negotiate upward, if necessary.

Many of my readers tell me, "I made a very low offer on a property, and I was amazed that the seller accepted it!" Most of these readers were afraid to negotiate. Yet when they threw out a very low offer, they were delighted to have it accepted.

Sellers *expect* you to negotiate. Don't disappoint them! You will even surprise yourself.

Ability to Get Two, or More Loans on a Property

If you bid on property having a high appraisal, you will almost certainly have the ability to get at least two—and possibly more—loans on the property. Why is this? There are a number of important reasons:

- Property with a high appraisal is desirable collateral for all lenders.
- Loans are common on valuable property.
- Lenders make money when there is more than one loan on a property; therefore, many lenders encourage second and third mortgages on desirable property.
- You will almost always use a second loan on a property when you mortgage out.

Further:

- Even in the toughest of times for residential real estate, lenders seek more loans (such as home equity lines of credit) on good properties because the collateral (the property) is safer and the interest earnings for the lender are higher than for many other types of loans.
- Residential properties usually suffer less in downturns during hard times, compared to commercial properties (office buildings, shopping centers, etc.), which often suffer much sharper losses in value and income; for this reason, second and third mortgages are relatively easy to get in even the most somber times for residential properties.

There was a time when a second mortgage was frowned on by many people. They felt that a second mortgage made someone an undesirable borrower. Not so today!

With the rise in the *home equity loan,* which is really a second mortgage, it is now fashionable to have a second loan on a property. It is this second loan which will enable you to mortgage out. So today you will hear many people boast about taking money out of a property instead of having a large amount of equity tied up in a building and not doing anything for them.

So always look at a property with the view of getting another loan on it. This loan can be a second mortgage, an equity loan, a property improvement loan, and so on. Regardless of the name of the loan, the objective is to put money into your pocket tax free while the building repays the loan!

And be sure not to overlook the "125% loan," discussed in Chapter 3 of this book. This type of loan can give you lots of cash for additional real estate purchases.

Possibility of Other Combined-Type Financing

You will almost always have more than one loan on a property when you mortgage out. So your search, when you're trying to mortgage out, will be for the second loan, usually the down payment loan. Why?

Good property will support the long-term mortgage loan that runs 15 to 30 years, depending on what you can negotiate. So your job is to come up with a new way to get the down payment money in the form of a loan. Here's a technique I developed a few years ago which does the job for plenty of my BWB readers.

Called the "reverse flip," this method gets *you* the property you want using that property as collateral for *your* down payment loan. It's the "leveraged buyout" for real estate. Here's how it works:

1. Find a motivated seller—one who is aching to get away from a property he or she has for sale.

2. Negotiate a price and a down payment. Don't push too hard on the seller; be willing to pay the asking price if the property will support all payments while giving you a positive cash flow.

3. When you know the amount of down payment the seller wants, make this proposal
    a. The seller will take out a home equity or property improvement loan for the amount of the down payment.
    b. You will make the monthly payments on this down payment loan and the seller will keep the cash from it, which will be tax free at that time.
    c. If you default on the down payment loan, that is, fail to repay it, you will "reverse flip" the property, and all payments made on the down payment loan will go back to the seller, as though he or she made them to the lender. This means the seller has the property back, plus all payments you have made on both the down payment loan and the long-term mortgage.

    What's in it for the seller? That person or firm gets its *full* down payment quickly from the loan. They are out of the property, as they wanted to be. Further, they have a sincere, hardworking person in you who will make a strong effort to repay the down payment loan and the long-term mortgage. And if you don't do as you plan, the seller has the property back again, with some paydown of the debt.

Jim K., a longtime reader, took over a beautiful garden apartment having 30 units by (1) paying the seller his asking price, (2) having the seller take out a $130,000 second mortgage on the property which the seller kept, and (3) taking over the second and first mortgage payments with a written agreement to return the property to the seller if one or more mortgage payments were missed. Jim has a positive cash flow from the property and does not anticipate missing a single payment. Instead, he looks forward to doubling up on some payments so he's "ahead of the game," should he ever run into a cash squeeze. Meanwhile, he's concentrating on improving the occupancy rate (the number of apartments rented) and raising the cash flow of the property. His reverse flip approach really appealed to the seller and got Jim the property quickly and easily by mortgaging out.

    NOTE: Jim's mortgaging out cash is the Rent Deposits Account for the building—some $18,000. This money is his now because it is transferred to the new owner on the sale of the property. (To figure the rent deposits, use 30 units × $600 per mo average = $18,000, with a one-month security deposit per unit.)

Other combined-type financing you might use to mortgage out with includes:

- Property improvement loans obtained by the seller
- Personal loan obtained by the seller using the property as collateral for the loan
- Additional mortgage, such as a third mortgage, which will provide the down payment to the seller while giving you the property to operate as a business which repays all its loans

What you may have discerned as we're talking about mortgaging out is an immense group of added features which can benefit many BWBs. These added features are:

1. The seller's credit rating is substituted for *your* credit rating when the down payment loan is obtained. So if your credit rating is a bit shaky, mortgaging out is an excellent way of sidestepping this problem.
2. As you repay the loans on the property, you improve *your* credit rating because you can point out to future lenders your excellent credit history with repayment of the debt on the property.
3. And, as you pay down the property debt, you increase *your* equity. This means that you can borrow against this equity and get more money in fist. As we say so often, in this business cash is king!

Real estate people are among the most creative in the world. That's why the term *creative financing* originated in the real estate field. *You* can use your creative powers to come up with new approaches to financing which will help *you* mortgage out—quickly and easily.

Your Ability to Repay All Loans

Mortgaging out is a great idea! You take over an income-producing asset and get cash for doing so. Could anything be sweeter? But, like all other good things in life, mortgaging out has its "costs." These costs are:

1. You *must* be able to repay *all* loans you take out to get control of the property.
2. You should have a monthly "cushion" of extra cash over and above your loan payments to provide money for emergencies.

3. You must be certain that you can keep the income stream (cash flow) under control at all times; this means that reliance on just one tenant could be risky, as compared to a number of tenants where the loss of one would not damage your cash flow too seriously.

If you haven't paid off many loans in your past business experience, you should proceed slowly with mortgaging out. Why? Because paying off a large loan can be one of the best educational experiences of your life. When you see how much interest you're paying each day of the seven-day week, you realize the true value of money. Unless you paid off smaller loans in the past, paying off a big loan can be a truly frightening experience. So start small and grow big as you gain more experience.

Joe T., a West Coast friend of mine, mortgages out regularly with expensive beachfront properties of all types—residential, commercial, and recreational. He summed up his mortgaging out experience with this advice:

> *Mortgaging out is one of the greatest experiences in life. But it does have its costs. And many of these costs can be hidden to the beginner. So my advice to every real estate entrepreneur seeking to mortgage out is: Start small; get the feel for what you're doing; then take on larger deals. You'll seldom run into problems if you proceed slowly; dashing ahead without much experience can get you into financial problems.*

Real-Life Mortgaging Out Deals for You

Let's look at some real-life mortgaging out deals. The only liberty I've taken in these deals is to round out the numbers so they're easier to understand. We'll show you several ways you might mortgage out in today's real estate markets.

Property-Improvement Loan: Jeff wanted to buy an income triplex (3 units) for $150,000. A local real estate lender offered him an 80 percent mortgage, or $0.8 \times \$150,000 = \$120,000$. This meant that Jeff needed $\$150,000 - \$120,000 = \$30,000$ down payment for the property. He called me and I suggested that he apply at a well-known and aggressive bank that makes $35,000 "Executive Loans" to people with good credit and a strong employment history, both of which Jeff has. Jeff applied for a property improvement loan, based on his future ownership of this triplex. He was approved within hours. Taking over the property, Jeff's numbers worked out this way:

Property cost	$150,000
Mortgage	120,000
Fix-up loan	35,000
Down payment	30,000
Net to buyer	5,000

As for closing costs, which are usually made up of such items as attorney fees, broker commissions, title insurance payment, deed recording fee, fuel-in-tank payment, and real estate tax payment, these were minimal for this deal. So Jeff mortgaged out with about $5,000 in his pocket.

Development Cost Mortgaging Out: While you may not yet be interested in developing real estate, that is, buying a piece of land and putting up a structure of some kind, many of my readers are. One, Bill P., in the Los Angeles area, drew up plans for a residential property designed to produce a yearly income of $200,000. He went to a lender and showed the building plans and annual income projections. The lender offered to capitalize the property at 10 percent, that is, lend on the basis of the future income stream of $200,000 per year. With a 10 percent rate, the lender offered $200,000/0.10 = $2,000,000 to buy the land and put up the building. Bill's total costs were $1,800.000. So he mortgaged out with $200,000 cash in his hand.

Seller Financing: Some sellers—particularly estates—are so anxious to get rid of a property that they're willing to finance your takeover. Thus, with a $500,000 office building that "wasn't going anywhere in the sales market," a reader, Tom L., negotiated a sweet deal by getting seller financing. Having an existing assumable mortgage on the building allowed Tom to talk the seller into giving him a second mortgage for the down payment. Here are the numbers on this office building:

Price of building	$500,000
Assumable first mortgage	375,000
Down payment loan from seller	125,000

As soon as Tom took title to the property, he refinanced it with an 80 percent loan-to-value mortgage and took out 0.80 × $500,000 = $400,000. He used $375,000 of this money to pay off the existing first mortgage, winding up with $25,000 mortgaging out cash.

HOW TO AVOID OVERLEVERAGING WHEN MORTGAGING OUT

You *leverage* an investment when you use a small amount of cash to control a large amount of value. Leverage allows you to increase your return on an investment, as compared to putting all cash into the deal.

Since most of my readers are *not* in a position to put all cash into any real estate deal, they must look to leverage to get control of suitable income properties. While leverage does have its advantages, it also has its disadvantages. You want to accentuate the plusses while eliminating the negatives of leverage. Here's how.

Know Your Finance Numbers—Money Costs Money

When you mortgage out you borrow 100 percent, 110 percent, 120 percent, and so on of the amount of money you need to get control of an income property. While this is a smart bit of business strategy, you *must* recognize that your borrowed money *will* cost *you* money every month! There's *no* way to avoid the cost of borrowing money unless you can get a 0 percent interest loan (which is possible) or a grant (which is also possible).

But for most BWBs, you must pay the cost of borrowing money. We'll talk about 0 percent money and grants later in this chapter. For now, let's see how you can control your cost of money.

Figuring your cost of money is easy. Just use Exhibit 4–1 and you'll have your cost in seconds.

Let's say you want to borrow $100,000 to mortgage out on a property where a $75,000 down payment is needed. The interest rate in your local area is 12 percent and you need the money for 10 years. From Exhibit 4–1 we see that the monthly payment for a $10,000 loan at 12 percent for 10 years is $143.48. Since you want to borrow 10 times as much, or $100,000, your monthly payment will be 10 × $143.48 = $1,434.80.

You can use Exhibit 4–1 for any of the interest rates given. And if you have a rate midway between two given rates, you can use the amount

Exhibit 4–1

MONTHLY PAYMENT FOR A $10,000 LOAN*

Interest Rate, %	Time to Repay the Loan, Years					
	5	10	15	20	25	30
6	193.33	111.02	84.39	71.64	64.43	59.96
8	202.76	121.33	95.57	83.64	77.18	73.38
10	212.48	132.16	107.47	96.51	90.88	87.76
12	222.45	143.48	120.02	110.11	105.33	102.87
14	232.69	155.27	133.18	124.36	120.38	118.49
16	243.19	167.52	146.88	139.13	135.89	134.48

*To figure your monthly loan payment, multiply the payment for the interest rate and term by amount of your loan ÷ $10,000. Thus, a $100,00 loan for 15 years at 10% interest would have a monthly payment amount of $107.47 × $100,000/$10,000 = $1,074.70.

that's half-way between the two given. Thus, a 13 percent loan would, for 10 years, cost $149.38 per month.

When you mortgage out, you'll usually have at least two loans on the property. The first is your long-term mortgage. This may be either a new loan or an assumed (taken-over) loan. The second loan is the down payment loan, which may be any one of several types mentioned earlier.

There are ways to reduce your present outlay for your second, or down payment loan:

1. Get a *standing loan* for your down payment loan. With a standing loan you pay interest only each month. At the end of the loan period, say, 3 or 5 years, you pay the principal on the loan. But if you don't have it at that time you can renegotiate the loan and extend it for another 3 or 5 years. Lenders like standing loans because they earn much more interest from these loans than from conventional loans where principal and interest (P&I) are paid monthly. The extra interest cost is tax deductible to you in your real estate business.

2. Get a *balloon loan* for your down payment. With this type loan you may pay interest only. But today many balloon loans are set up so you make a small principal payment along with your interest pay-

ment each month. At the end of the loan, you make your balloon payment. This final payment covers most of what you borrowed, plus any interest due. Balloon loans are usually renegotiable at the end of their term. Such loans—like standing loans—allow the lender to earn larger dollar amounts of interest.

Let's see how a standing loan might help your cash flow in a typical property on which you mortgage out. Here are the numbers from a recent actual transaction:

A BWB bought a $200,000 income property with an 80 percent long-term mortgage for $160,000. He borrowed $50,000 for 5 years using a standing loan. His interest rate on the standing loan is 12 percent. If he were to repay the $50,000 in 5 years in monthly principal and interest payments, his monthly payment, using Exhibit 4–1, would be $50,000/ $10,000 × $222.45 = $1,112.25. By paying interest only on a standing loan, his monthly payment for interest only will be $50,000 × 0.12/12 months = $500. So this BWB reduces his monthly expenses by $1,112.25 – 500.00 = $612.25. This can mean the difference between a positive and a negative cash flow on the property.

Remember that several important benefits are taking place while you're using a standing mortgage. These benefits directly affect your cost of money:

1. Your property is rising in value as time passes. So you have an asset that is improving your balance sheet, every day of the year.
2. Your equity (what *you* own) in the property is rising every time you make a payment on your long-term mortgage. This means that you have greater borrowing ability, every day of the year. So when your standing or balloon loan comes due you might

   a. Borrow against your equity.
   b. Refinance the building to pay off the standing loan.
   c. Get a *wraparound loan* to cover both the long-term mortgage and the standing loan when it comes due. (The wraparound loan lender pays on both the existing loans while you pay only the wrap lender.)

Meanwhile, of course, you have the positive cash flow from the property. This cash flow can put you on Easy Street, compared to reporting to an ungrateful and angry boss.

As you know, 2-year subscribers to my newsletter, *International Wealth Success,* are entitled to apply to us for business and real estate loans* of all types from $1,500 to $500,000. Most of the readers who apply to us for real estate loans seek the down payment loan they need. Why is this?

- Long-term mortgages are easy to get on good income properties.
- Requirements for mortgage loans—even in the hardest and toughest times—are more liberal than for other types of loans (signature, business, education, etc.) because the property is the collateral for the lender.
- Our 6 percent interest rate on down payment loans is not a burden, especially when the reader asks for a standing or balloon loan, which most do.

You now know how to figure your finance costs using Exhibit 4–1. If you have any problems with figuring your costs, just give me a ring. I'll be glad to work them out instantly, if you're a subscriber to my newsletter or a reader of one of my real estate books.

Be Aware of Other Mortgaging Out Costs

You do have other costs when you mortgage out. We mentioned them briefly earlier. These costs are:

- Closing costs—present in every real estate deal
- Miscellaneous costs—you're almost certain to have them

Every real estate deal has some closing costs. But you can work to reduce the cash outlay for these costs in several ways.

1. *Get an estimate of the closing costs in advance.* Having the estimate will tell you what costs to expect. Further, the very fact that you ask for an estimate in advance will put the various people involved on warning that you're a smart BWB who knows the score.

2. *Avoid real estate brokers at all costs.* They get a standard 6 percent fee which can put the kiss of death on an otherwise viable deal. Buy directly from the seller or from a government or state agency that does not charge brokerage commissions. Likewise, banks rarely charge brokerage commissions.

---

* Where permitted by state statute.

3. *Get a broker (if you must work with one) to accept payment of the fee over a period of months* (say, 12 months or longer). This will reduce the "hit" on your cash flow when you take over the property. You may also be able to eliminate the brokerage fee entirely by making the broker a partner in your deal. Check with your attorney to see if this is permissible.

4. *Ask your attorney to accept a stretched-out payment for legal services.* Or offer a small percentage of ownership of the property (5 percent, or less) in place of the legal fees. Many successful attorneys are willing to take a "piece of the action" in place of legal fees when they know the property has a good income.

5. *Negotiate with any lender who wants to charge you points (1 percent of the loan amount per point) for a new mortgage loan.* While getting the loan *is* most important to you, points are *not* sacred. A lender can still make a profit without points. So don't be afraid to say to a lender: "Are these points really necessary? I think they're a bit excessive, especially in view of your high interest rates." While a lender may not eliminate points entirely, asking can get the points cut in half, thereby reducing *your* costs.

6. *Try to get any loan prepayment penalty reduced or eliminated.* Here, again, lenders may be willing to negotiate, if you ask. You'll never know what's on a lender's mind until you politely stand up to him or her and ask a sensible question. I've seen lenders drop a prepayment penalty on a long-term mortgage when they knew they were getting the new loan on the property. Yet if the BWB borrower hadn't asked that the prepayment penalty be dropped, the full amount would have been charged. As the man said: "You'll never know if you don't ask!"

7. *Reduce inspection and appraisal fees by negotiating them downward.* This may seem like a chore. But the money you save is cash in *your* pocket! You wouldn't pass up the same amount of money if you saw it lying in the street. So why not bend over a little and negotiate? It can pay *you* big hourly wages. Remember: In tough times (and in good times, as well) almost everyone expects you to haggle over prices. So don't disappoint anyone!

8. *Stretch out title insurance payments.* Many BWBs pay for title insurance in one lump sum. This isn't necessary. Get the insurance company to accept three or five payments. Then each payment will be less of a hit on your cash flow. There may be a small interest charge. But it will be so little you won't even notice it!

Be Ready for Some Miscellaneous Costs

No matter what type of property you take over to mortgage out with, you'll have some miscellaneous costs. What will they be and how much will they be? That's hard to say because they are miscellaneous, that is, undefined until met! But typical miscellaneous costs you might meet are:

- Auto expenses for driving to and from the property
- Accounting fees for tax advice
- Bookkeeping costs for multiunit rental properties
- Repair and renovation costs for special tenants
- Travel costs for visiting out-of-town properties
- Loan application fees in the $100 to $250 range

While most miscellaneous costs won't break you, it's best to be ready for them. Then you won't be hit between the eyes by bills you never thought would come in. Mortgaging out can be *your* private money machine if you're ready for the ins and outs of this way of building riches in real estate.

REAL-LIFE EXAMPLE OF MORTGAGING OUT

The best way to see how *you* might mortgage out is to see a real-life example. The numbers tell their own story and can suggest ways in which you might approach any deals *you* like.

Remember: It doesn't make any difference how large or how small a building you're considering. When you mortgage out, you get a property which you own and you're paid money for taking it over! And there are *no* taxes to pay on the cash you receive until you sell the property. And even then, you may not have to pay any taxes! Keep in mind that the selling price of a property and its fair market value may not be the same when you mortgage out. Its selling price will often be lower than the market value. In the foregoing case the selling price was the same as the appraised value. Appraised value may, or may not, equal the market value of a property.

A seller in a hurry to unload a property during tough times (such as the seller above) will often price the property at its appraised value. Why is this? Because the appraised value is almost an "official number" since it is given by a person having recognized credentials. So the seller can easily justify the asking price by simply saying "I'm only asking for the appraised value of this excellent property. It's really worth much more!"

Property type	250-unit residential building
Annual income with $1,000 per month average rental and 5 percent vacancy allowance	$2,850,000
Appraised value	$12,000,000
Asking price	$12,000,000
Mortgage available @ 85 percent of appraised value	$10,200,000
Rehab loan available with seller cosigning	$2,000,000
Mortgage out cash*	$12,200,000 – $12,000,000 = $200,000
Closing costs	$60,000
Miscellaneous costs	$25,000
Net to you	$200,000 – $60,000 – $25,000 = $115,000

* = Mortgage + Rehab loan = $10,200,000 + $2,000,000 = $12,200,000.

The whole key to mortgaging out is getting the money you need that takes you from the fixed rate long-term mortgage to the selling price. In the situation just presented, the seller was able to get a rehab loan which the buyer took over and is making the monthly payments on for the seller.

The buyer got the seller to take out the $2,000,000 rehab loan on these terms:

1. The property needed fixing up.
2. The estimate for the fix-up work was $1,000,000 to $2,000,000, depending on how much work was done and by whom.
3. The seller wanted out fast; the buyer convinced the seller it was a good deal all around, including cosigning on the rehab loan, with a "reverse flip," as explained earlier.

So concentrate on getting that second, or third, loan. It's the key to getting cash out of a property when you buy it. Now let's see how *you* can pay *all* your costs in mortgaging out, including the cash that goes into *your* pocket!

Closing costs, as listed earlier, cover your legal, title search, title insurance, deed recording, and similar fees. There may also be miscellaneous costs to you for fuel in the tank, water usage fees paid in advance which you will benefit from, real estate taxes already paid by the seller, and so on. So your actual closing and miscellaneous costs will vary widely, depending on circumstances. Further, you can negotiate many of the costs with the seller, to reduce their impact on *you*. The closing and miscellaneous costs given are the result of negotiations between the buyer and seller.

FINANCING YOUR MORTGAGING OUT COSTS

Never try to mortgage out with property that doesn't pay you an income. Why? Because nonincome-producing property:

- Is a drain on your regular earnings
- Will not pay for itself while you're holding it
- Can put you into serious financial problems

So you should avoid using raw land, unoccupied buildings, and similar nonincome producers as your mortgaging out vehicles. Turn, instead, to strong income producers, like the property discussed here. Let's see how it will finance your mortgaging out costs:

Income, from above	$2,850,000 per year
Expenses @ 40 percent of income	$1,140,000 per year
First mortgage payment @ 10 percent for 30 years	$1,074,000 per year, rounded off
Rehab loan payment @ 10 percent for 10 years	$ 317,184 per year
Total annual costs	$2,531,184
Annual cash flow to you	$ 318,816

It is this annual cash flow of $318,816 that you'll use to pay any other costs that may crop up. But with an income of this level, and ownership of the property, you should not have any difficulty:

- Getting additional loans you might need
- Establishing a line of credit at any lender
- Repaying small bills you might have run up while getting started in your real estate business

Thus, if you need interim money between deals you can easily get it from the commercial bank that handles your real estate business account. The fact that you're running some $2,850,000 through the bank each year will make you more friends than you ever thought possible.

Likewise, your $115,000 cash which you received at closing will be a nice nest egg in the bank. You can borrow against this, dollar for dollar, if you need other interim funds for any business purpose.

So your mortgaging out cash and your monthly positive cash flow from this property put you in an ideal position of power. You can go on to more income properties or just sit tight and enjoy yourself—free from complaining bosses!

And you can pick up more greenbacks from unusual sources once you have the income and cash from your property. These unusual sources are:

- *Lines of credit* on your credit cards—with a strong income and cash in hand, banks will beg you to accept more cards.
- *Second mortgage lenders* wanting to put out more cash to earn a higher interest income; they will package all kinds of unusual loans for you.
- *Investors wanting real estate* in their portfolio without the daily work of supervising the property will ask you to take their money and put it to work for them—and *you!*
- *"Hard-money" lenders* (high-interest-rate loans) who will make short-term loans (5 years, or less) to you to get you over some high-cost times.

Here are two letters from readers showing what people are doing today to mortgage out while still showing a positive cash flow from their property:

> *Since I've been subscribing to your International Wealth Success newsletter I've acquired two 5-plex buildings and realize a positive cash flow of over $750 per month using a low investment of plastic (credit card line-of-credit) money. Not bad for a beginner.*
>
> *   *   *
>
> *I would like to thank you for your monthly newsletter. I am just about to settle on my first income-producing property with over 100 percent financing being used.*

Repay All Your Costs as Quickly as Possible

The income from your properties will pay *all* your costs and leave you a positive cash flow each month. To ensure your steady business growth and improved cash reserves, take these simple steps:

1. Repay *all* your costs as soon as you can.
2. Budget a certain amount of money each month to be used to repay costs.
3. Make payments on costs *first* each month so you rid yourself of the burden of these expenses as soon as possible.
4. Remember that each payment you make reduces your debt while it improves your ability to borrow in the future.
5. Take pride in paying what you owe; each payment helps the person receiving it while making you financially stronger in their eyes, and on your credit report.
6. Recognize here and now that if you're going to rid yourself of the daily rat race of a job, you'll have to take on other responsibilities, such as paying off your costs as quickly as possible.

Use Notes to Repay Your Legal Costs

You'll have legal costs in *all* your real estate deals because you should *never* enter any real estate transaction without the advice and counsel of a competent attorney. If you can't find a suitable attorney, don't do the deal! Why? Because:

- Real estate transactions can be complex; as a businessperson you have enough to think about without having to worry about the legal aspects of a deal.
- Real estate is involved with the essence of wealth—land. So every deal is surrounded by legal considerations that are centuries old. You *must* know how to deal with these matters.
- Using a qualified attorney can save you much money and grief. Since the attorney's fee is legally deductible as a legitimate business expense, you'd be foolish to neglect having an attorney on your "case"!

Since attorney fees can mount up, they can be a burden to pay all at once. A way around this big financial hit of attorney fees is to give the attorney a promissory note for all, or part, of what you owe.

With a promissory note, you can pay the attorney over a period of time. Thus, you could pay an attorney $100 per month for several years. This makes it easier for you to pay. And the attorney is assured of a regular monthly payment which improves his or her cash flow.

To work out such a deal, suggest it early in your talks with the attorney. Most attorneys are willing to work out a suitable payment arrangement. Why? Because they know that if you don't pay they can always sue you!

EIGHT KEY IDEAS FOR EASILY PAYING YOUR COSTS

Here are eight easy-to-use ways to get more cash to pay your various costs. Use those ways that appeal to you. Or take some of the suggestions and change them to suit conditions in your area.

1. Give people you owe large sums of money a "piece of the action" in your project. That is, give them a 1 percent, 2 percent, and so on ownership in your property in place of paying them for the service rendered. You can offer a "sweetener" to attorneys, building rehab contractors, engineers, and so on for work they do for you.

2. Work out a reduced price for cash. See if the people you owe money will take 20 percent, 25 percent, and so on less if you pay quickly for their services. Some will agree to a reduced payment. You can then use the saving to pay off other bills you have.

3. Look into 0 percent interest loans available in some states to real estate owners who provide housing for the elderly, the low-income, or the handicapped. Such loans will reduce your interest cost while ridding you of big bills.

4. Seek real estate grants made by both public and private groups to provide needed housing to certain selected population groups. Grants do not have to be repaid if you do the work for which the grant is made. You can use grant funds to repay other costs if you make this part of your grant proposal. See the back of this book for helpful information on getting grants for real estate projects of all kinds.

5. Borrow against your rent security deposits to get funds to pay off other costs. Have your attorney see if this is allowed in your state. If such lending is not allowed, use the rent security deposit as a "friend maker" with your bank so they make you an unsecured loan.

6. See if a wraparound mortgage can be arranged on the property to give you more cash to repay debts, quickly. A wrap can reduce your monthly payments to free up more cash to repay other costs.

7. Put your mortgaging out funds in an interest-bearing insured account. Use the interest to repay other costs. Be sure not to invest your mortgaging out cash in any type of security that could go down in value.

8. Seek out foreign lenders where you have "trophy" type projects, that is, new buildings in highly desirable areas of a city. Such projects are easily financed with new money at values higher than the current market. This means you can get extra cash to repay some of your costs.

Mortgaging out is the way to go, if you want to build your real estate fortune starting with zero cash. You now have the tools you need to start. And I'll help *you* with advice, financing, and even hand-holding—if you need any of these. Try me and see!

SUCCESS STRATEGIES FOR BUILDING YOUR REAL ESTATE WEALTH IN GOOD TIMES AND BAD TIMES

1. Get down-payment loans—even with bad credit—by using the power of having a motivated seller cosign for you or having your motivated seller pledge collateral to enhance your credit so you get the loan you need. Remember: Sellers can use the equity in their property to get you the loan to buy the property. Most sellers have more collateral than buyers. Trade on this fact and you can get the downpayment loan you need for any type of income real estate. Never give up your search for the down payment loan you need to get your first income property. Why? Because once you have that first property it will be much easier to get new loans for your second, third, etc. property. Your assets zoom as soon as you start making regular payments on your first income property. If you can't get the loan you need from conventional sources, try IWS, as detailed in Chapter 8 in this book. It may be the answer you need.

2. Look for older sellers in a hurry to unload their property so you can negotiate a zero-down deal for the property. Seek properties having hefty rent security deposits which become yours as soon as you take title to the property. Your rent security money will be your mortgaging out cash because you can borrow against it—dollar for dollar—using it as your collateral. And this cash is tax-free to you because it is not income—it is cash held in reserve for any damages your tenants might cause to the unit they rent. Depending on the number of months' rent your seller took for the security deposit (usually 1 month to 3 months), and the number of units in the property you're buying, your security deposits can range from a low of $5,000 to a high of $100,000, or more. So the security deposits can get you the loan you need, can put you in a cozy position with your banker, and can rescue you from financial disaster. That's why I strongly urge you to keep a careful watch on opportunities offered by sellers who want to sell their property quickly. It could provide the "gold" you need for the start of a great life in income real estate!

3. Search for assumable-mortgage properties for sale which will allow you to take over an income producer without it showing on your credit report. Further, if the seller likes you, he/she may not even check out your credit. So you can take over an income producer even though your credit may not be the best. And assumable-mortgage properties often have a lower interest rate. This means your monthly mortgage payments will be smaller, allowing you to earn a higher profit from the property. So spend time looking for assumable-mortgage properties—they can make you rich! Just be sure to have a real estate attorney check out the assumable clause in the mortgage. You can get a copy of the mortgage from the seller. The assumable clause in a mortgage allows you to take over making the monthly payments on the mortgage with no change in the interest rate on the mortgage, no change in the term (length of time for payoff), and no change in the amount of the payment. You also assume the responsibility of paying off the mortgage in the time stated in the original document. There is seldom a credit check when you assume such a mortgage. Many FHA and VA mortgages contain an assumable clause in them. If an assumable clause does not exist, see if the seller will allow you to assume the payments on the existing mortgage. This is called *assumption of the mortgage*. You make the payments but the seller is liable until you complete making all the payments on the loan. Again, there seldom is a credit check when you assume a mortgage.

4. Get an anxious seller to take out an equity loan for the required down payment, plus 15 percent more. You assume the responsibility for repaying the entire equity loan, which includes your 15 percent mortgaging-out cash. For example, with an $85,000 required down payment, have the seller take out a $100,000 equity loan on the property. Of this amount, $85,000 goes to the seller as his/her down payment; $15,000 goes to you as your mortgaging-out cash. So you've provided a win-win situation for the seller and yourself. You will—of course—have to make monthly payments on the $100,000 loan. So you must be certain that the income from the property can support these payments, plus the first mortgage payment, and all the expenses associated with the property.

IMPORTANT POINTERS TO KEEP IN MIND

- When you mortgage out, you gain ownership of an income property and come away from the closing with cash money in hand. You're paid to buy an income property!
- Money you get when you mortgage out is tax free at the time you receive it.
- There is no standard mortgaging out deal—each one varies, depending on the property, the seller, and the financing that you can arrange.
- To succeed at mortgaging out, use the formula given here—high appraised value, reduced asking price, negotiated lower selling price, ability to get two or more loans on the property, possibility of other types of financing, and ability to repay all loans on the property.
- Use the "reverse flip" to get sellers to cooperate with you so you can mortgage out on properties you want to buy to get you out of the paycheck rat race.
- Paying off loans when you mortgage out can improve your credit rating enormously and get you many more loans than if you use only conventional financing.
- Other sources of mortgaging out funds are property improvement loans, development cost loans, and seller financing.
- Avoid overleveraging when you mortgage out by knowing that money costs money—get to know your cost of funds.
- Be ready for closing and other costs in every real estate deal. Paying these costs off quickly can get you free of debt to the point where your monthly cash flow zooms.
- When you mortgage out you can pick up greenbacks from unusual sources; this can increase your cash holdings enormously.
- To get more cash for your various loan payments, use the eight key ideas given at the end of this section of your book.

How to Buy Up to Two Properties a Month with No Down Payment

If you read the real estate news in hard times you might wonder how you can get an income property with no down payment. You see all kinds of negative-sounding words like recession, overbuilding, credit crunch, and so on in the real estate news. It's enough to discourage the most ambitious BWB.

Yet BWBs I talk to every day go right on buying no-cash-down, and little-cash-down, properties. And these buys give them spendable money in fist *every* month. If these BWBs can get profitable deals going in their spare time in bleak days, so can *you!*

Why? Because even with the gloomiest current news, most BWBs I meet have great ideas and little cash to put these ideas into action. If this applies to you then this chapter is for *you.* But if you're one of the few BWBs who *has* money, this chapter is also for *you!*

Why? Because smart BWBs keep their cash and earn safe interest from it. They use OPM—other people's money—for their investments. Using OPM *you* can take over up to two properties a month without investing a penny of your own. Let's get started making you a real estate millionaire before you leave your present job or business. And you'll do it in good times and in bad times—if you use my suggestions. The zero cash approach to wealth is the best ever invented by anyone!

WHY THE ZERO CASH APPROACH
WORKS FOR BWBS

In wealth building of any kind, you have two main types of action. These types of action are:

1. *Physical*—getting out and *doing* what needs to be done to build wealth safely and securely

2. *Mental*—the planning, believing, and commitment aspects of your mind which get the job done despite any setbacks you might meet

Doing the physical—such as making a phone call, visiting a building you're thinking of buying, getting a rundown on operating costs, and so on—is easy. You just make a list of what has to be done and do it!

Doing the mental work is easy, too, if you know how to control yourself. And one of the best ways to control yourself, I find, is to take on chores that must be finished to reach your goal of financial independence. Starting with zero cash, that is, on borrowed money, has several mental advantages which make you more successful without your knowing it! The mental advantages of zero cash building of real estate wealth are:

1. You get started without depriving your family of needed funds; that is, you have just as much cash as you did before you started your real estate wealth building.

2. Borrowing money motivates you to work harder (the physical) to repay your loans. This makes your properties more successful, helping you build major wealth more rapidly.

3. Money you borrow *must* be repaid. Figuring out how you'll do this gives *you* a good "numbers feel," which helps you understand what really works in *your* wealth building today.

In the zero cash approach you borrow the money you need to take over a property. So *no* money comes from your own bank account. True, you *must* repay every loan you take out to buy property. But the interest on these loans is provable and tax deductible. Further, having to repay these loans makes *you* more successful!

Let's take a look at two zero cash deals to see how they work for people like yourself, giving you:

- Control of an income property without your having to put up any cash

- Monthly income from which you pay for the property while getting legitimate tax deductions and a tax-sheltered positive cash flow

Deal No. 1. A 3-unit income building is available for sale for $350,000, with $50,000 down being asked. You contact the seller, who is the building owner. After visiting the building (your *physical* action), you go home and work the numbers on the building (your *mental* action). It appears that you can have a small monthly positive cash flow if you buy at the seller's price, instead of trying to get him to reduce the price by 10 percent, or more. So you go back to the seller and tell him that the property interests you but that you'll need a loan from the seller for the $50,000 down payment. In real estate parlance, this is called a *purchase money mortgage.* You will also assume (take over) the seller's $300,000 first mortgage which already exists on the property. Your purchase money mortgage (often shortened to PM) will have a term of 5 years while the first mortgage still has a 23-year term remaining on it. You get the property, the seller gets your monthly payments on the PM mortgage, and everyone wins.

What's the key to deals like these? The key is finding a seller who believes that you'll do a good job running his or her property while regularly repaying the money owed. Your biggest selling job in this type of zero cash deal is convincing the seller of your sincerity and your dependability.

My experience shows that if you *really* want to succeed in real estate, you can —and will—find PM mortgage deals. They *are* around. You just have to snoop them out! Later in this chapter we'll show you how—and where.

Deal No. 2. You find a parking lot in a medium-sized city that does a steady business 5 days a week providing space for the cars of local office workers. The seller wants to move elsewhere and is willing to sell the lot for $200,000. You ask how much of a down payment is sought and you're told $25,000. Since you don't have $25,000 you offer the seller a *land contract,* which is a way to buy land on an installment basis. Thus, you offer to pay the seller $2,500 for 12 months to give the seller the down payment, plus an additional $5,000. When the seller receives the $30,000, then you will be given title to the property with a long-term mortgage for the remainder, or $175,000 (= $200,000 − $25,000). You get the property and its income. The seller gets a dedicated person to run the business while paying for it. By retaining title to the property until the down payment has been made, the seller retains control. And, of course, the seller receives an extra $5,000 from the sale. The land contract is also called a *contract for deed and installment land contract.*

Here, again, you will "work" the seller to allow you to take over the income property with no cash down. Does it take work? It sure does! But think of the results. You get a regular income from a property that's rising in value while you sleep. Meanwhile, the property is paying for itself. Could you ask for anything better?

HOW, AND WHERE, TO FIND ZERO CASH PROPERTIES TODAY

You *must* look for zero cash properties. At the start, they will seldom fall into your lap. To find such properties today, you must build a list of local real estate data sources including:

- Your local newspapers—they can really help you
- Real estate brokers in your area
- Foreclosure authorities—see Chapter 3
- For-sale-by-owner groups in the area
- Apartment owners' associations
- Attorneys specializing in real estate in your area
- Any other local source of real estate information, such as the multiple listing newspapers published in many residential areas
- Internet websites listing foreclosure opportunities

Now don't scoff at this list. It works! I've had readers who—on their first look in a local paper—found a zero cash property. They visited the property, made an offer, and took it over within days. *You* can do the same—if you devote time to looking for what you want. Let's take a look at each source of wealth building information.

Local Newspapers

Look in the Sunday edition. It usually has more ads. Keep your eyes open for ads that say:

- Bank foreclosures available. No cash down. We pay closing costs. Call 123-4567.
- Desperate owner seeks quick sale of 3-bedroom beauty in the Knolls area. Owner financing available to qualified buyers. Call 234-9876.

- Estate seeks quick sale of 10-unit apartment house. Make offer. Financing in place. Call 345-7986.
- Take over existing payments on income building. No cash needed. We pay closing costs. Call 765-2345.

Each of these ads has promise for you. And you'll certainly find other versions of such ads. Learn to spot a seller who needs a fast sale. You can work a zero cash deal with such a person—if you try!

Local Real Estate Brokers

Most real estate brokers won't talk to you if you tell them you're looking for a zero cash deal. Why? Because their training is full of cautions that say:

- Qualify the buyer—he or she must have money to put down on a property.
- Earnest money is part of every successful deal.
- Your commission won't arrive on time if you do a zero cash deal.
- Getting paid your commission is the most important part of any deal you do.

But not every real estate broker lives by these cautions. Since the seller pays the commission to the broker, you *can* find deals where the seller is so grateful to get a property sold that a commission is paid. On such deals the real estate broker will be willing to help you find and negotiate the sale of a zero cash property.

So spend some time talking to local real estate brokers. Don't tell them you're seeking a zero cash deal during your early conversations. Just tell the broker that you're seeking deals with the minimum cash down, which is true. You want to pay zero cash down!

Foreclosure Authorities

Chapter 3 of this book lists the many foreclosure authorities you can contact locally. Just remember that some will advertise in your local newspaper. That's why it's important that you scan the "Real Estate for Sale" ads every Sunday in your local newspaper. There's gold in them 'thar ads!

For-Sale-by-Owner Groups

The for-sale-by-owner craze is popular all over. You can cash in on this craze by contacting groups of such people locally. Just remember these facts about for-sale-by-owner offers—the owner-seller:

- Seeks to sell by himself or herself to avoid the 6 percent broker's commission paid on the usual home sale.
- Saving 6 percent in commission means $6,000 more per $100,000 of the sales price.
- Sellers acting for themselves have almost always read a book or taken a course on selling their home; you can get an insight into their thinking by reading two or three such books yourself.
- To work a zero cash deal with such sellers you almost always must offer them their exact selling price. If you try to negotiate the asking price downward, your zero cash deal will go out the window!

For-sale-by-owner deals are almost always slower than sales from newspaper ads, foreclosure authorities, and so on. So be prepared for a longer—and possibly more painful—negotiation. But the results are worth the time and effort when you get the property you seek.

Apartment Owners' Association

Look in your local phone book for the listing of the Apartment Owners' Association. Call and ask about the membership requirements. Join, if you can.

Once you're in the association, attend meetings. Get to know older, about-to-retire, owners. Become friendly with them. Find out about their buildings. Ask about their future plans. Since few younger people pay any attention to older people, you'll find a ready welcome.

As time passes you'll find that older owners will call you and ask if you have any interest in one or more of their properties. When a seller comes to you, an immediate advantage develops for you. Don't rush into asking for a zero cash deal. Instead:

- Take time to carefully study the financials (income and expense statements) for each property.
- Point out to the seller any disadvantages you see that might grow out of the financials.

- Inform the seller that you're cash-short and that any deal would have to be based on minimum cash down on the property.

- Don't rush a sale; let it develop slowly. Remember that your seller probably has had the property for years and is reluctant to part with it unless the buyer is a person who will take as good—or better—care of the property as the seller.

Yes, older sellers can get you started. But it does take a lot of work on your part to build the confidence these sellers have in you. Yet the results can really be worth your effort!

Real Estate Attorneys

In any area you'll find a group of attorneys specializing in real estate transactions. These professionals can be a big help to you in locating zero cash-down properties. Since the attorney's fee does not come from a commission on a sale, there's less of a problem getting information than with a real estate broker.

The best way to get information from an attorney is by becoming friendly with the person. You can do this by consulting the attorney of your choice about specific real estate deals you have in mind. To learn which attorneys handle real estate transactions locally, call the bar association and ask for some recommendations. You'll be given the names of three to five locals who have real estate specialties.

As with members of the Apartment Owners' Association, you have to act slowly with attorneys. Why? Because if you try to rush ahead you may produce a false impression.

Convince the attorney of your sincerity and dedication to building your fortune in real estate. Then move in on getting property for the least cash down. Before you know it, you may have several zero cash deals!

Other Local Sources to Tap

Many residential areas have small magazinelike booklets advertising properties for sale. Some of these multiple-listing booklets will contain as many as 500 ads per month for properties. Almost all buildings for sale will be illustrated by a photograph.

While almost all these property ads will seek a down payment, you never know when circumstances will force a seller to accept zero cash down. So it will pay you to look over the ads carefully and check those properties for which:

- A very low down payment is asked
- Contain the words "Financing available"
- Depict the seller as desperate for a sale

While you may not find many zero cash properties this way, it's still worth a few minutes a month to look. When you do find a zero cash property through such a listing, it's likely to be an excellent one in superb condition. The seller just had to move fast for any of a number of unforeseen reasons.

Search the Internet for Zero Cash Properties

If you use a computer and have access to the Internet, look for zero cash properties which may be listed on various websites. You can contact the seller by e-mail for detailed information about the property being offered. If you don't own a computer you can visit your local library, high school, or Boy or Girl Scout troop and ask to use their computer to access listings of zero cash properties. Since the computer and the Internet have many uses in real estate, it is wise for you to learn to use a computer as soon as you can. *But it is not necessary for you to own, or use, a computer to get rich in real estate today!*

FRAMING A ZERO CASH PROPERTY OFFER

Once you find a suitable property for which you think zero cash will work, you're ready to frame an offer and make it to the seller. Key steps to take in framing your offer are:

1. Size up the seller's cash needs
2. Negotiate zero cash for the property
3. Substitute paper for cash
4. Convince the seller of your sincerity
5. Make a "low-ball" offer
6. Know your income and expense numbers for the deal

Let's take a look at each of these keys to see how it might work for you. Remember: I have only one thought in mind. That thought? *Your* outstanding success in real estate—starting this very moment. So let's make *you* a success by using these powerful keys.

Size Up the Seller's Cash Needs

When you free yourself from being a workhorse for someone else for a pinch of paltry hay a day, you take on certain duties at the start. One of these duties is meeting the seller of a property you want to buy. (Later on, after you own several properties, you can assign this chore to someone else, if you find it a bore.)

Meet the seller as soon as you can after deciding that a property has some income potential for you. When you meet the seller, *listen* more than you talk. Why? Because when you're listening, you *learn!* When you're talking, you seldom learn.

While listening, try to learn if the seller:

- Is under pressure to sell the property
- Whether the seller has external pressures on him or her to move the property quickly
- What cash needs, if any, the seller faces

Seldom will the seller tell you directly what needs for cash he or she faces. Such needs usually surface as comments about:

- Bills that must be paid
- Tax obligations facing the seller
- Other demands for quick payment the seller must meet

When you detect such needs, it's time for you to make a zero cash offer. But where will the seller's cash come from? It will come from the new long-term first mortgage you'll get on the property. The seller's existing mortgage, if any, will be paid off by the new mortgage.

If you assume the existing first mortgage, then the seller's cash will come from the savings made by not having to make a monthly mortgage and tax payment. Either way, the seller wins.

Knowing the seller's cash needs can put you in the driver's seat when it comes to buying property. So *listen* carefully. It could put big bucks into your pocket. Soon you'll be able to junk your threadbare worker's clothes for the snappy new designs worn by the wealthy! Be sure to make notes about your views of the seller's cash needs so you won't forget.

Negotiate Zero Cash for the Property

Few sellers will accept your first zero cash offer. What you have to do is *show* the seller why a sale to you is to his or her advantage. So you must convince the seller that:

- Selling quickly to you is a smart move.
- You're an ideal buyer for this property.
- You'll give the seller the best deal possible.
- There won't be any hassles during the sale.

It may take you three to five meetings with the seller to get your points across. But if you work at it, a zero cash deal *is* possible. You must keep your goal (getting the property) in mind at all times. And you must keep moving toward that goal every moment of your meeting with the seller.

But what if the seller refuses to budge on his or her cash down payment demand? When you see that the seller won't move from his or her stated position, just say, gracefully: "It's been great talking to you. As you know, I love your property and would be happy to own it. If you change your mind, just give me a call. I'll probably still want the deal."

You'll be surprised to find that you get calls from sellers a few weeks after you walk away from the deal. In a slow real estate market there aren't that many buyers around. When the seller realizes that your offer is really a good one, he or she will often give you a ring on the phone.

When the seller calls back, it will usually be with a reduced cash down payment demand. Stand your ground! Tell the seller that you're seeking a zero cash deal—nothing less.

The seller may cave in at this point. Or he or she may mutter some unpleasant remarks and hang up. Don't give up! Wait a few more weeks. You may get a call in which the seller reluctantly accepts your offer because none better has come along. This means you've won!

Substitute Paper for Cash

A promissory note, which commits you to repay a stated amount of money by a given date, is often called *paper.* You can substitute paper for cash. Thus, instead of giving a cash down payment for a property, you can give the seller a promissory note.

Such a note is "cash" of sorts. Why? Because the seller can take the promissory note to a bank or other lender and have it discounted for cash. When a note is *discounted,* it is sold to a buyer for an amount of cash less than the face value of the note. Let's look at an example:

> You buy a property for zero cash, giving the seller a promissory note for $25,000 for the down payment. The seller takes this note to a lender who discounts it 30 percent, or 0.30 x $25,000 = $7,500. Thus, the seller will receive $25,000 – $7,500 = $17,500 cash for the note.

The same procedure can be used for PM mortgages. Plenty of lenders buy PM mortgages. The usual price is between 60 and 80 percent of the face amount of the mortgage. Much depends on the maturity date and interest rate on the PM mortgage.

Knowing these facts about promissory notes and PM mortgages, you can urge your seller to accept either type of paper in place of cash. You will then be getting your zero cash property.

And if you want to work for commissions in real estate, instead of owning property, you can become a discount mortgage cashout broker. Full details are given in the kit of this name described in the appendix to this book.

Convince the Seller of Your Sincerity

Sellers are often nervous. Why? Because selling a property represents a change in their life-style. As you know, most people resist change. In resisting change, while knowing that a change *must* be made, people generate tension within themselves. This shows up as nervousness.

To convince a seller that you're sincere in wanting to buy a property, you have to relieve some of the seller's nervousness. Do this by:

- Showing the seller that you understand his or her nervousness
- Being "human" in your sympathy over the pressure the seller is under
- Comforting the seller and reassuring him or her that the course of action you suggest is the right one

You can do lots of convincing just by sympathetic listening! Most sellers have a tale of woe to tell. If you listen to what they say, you'll score lots of points. So learn to listen and nod agreement—silently.

You'll be amazed, again and again, by what "a little bit of listening" can do for you in getting properties you want. When you listen carefully, sellers may:

- Beg you to take their property with zero cash because "you're such a wonderful person"
- Help you get a loan to buy the property—either by cosigning for you or by taking out the loan themselves and letting you repay it, with you not having to put up one penny of cash
- Introduce you to their lender with a strong recommendation that the lender make you the loan you need—without you having to advance any money at all

The key here is to get what you want simply by being pleasant to, and considerate of, another human being. This doesn't require one penny of outlay on your part!

Make a "Low-Ball" Offer

Once you find a property you want, you're ready to make an offer on it—after you've checked out the numbers for income and expenses. Your best course of action, usually, is:

1. Figure out what price you can afford to offer for the property, based on your "numbers" work.
2. Reduce this price by at least 20 percent *before* you make an offer (thus, you'd offer no more than $80,000 for a property you think is worth $100,000).
3. Make your offer, being careful to stipulate *zero cash* down; don't overlook this important step in your negotiation!

Keep in mind—at all times—that you should not "collapse" if the seller laughs at your low-ball offer. Remember, good friend, you're *negotiating*. There's always some give and take when you negotiate. So don't look for instant acceptance of your first offer. You may have to go "round and round" before your offer is accepted by the seller—after some possible upward adjustments. For instance, a reader recently told me on the phone:

I made a "wild" offer on a residential property—never expecting it to be accepted. But the seller snapped it up! I offered $300,000 for a property worth $425,000, with the expectation that I'd be turned down. Today I took over the property and I'm sure I'll make money from it while I hold it because I've done my numbers work. And when I decide to sell this property, I'm sure I'll make a big profit because it's going up in value every day!

So never, never be afraid to make a low-ball or "bottom-fishing" offer! Sure, the seller might be insulted. But the seller might also be complimented because:

- Your offer might be the *only* one the seller received.
- The dollar amount you offer might be higher than the figure the seller planned to negotiate *up* to.
- All other offers the seller received were "tied up" with conditions unacceptable to the seller.

Remember this: *Any* offer you make to a seller is a compliment! It shows that you value the property enough to go to the trouble of making the offer. While the offer may not be acceptable at first, it may become more attractive as time goes on for any one of the three reasons we just gave you.

To show you how strongly I believe in making a low-ball offer for property you might be able to get for zero cash down, I make you this firm promise:

- As a reader of my *International Wealth Success* newsletter, I will be glad to analyze—free of any charges—any zero cash deal you're considering.
- All you need do is send me the income and expense statement or numbers, the asking price, your offering amount, and your phone or fax number. (You can, if you wish, fax this information to me, or you can mail it, if you prefer.)
- You'll have your answer within 24 hours, or less, if you allow me to call or fax you. By mail, the answer may take longer.

Why do I make this offer? Because I want to show *you* the many advantages of a low-ball offer. And I want to help you overcome any resistance you may have to making such an offer. You *can* survive and grow rich in tough real estate times. It just takes a little courage and smarts!

Know Your Income and Expense Numbers

You can't "wing it" and make money in a zero cash deal! You *must* know the numbers for every zero cash offer you make. Why? Because in a zero cash deal you:

- Are highly dependent on the income from the property because you use this income to repay the loans you take out to buy the property
- Can be put into a negative cash flow situation if your income from the property falls sharply
- Must look ahead and do "what-ifs" for the property to explore various potential problems that might occur in the future
- Should know—*in advance*—what you will do if you have an income shortage, expense increase, or other cash flow problems

Let's take a quick look at income and expense numbers of a typical property to see what we mean. All numbers are rounded off to the nearest thousand dollars. Here are typical numbers you might meet in your wealth building:

Annual rental income	$100,000
Annual property expenses	40,000
Gross profit before loan payments	60,000
Annual loan payments	48,000
Annual net cash flow	12,000

Now it might not seem that $12,000 a year net cash flow is much to have left from an annual rent roll of $100,000. But I'd like to remind you that this property:

- Is paying for itself
- Is increasing in value every day
- Is heading toward giving *you* a larger cash flow after you pay off your down payment loan (the usual term of such a loan is 5 years)

Let's now do some "what-ifs" for this property, remembering that you'll ask the same, or similar, questions for any property you're thinking of taking over for zero cash:

1. *What if* my annual net cash flow goes down (decreases)?
2. *What if* my property expenses rise (increase)?
3. *What if* the property does not increase in value as fast as I expect it to?

We'll now "do the numbers" for these three *What if* questions:

Q. What if my annual net cash flow goes down (decreases)?

A. You have $12,000 annual net cash flow from this property. So your income could go down by $12,000 before you would have a serious problem. This $12,000 decrease would be a 12 percent fall (=$12,000/$100,000). A fall of this size would probably take place only in a very sharp recession or depression. To figure the chances of such an income drop, get data in your local library on the last recession in your area. It will show you how much *vacancy rates* increased during the recession. Apply these rates to the property you like and see how much your income might decline.

Q. *What if* my property expenses rise (increase)?

A. Your annual property expenses are $40,000. not including loan repayments. These expenses could rise to $52,000 (=$40,000 + $12,000 cash flow) before you'd have any serious problem. Since a rise of this amount would be 30 percent (=$12,000/$40,000), which is a very large number, you are reasonably safe. Where your property could stand only, say, a 5 percent rise, you could have future problems. As a guideline, your property should be able to withstand a 15 percent cost increase before its cash flow becomes zero.

Q. *What if* the property does not increase in value as fast as I expect it to?

A. You are *not* spending your rise in value on a daily basis. So you really don't need the value rise in your operations. Instead, you'll spend the value rise *after* you sell the property—which could be several years from now. So a slower rise in value really doesn't affect you day by day. All you have to do is wait for the property to reach the value you seek, before you sell it!

PROVEN WAYS TO NEGOTIATE WITH SELLER OR BROKER

Your goal, remember, is to get up to two properties a month with zero cash. So you'll have to learn how to negotiate because:

- Almost all sellers seek some cash from a deal.
- Brokers think that there must be cash passed or they won't get their commission (this is *not* so!).

To be able to negotiate more forcefully, and more successfully, you must prepare yourself. Here are the essential steps in negotiating any zero cash real estate deal:

1. Know market conditions in your area.
2. Research local property sales.
3. Never pay the asking price or asking cash down.
4. Clue yourself in to national real estate trends.
5. Convince the seller of zero cash advantages.
6. Take advantage of any time pressures on the seller.
7. Never be afraid to walk away from a deal.

Let's look at each of these essential steps to see how you can apply them. The negotiating techniques you'll learn can put you into the million-dollar class in both good times and bad times!

Know Market Conditions in Your Area

If sales are tight in your area, you must know this! Why? Because knowing that sales are tight (difficult) can put you into a powerful negotiating position. All you need say is: "Real estate sales are down 30 percent in this area, Mr. Seller. You have a great chance to sell to me. You should grab my offer while you can. I may find better deals on the way home today!"

To learn local market conditions in your area, look in your newspaper—especially on Sunday. The real estate section will tell you exactly what's happening. Look at the ads listing properties for sale. In hard times you'll see words like the following in some of the ads:

- *High assumable mortgage.* This means you can get in for zero, or very little, cash.

- *Motivated seller.* This seller wants out. You can get him or her out easily—on zero cash!

- *Owner financing available.* The seller will sell to anyone (almost) because he or she recognizes that a creditworthy buyer is hard to find. So if your credit isn't the strongest, or doesn't exist because you're a beginner, your chances of getting the property are excellent.

- *Priced to sell.* This owner really wants out. Why don't you help him, or her, to get out?

- *Must go (or be sold) this week.* This is a desperate seller. You should come to the seller's rescue and take the property for zero cash down!

- *No cash down; owner financing.* Your answer is staring you in the face. Call the owner—fast!

All these lines are from actual real estate ads in a recent Sunday paper. What do they tell you? They say both directly and indirectly that the sellers in the area where this paper is published are hungry to close a deal. Knowing this you can push hard for *your* no-cash deals! Remember: Knowledge is power. Get knowledge and you—too—can be in control.

Research Recent Property Sales

There's plenty of reliable information on property prices available to you in your area free of charge. This free information can be obtained from:

- Real estate brokers in your area
- Tax records offices
- Local attorneys
- Newspaper listings of sales
- A local Internet website

What use can *you* make of sales price information? Plenty. Thus, you can:

1. Use a low price for a similar property as a bargaining tool to have the asking price of the property you want reduced to a level that you can make money on.
2. "Read" a seller's offer to see if the asking price is sensible in view of similar properties in the area.
3. Show a seller how generous you are by citing actual selling prices for similar properties in the area, comparing your offer to those prices.

Just the very fact that you *do* know the selling prices of similar properties in the area will alert the seller to your knowledge. Any seller will be less likely to try to extract from you more than the offered property is worth, once he or she knows what you know!

You can even get data on the down payment amount. Sometimes this will be available directly. At other times you'll have to figure it out as the difference between the long-term recorded mortgage and the selling price. Concentrate on the low-down payment properties. These allow you to work a sharper deal with the seller, by pushing down the cash needed for the deal. If you find any zero-down deals, use these as your negotiating tool.

The key idea here is to use *all* the data that's available to you. It's free and it's there for the asking. Your attorney or a local real estate broker will be glad to give you the address and telephone number of your local tax assessor's office, plus the county clerk and other officials who are involved. Since the procedures for listing sales data vary a little from one community to the next, you must consult locally. Just remember this: Research *does* pay off!

Never Pay the Asking Price or Cash Down

Sellers always ask for a higher price than they expect to get. And they always ask for more cash down than they believe someone will pay.

Why? Because by being able to negotiate a selling price and cash request downward, sellers know that they can make a buyer feel that he or she is getting a bargain—as a result of their great negotiating skills.

Since you *know* that a seller expects to reduce the price of the property before it is sold, you'd be foolish to pay the asking price and the requested cash down. There is only one instance in which you should consider paying the asking price for a property. This instance is:

> Consider paying the full asking price when by doing so the seller will agree to zero cash down. Getting a property for zero cash down can make it worth your while to pay the asking price.

When you're working on a salary and are cash short—as most BWBs are—it's more important to build up your assets than to worry about the price you're paying for an income producer. Keep these important facts in mind at all times:

1. As long as a property can pay for itself, plus give you a positive cash flow, its actual price is not too important so long as it reflects fair value.
2. Once you own several income properties giving you a regular monthly income, you can then start to negotiate from a position of power. But, at the start, your most important goal is getting the most property for the least money down.

Your future is bright if you look for, and close on, up to two properties a month on zero cash. If you start with zero cash properties, as almost all my successful readers do, you're almost certain to break into the big money. So look for zero cash first, property price second! And if you can get the asking price reduced while putting zero cash down, go for it!

Get to Know National Real Estate Trends

The price you pay for a property in your area is influenced by what's taking place in the national real estate market. So you should know what's going on throughout the county, and the nation. The best way to keep informed about national real estate trends is to:

1. Read a national newspaper's business section every day
2. Get copies of national real estate magazines and read them regularly
3. Watch national TV programs having real estate and business coverage—make notes on key ideas presented about new trends in property values and sale prices

4. Access real estate websites on the Internet for developments in commercial real estate, financing trends, and properties available

Knowing what's going on in real estate nationally can help you work better deals with sellers. It also helps you spot areas where there are great values for zero cash down. Then you may write a letter such as this reader's:

I've been a reader of yours for several years. I find your books enjoyable and lucrative and informative. Seven years ago my wife and I started buying single-family detached homes here in the Washington, D.C., area (mostly in the Virginia suburbs). We also own rental properties in Texas and Pennsylvania. The totals are 11 single-family houses, 1 mobile home, and 1 RV park in south Texas. All the houses provide a nice positive cash flow.

Knowledge—as we all know—is power. You can become a more powerful BWB if you get knowledge of what's happening in real estate, both nationally and worldwide. And now's the time to start acquiring that know-how, both nationally and worldwide!

Use All Your Favorable Data

You're building your real estate know-how to get results. These results are:

- To buy up to two income properties a month using zero cash
- To have a positive cash flow from these properties
- To go on building your income property holdings until you have the level of positive cash flow that gives you the income you seek

Knowledge without action is useless. So you must use your know-how to get the zero cash properties you seek. To do this:

1. List those conditions that make your offer attractive to the seller.
2. Prepare a "seller's benefit list" which gives the seller a picture of the benefits he or she will obtain by dealing with you.
3. Use sales prices of similar properties as an example of why your offer is so fair to the seller.

What you're doing is preparing your "sales pitch" to convince the seller that a deal with you makes real sense. Now I know that making such a sales pitch may turn you off. You might prefer to put down some cash and not have to negotiate.

I fully respect such feelings, good friend. But what I'm trying to do is to show *you* how to conserve any cash you may have and get properties for zero cash. Further, most of my readers don't have that much cash to invest. So the zero cash route is the only one they can follow. And they're willing to sharpen their negotiating skills and do their homework to get the results they seek.

Remember this: Most buyers of income real estate are not too well organized. If you follow the guidelines I give you here you'll impress sellers so strongly that they'll hardly be able to refuse your request for a zero cash deal! As one reader wrote:

> *We prepared our real estate loan package in accordance with your examples in How to Borrow Your Way to Real Estate Riches. The man at the bank who approved our loan request said "This is the best loan package I've ever seen." Thanks for your help.*

If you can impress a banker with the results of your know-how (as in this letter, the loan package), you can certainly woo a seller to agree to your offer. So concentrate on using *all* your favorable data to convince your seller that your seriously thought through deal is the best he or she will ever get!

Take Advantage of Seller Time Pressures

Many sellers must sell fast. Why? For any number of reasons:

- A divorce situation requires quick cash.
- Seller "has had it" with the building, the area, the tenants, and so on.
- Winter cold has the seller so depressed he or she wants to flee to a warmer climate—yesterday.
- Death in the family has changed the seller's outlook.
- New interests have grabbed the seller's attention, so there's no time to "mess with" a building.
- And so on.

Most sellers will tell you about their time pressures. Or they will hint that they want out—fast.

Once you sense this time pressure on the seller, you should take action to move in on the seller. How? By:

1. Listing why *your* offer will let the seller get away quickly and easily
2. Searching for ways to get the seller out of the property faster than with conventional financing methods
3. Taking the stance that you're the seller's "savior"—that *you,* and only you, can take him or her out of the property quickly and easily

In acting this way you *are* helping the seller. And if you frame your offer so that you provide speed of sale, the seller will probably go along with your zero cash offer. You set up a win-win situation in which the seller gets what he or she seeks and you get the property you want.

Taking advantage of a seller's time pressures is a great way for you to help the economy while helping yourself. So don't be afraid to use your wits to help a seller while you help yourself!

Never Be Afraid to Walk Out

There will be times when a seller scoffs at your zero cash offer. We're all rebuffed at one time or another in life. Don't give up—as long as you're talking there's hope!

When a seller becomes abusive over your zero cash offer, pick up your papers and walk out. It's a great technique that can win you properties faster than you ever thought possible! Why? Because:

1. Often, there are many fewer offers on a property than a seller would have you believe
2. Your offer may be the only one on the table
3. When you walk out on a seller you transmit a clear and quickly understood message—that you're out of the deal
4. A motivated seller who planned on "playing with your offer" may panic when you walk

Making big bucks in real estate in good times and bad times takes work. And part of that work may be acting out a role that convinces people you know what you want. So don't hesitate to walk out on a deal—if your gut reaction tells you that's what you should do.

In years of real estate dealing I see—almost every time a property is for sale—that if one deal falls through another surfaces almost immediately. And the new deal is often better than the one you walked out on! So have faith. You *will* get the financial independence you seek, if you wheel and deal like a pro.

Make zero cash with positive cash flow your goal. Keep that goal in mind at *all* times. Why? Because you'll get what *you* want if you keep searching for it. Just yesterday a reader called me to say:

> *I'm taking over single-family homes in the Midwest. The typical price ranges from just $20,000 to a high of $55,000. I take them over with zero cash down from my pocket and mortgage out with $1,000, or more, at the closing. And the rental income more than pays for the mortgage, real estate taxes, and my closing costs. While I do risk vacancies, I haven't had one yet. My plan is to get enough of these single family homes to build my positive cash flow to a level where it will cover the few vacancies I might have. Zero cash does work—if you work at it!*

In working with BWBs and helping them complete deals I'm continually amazed at the great creativity and drive people like you have. Just glance at this recent letter from a reader:

> *Since buying and reading your book How to Make $1 Million in Real Estate in 3 Years Starting with No Cash, I have gone out and purchased rental income property by borrowing money only. My first purchase was for $45,000 for a duplex, borrowed (money). Working in Mexico through the week leaves only weekends to shop around for property and money availability. I am looking for properties with separate utilities, very little maintenance or upkeep, and occupied. Assumptions, zero, or very little down are also priorities.*

This BWB, who travels from Indiana every week to work in Mexico, still succeeds! He has my utmost admiration. And in his short letter he outlines his goals:

- Separate utilities—that is, the tenant pays for heat, electric, water, air conditioning, and so on.
- Little maintenance or upkeep—this keeps bills low.
- Occupied—you get income the day you buy the property.
- Assumable mortgage—you don't have to go begging for a new mortgage.
- Zero cash—what we've been urging on you for this entire chapter.

SET YOUR TWO-DEALS-A-MONTH GOAL

With a clear goal you can take over two zero cash properties a month. Without such a goal, you may drift.

To achieve your two-deals-a-month goal, take these fast steps:

1. Build a file of "next properties" as you work.
2. Work on one deal at a time at the start.
3. Be alert at all times to the next deal, and the one after that.
4. Keep score on your deals and use the results to spur you on.

Let's take a fast look at each of these steps to see how you can use them to build your wealth. I'll get you into up to two properties a month somehow! Here are your easy steps:

1. Build a File of "Next Properties"

You'll be generating lots of leads and ideas as you work. It will be easy for you to forget these if you don't note them down.

Your file need not be elaborate. A simple file folder marked "Future Deals" will be enough. Just throw the ad, broker's data sheet, or other information you have on the property into the file when you receive the information. Having such a file on hand will make you feel comfortable. Why? Because you'll know that you'll never run out of good leads!

2. Work on One Deal at a Time at the Start

If you try to work on more than one deal at a time at the start, you may find you become confused by the numbers and the differing time schedules you must meet. So, at the start, keep it simple! Work on only *one* deal at a time. This way you'll be able to give each deal your full attention. Further, you'll improve your chances for outstanding success because your mind will be directed at the one most important deal of your life.

It may seem more romantic to be juggling six deals at once. But romance seldom pays the bills. What you want is MIF—money in fist. You'll get it by working on one deal at a time at the start. Hear me—I speak from experience!

3. Be Alert at All Times to the Next Deal

While concentrating on one deal at a time at the start, there's *no* harm in keeping the next deal in view. That is, you can:

- Have notes handy about your next deal
- Allow your subconscious mind to work through the details
- Be lining up the players who will be in on the deal

By keeping the next deal in mind and being alert to new opportunities you keep your forward motion going. The result is that your wealth builds quickly—faster than you ever thought possible. And that, after all, is why you're reading this book. I want to make *you* rich!

4. Keep Score on Your Deals—Use the Results

Early in this book you started your riches notebook. Use it to keep track of the properties you take over, their market value, your monthly income, your monthly expenses, and so on. Review your holdings *every* month. Just looking over your asset buildup and your monthly income will make you feel good.

If you're into computers, you can put your riches notebook onto a spreadsheet for easy look-up. Having a laptop you can carry around can save you lots of time!

What's more, as your holdings grow you'll become more "wanted" by banks, mortgage companies, and private lenders. Why? Because you're a producer. Such organizations *want* to lend *you* money to put it to work to earn a safe income for the lenders. My organization, IWS, Inc., may even knock on your door to see if you—my good friend—can put some of our money to work for you—to earn us some interest!

NINE GUIDELINES TO GETTING FAST CASH

When you take over zero cash properties you're certain to have what are called "other expenses." These expenses can be for repairs, labor, taxes, and so on. Here are nine ways to get cash quickly to pay for your other costs:

1. Borrow against your rent security deposits. Most lenders will loan dollar for dollar.

2. Use current rental income to pay for some of your other costs. This will keep creditors off your phone.

3. Get a larger than needed property improvement loan. Use the excess cash to pay current other costs. Just be sure that the income from the property can repay all loans, with cash left over.

4. Refinance the long-term mortgage on the property to give you cash while reducing your monthly payments. You can often do this when you assume a mortgage on taking over a property. Lenders are usually happy to refinance an assumed mortgage.

5. Get company credit cards for your real estate business. Use the line of credit to finance your other costs. This will give you fast cash and the interest cost will be deductible as a business expense.

6. Set up a personal line of credit based on your new and stronger financial statement because of your property ownership. Borrow against this line of credit.

7. Bring in a silent partner for a small piece of the action in the property. Give the partner up to 5 percent of the ownership and income for a cash infusion to pay other costs. Be certain to have an attorney prepare the partnership papers.

8. Raise rents to increase your cash flow. Use the extra cash to pay other costs.

9. Get tenants to do work you would otherwise pay outsiders to perform. Use the savings to pay other costs.

You *can* get zero cash properties. They're being sold every day—almost everywhere. Use the tips in this chapter and you'll soon be free of wage slavery! You *can* do it. And I'm ready to help *you*—every day.

SUCCESS STRATEGIES FOR BUILDING YOUR REAL ESTATE WEALTH IN GOOD TIMES AND BAD TIMES

1. Line up down-payment loan sources you can use quickly and easily. Such sources should include (a) your credit-card lines of credit, (b) personal-loan sources (banks, credit unions, finance companies, insurance policies you own, etc.). Know—in advance—the acceptable reasons for which you can obtain your needed down-payment loans to take over two, or more, properties per month. Just remember that few lending organizations will lend you money for real estate down payment. Almost all lenders want you to have some of your own funds in every real estate project because they believe you'll work harder if you do. And their belief is correct for most people!

2. Find suitable zero-down takeover properties by using unusual sources to locate buildings or land to buy. Thus, regularly read ads in (a) newspapers featuring real estate for sale, (b) real estate magazines (both local and national), (c) Internet sites featuring real estate for sale, (d) bank flyers offering REQ (Real Estate Owned) properties, (e) sheriff and tax-sale bulletins offering foreclosed properties. Get on real estate broker lists for free information and leaflets on available properties. Join an apartment owner's association and study their publications for available properties. Using this approach you'll locate more zero-down properties, sooner.

3. Write up a zero cash offer you can send to sellers who want to get out of a property they've held for too long. Your offer can read thus:

> Do you want to sell your property at 10 percent more than your asking price? You can—if you sell it to me! And who am I? I'm a hardworking, honest, reliable Beginning Wealth Builder (BWB) who loves real estate. And I'm dedicated to upgrading and improving every piece of real estate I own. Call me at 123 4567 and I'll show you how you can sell your property in just days. Your Name.

4. Build your negotiating skills by reading books on the subject. Or take courses on negotiating real estate deals. The more skillful you are in negotiating, the better your chances of convincing a seller to sell his/her property to you for zero cash down. Remember—the better you are as a negotiator, the more zero-down deals you can put through. So become a sharp negotiator; it can make you a zero-down real estate millionaire sooner than you think!

IMPORTANT POINTERS TO KEEP IN MIND

- The zero cash approach can make *you* more successful while getting you started faster.
- Zero cash deals give you control of valuable property while you build a steady monthly income.
- Deals with zero cash down will *not* chase you. You *must* look for such deals.
- There are plenty of places and people that can give you access to zero cash deals—everywhere.
- Frame every zero cash offer to meet the seller's needs while getting you the property you seek.
- You will have to negotiate for zero cash property, almost every time you work a deal. But it can be fun and wonderfully profitable.
- Never be afraid to make a low-ball offer or use paper instead of cash.
- Become an expert on income and expense numbers. Not knowing these numbers can make your life more difficult.
- Get to know both local and national market conditions—your know-how will pay off in great deals for yourself.
- Never pay the asking price or cash down if you can work a better deal.
- Use favorable information and take advantage of any time pressures the seller has.
- Never be afraid to walk out on a deal when the terms aren't to your liking. Another deal will come along soon—or the seller will accept your offer.
- Work only one deal at a time when you're starting out.
- Develop creative approaches to paying your other costs.

Smart Ways to
Build Real Estate Riches
with Any Property

6

When tough, tight, money-scarce times strike real estate, you *must* manage your way through the minefields. While management may look like a big, frightening word, it really isn't!

Managing real estate properly in terrible times just takes some common sense. You aim at keeping your real estate income high and your expenses low. You don't have to be a genius to figure this out or to do it. Through dozens of real estate downturns it has been proven, again and again, by BWBs that you *can* make money from almost any real estate property, if you manage it properly. Poor management can drive any property into the red. You don't want this to happen to *your* properties. In this chapter we show you smart ways to squeeze every profit dollar possible out of any property you own or lease for income use.

KNOW YOUR INCOME—TOP-LINE
MANAGEMENT PAYS THE BILLS

You'll often hear the expression "It's the bottom line that counts." What the person saying this means is that it's the profit from a business that's important. This is true.

But how do you get to the bottom line? By starting at the *top line!* Because without a top line there won't be any bottom line. That's why I urge all real estate BWBs to emphasize top-line management first.

Why? Because when you have real income from your properties you can manage them to produce a suitable profit.

145

But without income—the top line—it's impossible to produce a bottom line. So look for the top line first. After you get your top line, it's easy to manage your money to produce the maximum profit.

There are a number of ways to build a strong top-line income. Let's look at them to see how *you* can get the most profit from every property you own or lease.

BUILD YOUR INCOME FROM RENTS, SERVICES, PARKING

Your largest source of income from most real estate properties will be the rents you are paid by tenants. Knowing this, you must:

1. Keep your vacancy rate at zero, or as close to zero as possible. The lower your vacancy rate, the higher your rental income.

2. Collect your rents *on time*. Every day you miss on a rental payment is money *you* lose. So don't put up with slow pays—get them on schedule or get them out of your property!

3. Raise your rents as often as the market will allow. Be aggressive—don't be timid about getting more for the excellent rental space you provide your tenants. Today's almost universally higher rents help you show a higher profit from almost every property.

4. Knowing that rental income provides 95 percent or more of your income, watch every payment you receive. Charge for late payments; sock a big extra charge for bounced checks or money orders. Don't be a charity! Your property is providing clean, well-kept space for tenants. They should pay for the rental of this space on time with good funds.

While your rents are your largest source of income, services may be the second largest source. Such services might include:

- Washing machines and dryers used by tenants
- Beverage and cigarette machines
- Game room facilities
- Swimming pool or health club services
- Cleaning, decorating, or catering services

While such service income will never equal your rental revenues, the service funds can provide some nice extra cash flow. And it is true, of course, that the name of the game in real estate success is cash flow! So take steps to increase every source of cash flow you can find.

Parking fees are important for some property owners. While you'll have to provide free parking for your tenants, there are times when you can convert your free space into money. For instance:

- Where you have large daytime demand for parking space in the vicinity of your property, it may be possible to rent part of your space. This is often done to accommodate the cars of local workers when your property is near a large facility—such as an industrial plant, central postal facility, and so on.

- Check with local law enforcement agencies to see if they need temporary storage space for seized vehicles, trucks, and so on. They pay well—and fast!

Being creative about parking income can pay you big rewards. Not only do you get cash income now, you will also meet people who can be important to your future real estate career. So take a creative approach to your parking income possibilities.

Never delay *any* income from your properties! Get your money *now.* A dollar today is more valuable than a dollar tomorrow. Why? Because if you follow my tips, you'll:

- *Invest short-term funds in a "sweep-type" account where all monies are swept into an interest-bearing account every day.*

- *Use an interest-bearing checking account* so you earn interest on business funds every day.

- *Manage your business cash so it generates the largest* amount of income possible for you and your business.

- *Never pay a bank for handling your money.* Make the bank pay *you* for the right to handle *your* business funds.

- *Deal with a large commercial bank.* Ask the manager what you have to do to get a *free* business checking account that pays interest. Sometimes all it takes is keeping a certificate of deposit (CD) at the bank. Since you'll often have extra funds to put to work, you might as well do it at a bank where you get other benefits.

Managing your real estate money is both fun and interesting. So what if you "only" earn $60 a year (or some other small amount) from your business checking account? It's still money you did not have to work for. Further, it adds to your top line. And that, after all, is what you're trying to do! Remember: Get the money on the *top line*—that is sales income from the space you rent, services you provide, and so on—and you can *manage* the money to give you a *bottom-line* profit.

MARKET YOUR PROPERTIES
FOR ZERO VACANCIES

When a property, or part of it, stands vacant, you're losing money! Sure, you may be getting ready to sell the property at a big profit. But if you're not getting income from it, the property is almost certainly causing *you* to lose money.

To maximize your top line, you *must* strive for zero vacancies in every rental property. For with every square foot of available space rented, your top line is certain to give you a rich bottom line!

Now you won't be able to achieve zero vacancies every day of the year in every property. But if you strive for that zero rate, you're certain to reduce your vacancy rate to close to zero. And that is the goal you're seeking to reach.

How do you achieve a zero vacancy rate? By using low-cost marketing methods that get your property data in front of potential renters. Let's look at such methods and how you can use them.

BUILD LOW-COST MARKETING METHODS
FOR YOUR PROPERTIES

You can spend big money on marketing your properties and get people or firms to rent your space. Often the big-money ads don't produce results as good as low-cost ads. Sometimes *free* ads will produce better results than *paid* ads! Let's see how *you* can save money in marketing your rental properties. What we're talking about here is getting tenants—not selling the property to another buyer. Low-cost ways to market rental space include:

- Free store display bulletin boards
- Local pennysaver newspapers

- Religious group weekly and monthly bulletins
- Government agencies looking for rental units
- State agencies seeking homes
- Local flyers for people seeking space of some kind
- Ads on local Internet websites

Let's look quickly at each of these marketing methods to see how you can use it in your wealth building.

Free Store Display Bulletin Boards

Many stores have bulletin boards on which you can put 3" x 5" cards announcing availability of an apartment, a parking garage, a parking space, and so on. For the cost of a 3" × 5" card you can get your message in front of a large local audience. You can change the message as often as you wish.

Some stores may limit the length of time your ad can run. Thus, some stores have a 2-week limit for ads. Others allow ads to run 1 month. From what I see, the time limit is not too strongly enforced by most stores.

Typical ads you might run on free bulletin boards include ones like these:

4-room apartment in lakes area available. Pretty view. Rent $985 per month. Call owner at 1 23-4567, day or night.

1-room studio for rent; $580 per mo. Excellent building. Call 234-9876.

In my own real estate activities we've kept all our properties fully rented using low-cost bulletin boards. You'll never know their power until you try. So start with your first property—now!

Use Local Pennysaver-Type Newspapers

There are thousands of local weekly and monthly newspapers having strong pulling power for real estate. And their ad rates are low. So you really can't lose by advertising in such papers.

Some local papers will run your ad free. You pay only when you get results, that is, sell a property, rent an apartment, and so on. So you really can't give any excuse for delaying to run an ad when it's free!

For best results, try several local papers. Compare the number of requests you get for more information. Expand your ad in the paper or papers giving the best response. With such an approach you're sure to get results in your search for a sale or a tenant.

Religious Group Weekly and Monthly Bulletins

You can get faster results for some offers by running your ad in a local religious group bulletin. Such groups rarely charge for the ads they run. Instead, they look on the ads as a service to their congregation.

Keep your ads for such bulletins short. Why? Because space is often limited. Long ads may be shortened by the bulletin editor. It's better for you to write a short ad giving the facts you regard important. Then it won't be cut by the editor. Your ad will run as *you* wrote it, not as someone cut it!

Government Agencies Looking for Rental Units

If you own residential units, don't overlook federal government agencies looking for rental units. Why? Because they can be an important source of income for you. Further, your property is safer because:

- Rents are sent directly to you, the owner, instead of to the tenant
- There's no chance of the rent money being "lost" when it comes to *you* first, instead of the tenant
- The rent you'll receive is often several dollars above the equivalent market rent
- Currently offered rates for the Section 8 federal government program range from about $800 to $1,200 per month per unit, depending on the number of bedrooms in the unit

When you rent out Section 8 and similar housing, you are guaranteed to receive rents for a stated period if the tenant remains in the unit. With such a guarantee of income, you can easily get property improvement funding or other types of needed financing.

Call, or visit, your local federal Housing and Urban Development office. You'll meet cooperative people who can give you a quick education in what's available for you locally. Then take action to start the income flowing into *your* bank account—fast!

Contact State Agencies Seeking Homes

With residential property you have opportunities with both federal and state agencies to obtain guaranteed rental income. Some state agencies will even agree to direct deposit of rental income into your business checking account. So you don't even have to endorse your monthly rent check! It goes directly into your account. And my experience shows that your money usually arrives a day or two early. So you have your funds faster.

State agencies to contact include those with the word "Housing" in their name. Look in the back of your local phone book for a listing of your various state agencies. Contact them by phone or mail, asking for information on their housing programs. You'll be surprised at the friendly and helpful responses you'll get. Why? Because such agencies *need* and want what you're offering!

Use Local Flyers to Promote Your Space

Not everyone is into residential real estate. Some people prefer industrial or commercial properties. If this fits you, then consider using flyers distributed to local industries advertising the space you have for rent or for sale.

In the area where I have real estate holdings, people send their flyers to local businesses. The hope is that the business owner needs more space of some kind and will react to the flyer.

Results in many parts of the country show that such flyers work. And the cost of printing 500 or 1,000 flyers is low compared to the results they can bring in. Try them and see for yourself!

Offer Your Residential Units on the Internet

Use the Communities Across America, Inc., website for your community to publicize the availability of your rental units. This organization is a publisher of community websites on the Internet. If you have a business listing in your community, you will—in general—be listed free of charge. Look for the web address of this publisher on the Internet or in any of the many *Yellow Page* directories of Internet websites. You can get excellent publicity for your local rental offerings using this approach.

GET YOUR COLLECTIONS IN ORDER

People will often "hang you up" for your rent payments. They'll give you all kinds of excuses like:

- The check is in the mail.
- There's been an illness in my family.
- The bank made a mistake with my checking account and it will be cleared up in a few days.
- I sent out the check two weeks ago—it must be lost in the mail. I'll send another soon.
- And so on.

Learn now: *Don't accept any of these excuses!* The first time a tenant gives you such an excuse for a late payment of rent, tell the person:

- I'm taking the late payment out of your security deposit and you'll be charged interest of $—per day until I receive the full amount of the rent from you.

Tenants will test you to see how late they can be with their rent without getting you angry. Not every tenant will do this. But a few are certain to try. Don't tolerate such tactics. Take these positive steps:

1. React quickly to the first delay. Don't let the rent be more than two days late before you contact the tenant by phone, fax, or mail, expressing your extreme disappointment.
2. Tell the tenant exactly what penalties you will impose on each and every late payment. Be certain to do this in a businesslike and professional manner. Let the tenant know that you expect—and demand— that rent be paid exactly on time.

3. Charge a stiff penalty if a rent check bounces, as they may now and then. If your bank charges you for a bounced check, multiply your cost by at least three, or more. Why? Because it *costs* you money in time and phone calls to inform a tenant about a bouncing check. You're entitled to be paid for this time.

4. Hire a collection agency to go after your tenants, if they resist your efforts. It won't cost you anything up front to employ a collection agency. They charge only when they collect. While you can use the standard preprinted notice letters to jog your tenants into paying past due rents, my experience with them hasn't been too productive. Bringing a third party (the collection agent) into the picture usually gets quick, and positive, results.

5. Go after *all* income due you! Don't let a single dollar fall behind. You lose money every day you don't have money rightfully yours in *your* hands. Remember: Tenants are different from one-time business customers. Tenants are usually with you for years. Get them started paying on time and your business will boom.

I never get used to the amazing things my readers will do in real estate. A call from a reader in the Northeast opened my eyes to the power of creative thinking in real estate. This reader says:

> I got into real estate through reading your books after I had decided to study medicine and become a doctor. This was after I married, fathered four kids, and had another career. To pay my medical school tuition I bought 21- and 24-unit buildings without putting up one penny of my own cash. In fact, I came away from each closing with money in hand. Simple arithmetic showed me I had to have my rents on time if I were to pay my medical school tuition when it was due. So I set my tenants up to pay a few days before the first of the month so I would not be delayed by any of the usual excuses. Soon I'll be graduating from medical school, thanks to my zero cash real estate and timely rent payments. (This reader used his credit card line of credit and rent security deposits to take over income real estate on zero cash.)

Your key idea here is: *Get the money in when it's due.* With the money in hand, I'm sure you can figure out productive ways to use it.

BECOME A RENT EXPERT FOR YOUR AREA

Too many BWBs are left behind in the "rent race"; that is, they fail to keep up with the rent levels in their area. This can hurt you. Why? Because:

- Not knowing the going rates for rents can cause you to lose money.
- Every dollar in lost rental income can cause a further loss of interest income you might earn on the money.
- Lower than going rents might cause you to get less desirable tenants in your property, leading to increased maintenance and repair costs.

You can easily keep up with rents in your area. All it takes is a few minutes a week during which you:

- Talk to members of the Apartment Owners' Association in your area (or call them on the phone)
- Scan the Sunday papers for ads listing like properties and the asking rents for them
- Talk to rental agents in the area to see what your various units should bring in rental income

It's easy to get left behind if your property is fully rented and your income is strong. Don't let this happen to you! When you fall behind in rental income this year, it carries over to next year, and the year after. So you *must* be aggressive putting through rent increases to keep you up to the going rates in your area.

Many BWBs will give excuses for not raising rents. While I know that each property is unique, you *must* remember that real estate is a *business*. Once you start treating it as a hobby or other form of relaxation (even though it is, and can be, fun), you can run into trouble.

For example, raising the rent by $25 a month on a unit gives you $300 *more* per year income. Since almost every rental unit is tax sheltered by depreciation, this extra $300 is free and clear to *you*. Why give up such tax-free income when it could be yours for the asking?

You can earn *big* dollars per minute when you stay current on local rents. Not only will you make more each month—you might also come across some excellent units for sale for zero cash. It really pays to be involved in *every* aspect of real estate in your area!

To keep up with changes in commercial real estate, log on to the Internet website www.InternetReview.com. You'll get lots of useful information daily on this site.

KEEP YOUR EXPENSES TO THE MINIMUM

In any real estate property held for rental you have money coming in from rents—your top line. Then you have money going out in the form of expenses for fuel, electric, real estate taxes, trash disposal, labor, maintenance supplies, advertising, and so on. To maximize your bottom line— the difference between your top line and the total of the expenses—you *must* keep your expenses as low as possible. Ways in which smart BWBs control their costs in income real estate today include the following—all of which you can probably use in *your* wealth building activities:

- *Use automatic controls for fuel and electric services.* While such controls do cost money, it is easy to figure the savings they will produce. Knowing this, you can easily calculate how long it will take for the savings to pay for the controls. The makers of the controls will quickly show you the payoff time and the savings you'll get. They gladly do this at no cost to you! Some makers will even install the controls free, allowing you to pay for them out of savings.

- *Take an aggressive approach to your real estate taxes.* See if you can get these taxes reduced—even if they're low to start with. You can get real estate taxes reduced if you follow the correct procedure for your area. To learn what steps you must take to get your taxes reduced, contact your local collector of taxes. Most have printed procedures for you to follow. They'll send them to you free of charge. You don't even need an attorney for most tax reduction efforts. But if your situation is complex, call in your regular real estate attorney for help. The fee you pay could be recovered many times by the tax savings you get.

- *Get bids from several local trash disposal companies before you settle on one.* Why? Because rates can vary widely. Getting the cheapest rate saves you money!

- *Look for skilled maintenance personnel for your properties.* I use local police, and fire department personnel in their off hours. They do excellent work and the cost is only one-third of that of local mechanics. So more of my top-line income reaches my bottom line! You, too, can do the same. All it takes is a simple question to a local police or fire department member. The question? "Do you know where I can find some good mechanics to help me maintain my rental properties?" You'll be flooded with good volunteers who work hard and don't charge you an arm and a leg. Remember: Part-time labor is always much cheaper than full-time workers. Most part-timers are so grateful to get the work that they charge you reasonable and affordable prices.

- *Hook up with a local industrial supply house to buy your maintenance supplies.* We use a local supply house that sells only to other businesses. Our discount is 25 percent off the hardware store prices of the same items. So our bottom line is bigger because we use a shrewd approach to buying supplies. We had to register with this supply house by giving them our business card. But once on their computer we can order by phone and get these big savings.

- *Hire at least one rental agent to keep your top line big and steady.* You don't have to pay a rental agent anything. The tenant pays the agent for finding the unit he or she seeks. But you benefit by having a professional marketing your space to prospects. Since you're not paying anything for this effort, you benefit greatly. You get your tenants with little more than a phone call and a short description of the unit you're offering.

Keeping expenses to the minimum is one of the important keys to making it big in real estate in good times and bad times. In good times your profit zooms when expenses are low. In bad times you stay in business and show a decent profit when you keep your expenses down. Either way, you can't lose!

USE SMART FINANCIAL CONTROLS

Today there's *no* excuse for using outmoded financial controls for your real estate business. With the personal computer—from desktop model to laptop—available with fast and simple software for building and property control, you can easily run your business efficiently. Even if you can't afford a PC, you can use carefully planned manual controls which show you where every dollar comes from—and goes.

Cash management is the key to success in every real estate property today. Why? For a number of good reasons. Effective cash management:

- Allows you to pay your bills on time
- Tells you what profit to expect

- Helps you plan for future purchases of properties
- Keeps your business organized for success
- Warns you early on of possible trouble spots

It's not necessary for you to buy a computer to manage your real estate. Instead, all I ask is that you become aware of the importance of effective cash management to your future success.

Once you're aware of the importance of effective cash management, all you have to do is see a certified public accountant who knows real estate. Such a CPA will set up you books for you so you can control every penny that comes in and goes out. Here are a few tips on getting maximum income from money you hold for varying periods of time:

- *Rent security deposits*—These can vary from one month's rent to three months' rent. In some states you must pay a nominal rate of interest on such deposits. *You* keep the difference. *Strategy for you:* Invest your rent security deposits in insured maximum-interest accounts to provide the largest income possible to your business.

- *Repair funds*—Since you do not have to pay for repairs in one lump sum, put such funds to work as soon as you receive them, or reserve from other sources of income. *Strategy for you:* Keep repair funds in an interest-bearing checking account, ready to be paid out when needed.

- *Section 8 payments*—Made by the government, you should direct them to be paid into an interest-bearing account so you earn income from the moment the payment is credited to you. *Strategy for you:* Have Section 8 payments deposited directly in your interest-bearing company account. This way you don't lose interest while the check is in the mail or someone is struggling through traffic to get to the bank.

Shrewd cash management can make you richer than you might ever imagine, sooner than you think. But you *must* take effective cash management seriously! Gone are the days when you could manage a property out of your left-hand pocket. Today you must exert every skill you have to squeeze the maximum profit out of that top line. Now let's see how today's real estate successes grow rich through shrewd cash mortgage.

TEN UNIQUE WAYS TO MAKE ANY
INCOME PROPERTY SUCCESSFUL

An income property can become your personal cash cow, if you run it right. Here are ten effective ways for doing just that:

1. *Charge the maximum rent for each unit.* This is so for an apartment, a square foot of retail space, a parking space, and so on. Never make the mistake of charging too little for your space. Such an error can haunt you for life. And it can leave your bank account with a big hole in it if your expenses should suddenly rise.

2. *Keep upgrading your class of tenants.* Richer and more successful tenants can afford higher rents. And they'll give you fewer headaches with property destruction and vandalism.

3. *Market your property every day.* Keeping your property in front of people can mean that you'll have a lineup for any vacancies. This reduces any losses vacant units might generate. Some real estate BWBs are able to have zero vacancies because they market their properties on a daily basis.

4. *Never allow a dollar to sit idle.* With good cash flow, you should be earning interest 24 hours a day. There's nothing wrong with such an approach. The largest of companies and banks won't let a dollar be idle for a moment. Why shouldn't *you* do the same? It's legal, it's shrewd, it's sensible, and it's the approach all my successful BWBs use. *You* should, too!

5. *Use part-time maintenance labor.* It's cheaper and the work is often better than that done by high-priced so-called professionals. My experience with large-fee professionals is that their work is sometimes much less competent than that of part-timers. You must, of course, obey the law where licensed crafts people are required. But if you look around enough in your local area you will be able to find licensed part-timers. Why pay two to three times the price for work that's no better? It just doesn't make any sense!

6. *Hack away at fixed expenses.* Thus, do your best to reduce your real estate taxes. See how you can reduce other fixed expenses like electricity, water, fuel, and so on. Remember: Every penny you save in fixed expenses goes directly into your pocket in the form of tax-free profit. Fixed expenses can make a profitable property a loss property. So take every step you can to cut all your fixed costs. It really pays off!

7. *Refinance your mortgage to reduce monthly payments.* One of your largest fixed costs is your monthly mortgage payment. Reducing this payment can put many more dollars in your pocket—*every* month. If you agreed to a high-interest mortgage when you bought a property, keep a daily eye on interest rates in your area. As rates fall, you may be able to make a large saving on your monthly payment by refinancing (getting a new mortgage). You'll find that if you can get an interest rate that's 2 percent less than your current rate, the cost of refinancing is worthwhile. Be sure to review your options *before* you refinance. And get exact estimates of the cost, such as points, closing fees, and so on.

8. *Use your rent security deposits to advantage.* You often are restricted on what use you can make of your rent security deposits. But nothing stops you from transferring such deposits from one bank to another to get maximum service. Thus, some banks will happily extend you a loan if you transfer your rent security deposits to the bank. The bank knows that the money will remain on deposit for an extended period. So the loan officer will be much more friendly and cooperative with you. Such courtesy doesn't cost you a penny. And it can come in handy—especially if you need a loan for certain personal needs. Your property thus becomes your personal cash cow. And, as we all know, the proceeds of a loan are nontaxable. So you get *all* the funds you borrow. There are *no* deductions.

9. *Combine business needs with your "turn-ons."* This way, you get pleasure from doing things that bring in profits. Thus, if you must drive to your properties, make driving fun. You'll enjoy business more, do a better job, and have more fun—especially when your driving is a provable and legitimate expense for your business. There's no rule saying a business expense must be painful. So if you can enjoy what you do in your business while the expense is paid from income, you're doubly ahead! Just be sure that you carefully obey all rules at all times. Then you can easily combine your business needs with your "turn-ons" and have fun all day, every day.

10. *Build cash caches using smart refinancing methods.* As soon as you build substantial equity in a property, say from 25 percent to 50 percent of its market value, refinance it to take cash out to serve as a "cushion" for your money needs. You can use your cash cache for future buys of more income property, to treat yourself to a needed vacation, to pay for improvements needed by the property, or for any

other sensible purpose. The whole key here is to make yourself feel richer and more comfortable by using money that's available to you for just signing a few papers! Take my word for it, good friend, there's nothing as nice as having bundles of cash in the bank that come to you tax free.

Yes, *your* income properties *can* be your personal cash cow. You just have to arrange your affairs to take advantage of the many opportunities available to you. Be sure to have the advice of a competent real estate attorney and accountant when making your cash cow plans! Hundreds of my readers write to say, in essence, for different investments in various parts of the country:

> *I never knew my life could change so much for the better. Thank you for showing me how. Since I started buying income real estate my income has doubled, my savings have tripled, and my life-style has improved enormously. I dine in better restaurants, drive a luxury car, and have the longest vacations of my life. I could never achieve this level of success on a job which locks me into a payroll with a miserable 3 or 4 percent salary rise each year. Sure, I have some problems with my property now and then. But there's no business that doesn't have an occasional problem. With my big income I sometimes welcome the problems because they mean I'm earning my money!*

MULTIPROPERTY METHODS
TO BUILD YOUR RICHES

You will probably own more than one property if you want to build large riches in your own real estate business. Why? Because it is seldom possible to build large riches with just one property. Further, with several properties you:

- Diversify your investment risk. You don't have all your eggs in one basket.
- Reduce vacancy risks because diverse properties often appeal to different markets. Such markets seldom suffer downturns at the same time.

- Have cash coming at you from all directions. This is a wonderful feeling which can keep your bank account full and your spirits high.

There are a number of simple methods which can help you build maximum cash flow from multiproperties. Using these methods can build your wealth faster than you ever dreamed. Here are the key methods *you* can use to build *your* multiproperty wealth:

1. *Combine your management and maintenance staffs for all properties into one group.* This will save payroll costs, reduce duplication of efforts and help you control both income and costs more easily. There's no point in having duplicate staffs when one group can do the work of several.

2. *Remember—at all times—that real estate is a slow business.* You seldom have the rush deadlines met in other businesses. So you can afford to do work on regular hours, without the high cost of overtime labor. Knowing the slow nature of the business, you can avoid being hustled into getting work done quickly at higher than normal costs.

3. *Buy materials and supplies in bulk quantities to save.* By centralizing your buying you can negotiate lower prices on all your purchases. Every dollar you save this way is an extra buck that goes to the bottom line, improving your cash flow.

4. *Use a roving manager instead of individual property personnel.* This saves costs and gives you more precise control of property costs. And you get a greater uniformity of tenant treatment, leading to greater satisfaction with the services you provide.

5. *Pay your people well while demanding best performance from each person.* Build loyalty to yourself by getting to know each worker and his or her aspirations in life. Show each person how—by working hard for you—he or she can prosper while doing important work. Remember: In real estate people can be almost as important as the property they work with. So take time to give your people the feeling of importance they deserve when they do the outstanding job you expect of them.

6. *Bring in a professional manager to handle all your properties when your own staff can't deliver the results you seek.* One property management firm increased occupancy by 145 percent in an apartment complex, raised net operating income by 252 percent in another one, and raised rental rates by more than 25 percent in a 6-month period in

a soft market. The cost to you of such professional management is small compared to the re-stilts you get. And knowing that you have skilled professionals running your business allows you to concentrate on finding new and more profitable properties at a cost you can afford.

7. *Keep pushing every day until you reach your income goals.* You *can* build the wealth and freedom *you* seek by taking over profitable income properties. Knowing your goals—which you outlined earlier when making your career plans at the start of this book—you can steadily move toward them, if you push every day! Sure, it *does* take work. But it's work that's rewarding—work that pays its full benefits to you instead of a hard-driving unappreciative boss who's never satisfied no matter how much you do.

SUCCESS STRATEGIES FOR BUILDING YOUR REAL ESTATE WEALTH IN GOOD TIMES AND BAD TIMES

1. Explore the potential of rooftop rentals for satellite dishes, microwave antennas, radio and data transmitters, and similar electronic equipment. With the growing use of such devices, property owners in large cities are significantly increasing the income from their buildings. Large communication companies pay their bills on time with checks that don't bounce! Further, such companies are willing to pay more than fair rents for the space they occupy on your roof. And these firms pay all construction costs, even that of strengthening your roof, if necessary. So explore your potential for sizeable extra income from rooftop installations of electronic devices by communication and other electrical service companies. To get in on this new gravy train for building owners, contact telephone, television, Internet, cable, and wireless companies serving your area. You'll find them listed in your local *Yellow Pages.* Prepare a one-page description of your building giving its location, height, roof area in square feet, age, type of construction, etc. Send this by mail or fax to interested communication companies. Have your attorney approve any contract *before* you sign it!

2. Allow your tenants to improve your property at their expense for labor—and possibly—materials. Let them do the painting, plastering, sheet-rock work, etc. Where a licensed mechanic is required—for example to do electrical or plumbing work—be certain that the work is done by a qualified contractor—at your tenant's expense. If the tenant won't pay for this work, offer to share the costs with your tenant. Be certain—at all times—to have the job your tenant does inspected by a competent specialist in the work performed. And here's a little-known secret: *Tenants who do work in their own rental units stay longer.* Why? Because they want to get their money's worth out of the improvements they paid for. The only way to do this is to stay in the rented unit longer! Result? You have a more stable income from your improved property, and fewer costs to recondition the unit for a new tenant after an earlier one moves out.

3. Aim for a zero vacancy rate for all your rental properties. While the average national vacancy rate is computed at 5 percent, this need not apply to you! Achieve your zero vacancy rate by developing more effective ads and promotions for your properties. Aim at getting stable tenants for all your properties. Have each tenant sign a lease developed by your real estate attorney. Or you can use a pre-printed lease you can buy at any of the major office-supply stores. Start with reliable tenants and you'll earn more from every property you own! And when you get stable tenants, treat them well. Keep your property neat and clean. Be willing to allow the tenant to make minor improvements (see Item 2, above) to his or her unit at the tenant's expense. Don't pester a tenant whose rent is a day or two late for understandable reasons—illness, vacation, job loss, etc. But be strict and insist on the rent being paid every month. Tenants are like children: They enjoy being guided into correct behavior patterns and appreciate discipline because they know it is good for them!

4. Raise the rents in your rental units to the new highs being accepted worldwide today. Don't be afraid to break "barriers" such as $500, $750, $1,000, etc., a month. Rents for apartments in desirable areas of many cities are now $2,000, $3,000, and even $6,000 per month. Some extra-desirable penthouse apartments in high-rise buildings rent for $10,000 per month—and up! And covered parking spaces—such as in an underground garage—rent for as high as $1,000 per month for just one car! So, raise your cash flow and improve your life style by keeping up with the times and not falling behind in raising your rental income. Believe in yourself and your view of rent potentials. If you think you can charge a higher rent, hold out until you find tenants willing to pay the rent you believe your units are worth. Real estate rents seldom decline—they almost always rise with the passage of time. So wait it out until you get the rent you think you deserve!

IMPORTANT POINTERS TO KEEP IN MIND

- Top-line management—where you bring in the money first, and worry about how to spend it later—pays the bills best in any real estate business.

- Build income from every source—rents, services, and parking. Remember: A dollar is a dollar, no matter where it comes from in this business. Some real estate people rent a daily parking space to commuters for as much as $250 per month and are happy to get the revenue.

- Never delay income from your properties. Invest idle money in short-term interest-paying vehicles to derive the highest return you can from your business money.

- Keep your vacancies at the minimum by using shrewd low-cost advertising techniques.

- Rent units to government-paid tenants. You'll be paid directly by the government—promptly and accurately.

- Never accept rent delays. Go after your money as soon as you have a delay in the monthly payment.

- Don't let your rents fall behind the going rates in your area. You lose money quickly this way.

- Keep your expenses to the minimum at all times. Remember: The bottom line is the difference between the top line and your expenses. The lower your costs, the higher your bottom line.

- Use smart financial controls. They can save you money and help you keep more of the money from your top line.

- Use the 10 unique ways given here to make any income property successful. Then you'll have a personal cash cow.

- When you own several properties, as you probably will, use the multiproperty methods given here, in this chapter.

How to Make Your Real Estate Fortune While Fully Employed

Having read this far in this book, I know that *you*—my reader friend—are different from millions of other would-be BWBs. Why do I say this? Because, having spent this much time reading tells me that you're a dedicated wealth builder. You're ready to challenge tough times, ready to prove the doomsayers wrong! Like me, *you* believe that real estate *always* bounces back.

You, like me, believe these negative thinkers are dead wrong. And you're ready to launch your real estate career no matter what others may say about the poor state of the economy. You're even ready to spend dozens of hours a week in bad times on your future real estate success. Yet it's *not* necessary for you to put in large blocks of working time on your real estate.

Why? Because real estate is *not* a full-time occupation! You can build millions in real estate in your spare time. Plenty of my readers are doing this right now. And plenty have done it in the past.

I want *you* to be my next millionaire. And I'm so sure you *can* build real estate riches in the millions that I'm ready to:

- Help finance your future wealth through my industrial lending company, where permitted by statute
- Answer any questions you may have, as a subscriber to my monthly newsletter, which covers many important real estate topics
- Analyze—free of charge—any income and expense statement you have for a property you're thinking of buying

165

- Have you visit me in my New York office for lunch to discuss your real estate goals and plans

How can I say that real estate can be a spare-time activity for you? Because I invest in real estate in my spare time and make money from it while:

- Serving as director of a large real estate and general-purpose lending institution
- Writing a number of well-received books on wealth building for my favorite people—BWBs
- Authoring several large handbooks which are used by engineers throughout the world
- Publishing two newsletters for BWBs on wealth building and financing sources
- Running my own industrial lending company which makes loans* to BWBs needing down payment and other types of real estate and business financing
- Enjoying several hobbies, bringing up three kids, and having a happy wife

If I can do all these things, I'm sure *you* can do better—in your spare time! Why do I say this? Because I'm not the smartest guy I ever met. Just the fact that you're reading this book shows me that you're smarter than I am. And you'll soon be writing me a letter like this one which arrived today from a reader who says:

> *I've benefited substantially from many of your real estate books. I now own 20 properties (78 units) with a value of over $1.2 million. All these properties were purchased with little or no money down. It's good to hear what a professional banker like yourself has to say about real estate.*

This reader built his real estate wealth in his spare time—and *you* can do the same. You don't even have to quit a job you hate—until you're sure your real estate income can support you and your loved ones. Let's see what this approach can mean for your financial future.

---

* Where permitted by state statute.

RECOGNIZE THAT REAL ESTATE NEEDN'T BE A FULL-TIME OCCUPATION

By approaching real estate as a spare-time activity, you arrange your life to get more done. Thus:

- Weekends are great for seeing tenants, suppliers, and contractors
- You can run dozens of properties without taking a moment off your regular job
- Your real estate profit dollar is a very powerful one because it's on top of your regular job income
- Doing spare-time real estate investing can enlarge your life, bring you into a new circle of friends, and put a big bulge in the cash side of your wallet
- By starting in your spare time you don't risk your main income source—your job. Instead, you get to see—at almost *no* risk—the advantages of your own profitable real estate business
- All these advantages are available to you on borrowed money! Thus, you don't have to invest a penny of your own. Could anyone ask for a better deal?

For most income properties in good condition you won't invest more than 2 to 5 hours a week in management work. Since you probably don't work on your job more than 40 hours a week, you can own and manage 4 to 10 properties and still put in only 60 hours a week of work. Yet your real estate income could run from $40,000 to $100,000 per year, depending on the types of properties you buy.

Residential real estate—called garden apartments, apartment houses, multifamily housing, and so on—takes the least amount of your time. Why? Because, as we'll see later in this chapter, you can easily arrange for low time involvement on your part. Yet residential properties promise the greatest investment rewards for BWBs today—and in the future. Why? Because:

1. Reduced building starts in recent years have shrunk the supply of apartments available.
2. An uncertain job market has led families to either delay or forgo home ownership—so more people seek rental units than ever before.

3. Slowness in raising rents in recent years means there's plenty of room for future rent increases; this will benefit *all* owners of multi-family units.

4. New properties are charging sky-high rents. This means you can raise the rents of your existing properties to new levels, increasing your income markedly.

With these four favorable factors in view, and knowing that residential property requires the least time involvement, I see many of my readers opting to take over such properties for their spare-time wealth building. And you—good friend—*can* do the same!

Don't moan and groan "It's just more work, and I'm tired of working!" Real estate is *fun*. It's especially great fun when you're dropping several thousand dollars a month into *your* bank account. The rewards for just a few hours a week of work are enormous.

To get to my New York City office I ride the Long Island Rail Road from my home. Each day I have a fat envelope of income checks to deposit in the bank. Yet many of my fellow train riders who are overimpressed with their own importance because they have a fancy job title at some large corporation often come to me and say: "Ty, the firm I work for is downsizing. So I'm being excessed. They're asking me to leave and they're offering a nice package. What should I do? I still have two kids to put through college."

These people watch TV every night. They spend weekends goofing off while they get fat and sloppy. Then, when the crunch comes, they're unprepared.

Better they work an hour or so each evening to make some spare-time money. They can even watch TV while working. Then if a crunch comes they can leave their job gracefully because they know they have a steady, dependable spare-time income.

In my own life, my spare-time income often exceeds my regular income. And the same happens to many of my readers. I want it to happen to *you!* It can if you:

• Recognize that real estate *can* be a profitable spare-time activity for you, at the start.

• Set your mind to working a few extra hours each week to bring in those highly powerful spare-time dollars.

• See your money making as fun—instead of work. It will certainly provide you with the money you need to have any extra fun you seek.

Now let's see how you can find, and evaluate, low-time-involvement (I call it LTI) real estate to make your fortune. You'll see how much fun and how profitable it can be.

WHERE, AND HOW, TO FIND LTI REAL ESTATE

Your best source of low-time-involvement real estate is your local area. Why? For a number of good reasons. Local property:

- Is easier to evaluate quickly and cheaply
- Is offered by people who "speak the same language" you do
- Can be financed faster because conventional sources are more willing to work locally than at a distance

Look in your local newspapers first. They carry the newest ads for properties being offered for sale. Contact the seller quickly—don't let time drag—you may lose the property.

Next, check local real estate magazines, the Apartment Owners' Association, and nearby realtors. All can lead you to hot properties that can help you build your fortune in your spare time.

At the start, stick with local properties. In some areas it may take you a while to find the right income property. But its local location makes all steps in the deal much easier for you.

And in case you're wondering if my lending firm can work in your area, the answer is yes—we can work (and do) anywhere in the world. So don't let the possibility of having trouble with financing stop you. The money is available for good properties bought by 2-year, or longer, subscribers to our newsletter. While we *do* have loans with nonsubscribers, it is our belief that subscribers benefit from many of our financing ideas and methods.

So look locally, in publications and with realtors. That's your *where.* Read *every* ad for the type of property you seek. Inspect the property. Do your "numbers" work. Then make an offer. That's the *how* of getting LTI income property of any type.

Likewise, check any local websites on the Internet. Some list local real estate for sale. You can easily download photos and data to determine if the properties offered are LTI types.

MEASURES TO USE TO JUDGE LTI PROPERTIES

Some properties *are* low time involvement; others aren't. To decide which are and which are not, consider:

1. Ease of rent collection
2. Tenants pay utilities
3. Freedom from costly maintenance
4. Low labor requirements
5. Ability to use management firm
6. Property suitable for local market

Let's take a quick look at each of these measures and see how you can use it to judge your future properties. You can build your future wealth using just a few of these measures.

Ease of Rent Collection

Can you collect rents by mail—the easiest way—for the property you're considering? Some people are more mail-oriented than others. Or can you have your tenants make a direct deposit of their rent into your business checking or savings account? This is another easy way to collect rents. What about government payment of rent directly to you?

Each of these ways means less time involvement on your part. And the less time you must spend on a property, the better your chances of making money from it in your spare time.

So look for ease of rent collection. It will save you time, gas, and shoe leather!

Tenants Pay Utilities

If the property you're considering is arranged so your tenants pay fuel, electric, gas, and other utility bills, then it's LTI. Why? Because when tenants pay utility bills it means that they call the utility when power goes out. You don't have to make that call!

The fewer calls you make, the less time involvement. What's more, you keep more of every rent dollar when tenants pay utility bills. Instead of saying that 5 cents of every rent dollar goes to pay for fuel and electric, *you* keep that 5 cents.

As a general guide, properties in which tenants pay utilities are a better buy than those in which they don't. But you *must* look at *all* the numbers before buying any property—including those in which your tenants pay utilities.

Freedom from Costly Maintenance

Some properties are easier to maintain than others. Thus, wooden structures usually require *more* maintenance than stone or metal buildings. And structures with metal or plastic siding usually cost less for upkeep than wooden ones.

So take time to analyze your future maintenance costs. Get figures from the seller covering past maintenance costs. They may be somewhat understated so they make the net income of the property higher. Knowing this, you can look for areas of "fudging."

As a general guide, low-maintenance properties will take less of your time. But the numbers *must* work out. Why? Because the price you'll be asked to pay for a low-maintenance property will be higher than for one having large maintenance costs. It will be necessary for you to balance the numbers.

Low Labor Requirements

Some properties "run themselves." Others require large staffs. The property with the smaller staff will require less supervision from you. So your time input will be lower—LTI again.

Be careful to distinguish between steady labor and part-time labor. Steady labor is that which is required 7 days a week, 365 days a year. Typical of this labor type is elevator operators, doormen (or women), security guards, and so on. Part-time labor is maintenance workers, painters, plumbers, and so on.

Large steady-labor crews can drain you financially. So look for the property that runs itself. While this is almost an impossible dream, there are a number of properties that require hardly any labor at all. These are the properties to invest in—if you want to run your business in your spare time.

Ability to Use Management Firm

You can have your property run by a management firm and save lots of your time. The usual fee you'll pay is 5 percent of the total rental income. On top of this you'll have to pay for any special maintenance, for fuel, electric, and so on, unless your tenants pay for these.

A management firm can take much of the burden off you. And the fee you pay is provable and tax deductible. What's more, a good management firm can get rent increases and other fee rises for you without any grief on your part.

To increase your income with a management company, insert a clause in the contract which says:

> For every one-percentage-point increase in the rental rate above 95 percent, XYZ Management Co. will be paid a 0.5 percent bonus in its management fee for the year in which the rental rate exceeds the 95 percent goal.

Some management firms maintain nearly a 100 percent rental rate (also called occupancy rate) when they have such a clause in their contract. You should, of course, have an experienced attorney prepare the contract for you.

Property Suitable for Local Market

Most of your tenants will come from your local area. So the property you invest in should be suitable for such people. If it is, your time investment will be low. It if isn't, you may have to spend weeks making the property suitable for locals. Thus, a reader tells me:

> *I have options on several floors of office space containing 50,000 sq. ft. per floor. In trying to rent these floors out I found that they're not suitable for law firms because there isn't enough window space. Law firms want each partner to have a window office. My floors don't have enough windows in relation to the floor area. So I must find local firms having a large staff of "bull pen" workers needing few private offices. I'm lucky because there are a number of local firms needing large areas for huge numbers of clerical workers having few bosses in private offices.*

Getting property suitable to local needs will cut your time investment enormously. The time you spend "sizing up" a property *before* you buy it can pay big returns to you after you take it over. Why? Because if the property is suitable for your local area, you can rent it fast. Your time will be saved for other things—like earning more money from other good investments!

SCHEDULE YOUR TIME TO EARN MAXIMUM DOLLARS PER HOUR

You work 35 hours, 5 days a week if your career is in an office. On the production line, or in a service business, you work 40 hours, 5 days a week. With 168 hours in the week, you have plenty of spare time to run your wealth building real estate business. All you need do is schedule your time to collect the income from the money machine you're building. Here are some practical suggestions for setting up *your* schedule:

1. Saturday morning is a great time to meet sellers, visit properties, talk to your attorney about the properties you plan to buy.
2. Sunday afternoon is a good time to visit properties that interest you.
3. Sunday morning is a productive time for visiting realtors to review properties they have available for you.
4. Any evening, after your regular work, is a suitable time for calling tenants, discussing prices with sellers, or getting points straightened out with your attorney.
5. You can go online to the Internet 24 hours a day to get real estate information from local and national websites. If you use a computer on your job you can access the Internet from it. Or use a local library's computer.

Meanwhile, of course, you'll carry on your regular job, bringing in a steady income. And while you're working, your real estate will rise in value, every second of every minute. True, during hard times, your rise in value may be less. But real estate values *always* recover and surge ahead again.

So you can't lose when you run your spare-time real estate ventures. The demand for good space, along with the upward push in prices produced by the rise in all costs, just makes *your* properties more valuable every day. True, you may miss a few TV programs during the week when you do some evening work. But the financial freedom you obtain is well worth missing a few TV programs. What's more, you can record them on your VCR for later viewing. So you really don't miss anything—except being poor! I'll take rich any day over poor.

One reader BWB recently told me on the phone about his real-life schedule for his real estate wealth building:

> *I work 35 hours in a big bank. So I have to take care of my real estate business on weekends and holidays. Even so, I still take a 2-week vacation every summer and "sneak" plenty of time off during the rest of the year. I collect rents by mail, which is sent to my home. Since I buy only two properties a year, I meet with sellers and realtors only three or four times on a Saturday morning. The sale is often done in the evening in my attorney's office. Again, this is only once or twice a year for a few hours. If a repair is needed, I have the mechanic call me at home in the evening. While I could have tenants and mechanics call me at my job phone, I prefer to keep my real estate business separate from my regular job. For me it seems to work best that way.*

You can easily work your time needs around your job and real estate. You just make a few guiding decisions and follow them. If they work as you planned—fine. If these decisions don't work as you planned, just alter them, based on your findings. Typical decisions you can make are:

1. You will, or will not, take calls from your real estate activities at your regular job. (Some jobs are such that you *can* receive such calls and conduct lots of business on site. Others prohibit such activity altogether.)

2. You will, or will not, work a few hours on the weekend to manage your bargain-basement properties to deliver maximum profit to you. (To some folks, the weekend is sacred and must not be sullied by work. If you're this type, I respect you! So you'll do your real estate business during the week.)

3. You will, or will not, work one or two evenings a week on your real estate. Since just an hour or two is usually enough to take care of the work, you really should consider putting the time in. Few real estate wealth builders spend more than 5 hours a week on their business, once they have their properties upgraded to a level where they yield lush green profits every minute of the year.

These decisions will help you work your time needs around your job and your real estate. So make those decisions today—there never was, and never will be, a better time!

SIX MAGIC TIPS FOR GETTING MORE FROM EACH HOUR

You hear lots about productivity and how it influences the success of nations. The same is true for yourself. The more you can produce in one hour, the greater your personal productivity. And, likewise, the greater the amount of wealth *you* will build! Here are six magic tips for raising your productivity so you get more from each hour:

1. *Plan your day.* Know what you must do—and do it! Don't waste time—you can never get it back once it has slipped through your fingers.

2. *Use to-do lists for each day.* They help you plan the day and you'll get an emotional charge when you check off a job that's done.

3. *Do the most important things first.* This is called *prioritizing*—a big word that simply means just do what's most important first, what's next in importance, second, and so on.

4. *Use modern tools to save time.* Thus, you may need a fax machine, a cellular car phone if you drive around to manage your properties, an answering service that can keep a suitable distance between yourself and your tenants, an accountant to prepare your annual tax returns and any quarterly reports to both relieve you of details and save you money in operating costs, and a personal computer to help you keep track of income while making projections for the future.

5. *Get reliable legal and accounting assistance.* You *will* need competent legal and accounting advice. Why? Because when you rent to tenants there are always questions which arise over leases, contracts, and other agreements. Without good advice you can run into problems. And remember this: The cost of such advice is provable and tax deductible. So why worry and fret when relief is as close as your phone?

6. *Do a little each day to reach your financial goals.* Making daily progress can bring your financial goals within reach much sooner than you ever thought possible. While giant steps are nice to think

about, in real estate progress is often made in small steps. So take that one small step every day and before you know it you've progressed a mile toward your goal! What's more, every hour will be more productive for you!

GET—AND STAY—FREE OF TENANT DEMANDS

Some tenants are a "dream," others can drive you crazy. The key to a happy existence with any tenant is to get free of unwarranted demands. You can take several steps to achieve this. These steps are:

1. *Don't answer tenant demands yourself.* Have someone between you and the tenant. That someone can be a secretary, a telephone answering service, or a phone answering machine. Using such an intermediary helps to defuse a tenant's anger and frustration. Further, when you call back, the tenant is impressed that you care enough to do so. This helps reduce any anger the tenant may be feeling.

2. *Keep as great a distance as possible between tenants and yourself.* Don't socialize with tenants. Keep your relationship one of strict business. Being remote from your tenants makes them think twice before complaining.

3. *Be fully attentive to your tenants*—when you want to be. That is, *Never* ignore a tenant's request or complaint. Just get to it when *you* want to, not when the tenant demands you give him or her attention. Be considerate, understanding, and fair at *all* times! It pays off in better rent collections and fewer vacancies.

4. *Have tenant requests answered quickly.* Fast response gets you lots of goodwill. Quick answers can defuse strong complaints. What's more, your fast response can stop complaints to local rent authorities. This can save you lots of time and unnecessary paperwork.

5. *Keep promises to tenants.* If you say work will be done by a certain date, get the work done on time. If there are delays beyond your control, explain these to the tenant either yourself or through an employee.

Getting and staying free of tenant demands can make your real estate life a lot happier. All it takes is some sensible planning. There's *no* point in allowing others to run your life if you can take charge by just making a few changes in your work habits!

GROW RICH IN YOUR SPARE TIME

The U.S. government has its Section 8 program wherein you're paid rent for providing good rental units for residential purposes. So if you own such units, or you're thinking about owning them, you should check out the going rents in your area. Do so by looking up in your telephone book under "U.S. Government Offices" (usually blue-colored pages) the listing for the Department of Housing and Urban Development (HUD). Contact the HUD and ask for their free information on the Section 8 program. They'll send it to you quickly.

Do the same for your state. Each state has some type of housing department. The one in my state is called Division of Housing & Community Renewal. Yours may have a different name. But you will, in general, find it listed under some variation of the word *housing*.

Large cities also have housing groups. You will also find them listed in the blue pages of the phone book.

All it takes with any of these groups is a phone call or letter asking for information. You'll soon receive the numbers giving typical rents paid for various sizes (number of bedrooms and baths) of units.

The rents paid by government agencies will equal—and sometimes exceed—going rents in the local area. Try to get government-supported tenants for these good reasons:

1. You are paid your rent directly.
2. Your rent check arrives on time—every month.
3. When local rents increase, your rent payment will rise.
4. You never have to worry about late, or missed, payments.
5. Your units are needed; so your vacancies are lower.

KEEP YOUR PAPERWORK SIMPLE

When you're running your real estate empire in your spare time, you want to keep everything as simple as possible. One important area to keep simple is your paperwork—where you record income and expenses.

Exhibit 7–1 shows a simple form you can use for keeping your rent records. Use such a form and your part-time staff can keep an accurate record of all the income and expenses associated with each property you own.

Exhibit 7–1

**INCOME AND EXPENSE RECORD
123 MAIN ST., ANYTOWN 00000
DATE**

RENTS RECEIVED

MONTH	J	F	M	A	M	J	J	A	S	O	N	D
Apt. No.												
123	$495	495	495	495	495	495	525*	525	525	525	525	525
456	325	325	325	325	325	325	450*	450	450	450	450	450
789	800	800	800	800	800	800	875*	875	875	875	875	875

EXPENSES PAID

Apt. No.												
123	12	—	—	18	—	—	22	—	—	15	—	—
456	—	—	—	—	23	—	—	—	—	—	14	—
789	246	—	—	—	—	—	—	—	—	12	—	—

*Rents increased July 1, Year _____

There are computer programs for managing real estate. If you enjoy computer control of your business, choose a program that gives you the desired control with the least time input. This may not be the cheapest program available to you. Such programs are especially useful when you have tenants whose rent is paid by some branch of the government. Thus, one reader tells me:

> With the Section 8 Program I have almost an automatic income because the rents come in right on time. In fact, some rents arrive one or two days before they're due. We hold the checks until the due date and deposit them early in the morning. This way we have the cash sooner. Each payment is recorded in our computer so we have a real-time picture of our cash flow and balance sheet. Positive control of guaranteed rents lets me spend more time planning for the future instead of worrying about daily problems.

FOUR KEY RULES FOR GETTING RICH
IN YOUR SPARE TIME

Millions of people get rich in spare-time real estate. You, too, can do the same. Here are four key rules that almost guarantee your success in this great field:

1. *Buy zero cash properties whenever you can.* Why? Because such properties help you avoid a credit check, a loan application, and so on. You don't take up your valuable spare time with a lot of work that may be wasted if your loan is turned down. With zero cash properties you almost always have owner financing. This type of financing is free of credit checks and other hurdles.

2. *Buy only positive cash flow properties.* Never, never take money out of your job salary to support a real estate project! Such action can cause you all kinds of losses. *Every* property *must* deliver a positive cash flow *every* month. Never vary from this rule!

3. *Get part-time help to run your business.* This will allow you to give full attention to your job while you continue to hold it. Having the help will also allow you to have some free time. Remember: Your business should be fun! You should get something out of it that you value beyond money. This "something" can be any form of recreation you enjoy. If you do all the work yourself—without helpers—you won't have any time to relax.

4. *Keep planning for your release from your job.* Use your paperwork controls (mentioned earlier) to point the way to the day when you can shuck your job and run your real estate full time, as a free person. Having your "release" plans will motivate you to move ahead to do more for your future. The result? You'll be more successful!

Readers write me almost every day telling me how they're building wealth in real estate in their spare time. Here's a letter that arrived from a BWB in Florida:

> I must share with you my two best recent deals. You'll remember that it was you who got me started in real estate some years ago.
> While taking over a foreclosure from a bank, I noticed a ratty looking sign on a building a few doors away. I called

the telephone number on the sign and had a good conversation with the seller. There were 19 properties involved, with a total of 29 units. Most had positive cash flows. The seller and his partner invited me to take over all the properties provided I would handle rent collections and maintenance. I agreed and spent 2 days writing "agreements for deed" with zero cash down. Now all I do is collect rents and make payments. My positive cash flow is about $2,000 per month. Now my property portfolio totals about $800,000.

The second recent deal for this reader allowed her to mortgage out:

We just had an opportunity to buy from a mortgage company four fixed-up and ready-to-rent houses for $500 each toward closing costs. They wouldn't sell the four we wanted unless we took a fifth one. This was a nice 3-bedroom home having 3 units at the back that looked like they'd been hit by a bomb. It looked like there would be about $10,000 worth of repairs needed. But once these repairs were made we'd have an additional $900 per month rental income. So we decided to do the deal—but only if they'd give us $20,000 to do the repairs. They balked, saying the most they'd pay would be $18,000. We accepted their offer. So we'll have a profit of at least $8,000 if we have an outsider do the repairs. If we do them ourselves, the profit will be even higher because we can save money on the repairs! In both these deals I became an instant landlord.

MAKE LOWER PRICES YOUR PATH TO WEALTH

In bad times real estate prices are lower. You *can* make such prices your spare-time path to real estate wealth. How? Recognize here and now that:

- *Down markets are really up markets for you.* Lower prices mean you can grab off the bargains and jewels at deeply depressed prices because you have the freedom and independence to wait because your job income yields enough money to pay your basic expenses. You get below-market "steals" that can only go *up* in value as time passes.
- *Lower prices mean bigger income in your pocket.* When you pay a lower price you finance a smaller debt. So your monthly mortgage

payments are lower. This means *you* keep more of each income dollar that flows into your business. So your profitable cash flow is higher and gives *you* greater freedom and earlier release from the job "prison."

- *Controlling costs puts more money into your pocket.* On your job you may get a pat on the back when you cut costs and save the boss some money. Or the boss may ask you, in a surly tone, why you didn't cut more costs. In your own business you benefit from every cost cut you make. You see the results in your upward surging bank account. Your take-home pay—even if you leave it in the bank to earn interest—is higher because *you* cut costs. While you may miss the pat on the back, money in the bank is a lot more rewarding. As the famous saying goes: "I've been rich and I've been poor. Rich is better!" A pat on the back won't make you rich; money in the bank will. So use a sharp pencil to keep your costs as low as you can.

- *Use your mind to earn income while others flee in panic.* You can easily substitute your ideas for cash. Coming up with creative ways to get properties during hard times while you still hold a job can easily make *you* a millionaire. So don't flee the scene when things get bad. Stay in the battle. The few warriors who remain will reap the rewards of a gallant fight. If you want the rewards of financial freedom you *can* get them when you actively seek bargains in both bad times and good times! Keep thinking *how* you'll get the properties you want in your spare time without putting up a penny of your own money.

Remember: If all else fails, I'm as close to you as your telephone, if you need advice and you subscribe to my newsletter. What's more one of my financing sources may be able to help you get the funds you need for your wealth building. You're my friend and I want to help *you* get rich in your spare time while you use your regular job to meet your normal living costs.

SUCCESS STRATEGIES FOR BUILDING YOUR REAL ESTATE WEALTH IN GOOD TIMES AND BAD TIMES

1. Get part-time managers, mechanics, and business people to operate your properties while you're at your regular job. Allow these people to answer calls from tenants, suppliers, city officials, etc. Have your part-timers do as much of your work as possible when dealing with such contacts. Set up a system of recording messages received, actions taken, and any further steps required; use a computer or paper forms to track the required work. Review this information once or twice a day so you're fully up to date on all your properties. Arrange vacation schedules for yourself so you can get away from your business and have time to refresh your thinking and viewpoints. When your real estate income reaches a level where you can leave your regular job, do so. But review the future potential for your real estate before taking the big step of leaving your job. Building a solid income in real estate takes time. So don't rush leaving your regular job until you're certain that your real estate can give you the income you need for yourself and your loved ones!

    2. Obtain suitable machines to help you run your business. Thus, you'll find that a fax machine, telephone answering machine, cell phone, laptop computer, and e-mail will all help you run your business more efficiently with less time and energy investment on your part. At the start, you can lease such machines, reducing your cash outlay. As your business grows you can gradually buy each of these units. Your cost and lease payments—of course—are provable and tax deductible! Be certain to make full use of all the machines you lease or buy. Why? Because they will simplify your life while increasing your income! Also, you'll be using your equipment to generate more income. But if the equipment just sits idle, you are actually losing money on it. For example, you can even use your computer to generate your monthly rent bills to send to your tenants. This will save you time and get you your monthly rent payment sooner. With the widespread computerization of bills and statements, tenants react faster—and pay sooner—when they get a computer-generated bill or statement from you. You can access the Internet with your computer and visit the many real estate sites that are available. Technology has really arrived in the world of real estate and you should be part of it—for your own future wealth!

    3. Collect your rents without ever having to see a tenant, ring a doorbell, or visit a property. Use mail-in addressed envelopes with a bill giving the amount of the payment, the month covered, the apartment or suite number, and the property location. Or, accept credit-card payment of the rent due, putting the charge through your own merchant account. And—if you wish—you can arrange with each tenant a monthly automatic rent charge to their credit card. This will simplify your life, and theirs.

If you prefer, you can take a check by phone payment and process it through your merchant account—again without ever seeing your tenant each month. You can arrange to do this automatically, on the first of each month. (See the back of this book for the *Merchant Account Kit* to learn how to get your own credit-card and check processing facility.)

4. Visit your properties on weekends, or at other times when you're off from your regular job. Arrange to see your part-time managers and contractors at this time. While it may seem that you're working long hours, the extra income you receive from your real estate investment will—I'm sure—make you very happy. And your improved lifestyle will reward you and yours with pleasures and opportunities you never thought possible! By visiting your properties on the weekend you'll have a better chance of seeing your tenants and letting them know that you're really interested in providing them with neat, clean, and safe housing or business facilities. There's no substitute for one-on-one meetings with tenants!

IMPORTANT POINTERS TO KEEP IN MIND

- Real estate is *not* a full-time occupation: you *can* build millions in net worth in your spare time.
- Weekends and evenings are great times for you to find, and buy, income property of all types.
- By starting your wealth building in your spare time you don't risk your main source of income—your job.
- By holding your job you put yourself in a better position to borrow money to get the real estate you seek.
- Most income properties don't require more than 2 to 5 hours a week of work on your part.
- For most BWBs, residential property requires the least time input.
- Use your head and ideas to make money in real estate, and your spare-time income can exceed your regular job income.
- Seek low-time-involvement real estate because it allows you to have a freer life.
- Seek LTI properties which feature ease of rent collection, tenants pay utilities, low maintenance, low labor bills, use of a management firm, and property suitable for your local market.

- Work your time needs around your job *and* your real estate.
- Plan to get more from each hour you spend on your real estate wealth building.
- Get—and stay—free of tenant demands on your time and attention.
- Use government programs to fill your residential properties with tenants whose rent is paid in full—on time.
- Aim, every day, at building your real estate fortune in your spare time. Don't leave your job until you're sure your real estate income can support you!

How, and Where, to Borrow Millions for Any Real Estate Deal

8

It may seem that hard times in real estate make borrowing money more difficult. There's some truth to this. At the same time, though, money for real estate continues to be loaned—even during the bleakest days.

To get *your* hands on some of the money that is always being loaned for real estate, you have to approach the *right* lenders for the *correct* amount of money for a *specific* property. This chapter shows *you* how and where, to find money for *all* your real estate deals. You'll quickly see that real estate is the world's *best* borrowed money business! It's also the world's *biggest* borrowed money business. So if you're cash short, real estate *is* the business to get into.

And my reading of the thousands of BWBs I meet every year is that almost every one of them *is* cash short, especially those who say they have "good" jobs! In my view there really isn't any good job. Why? Because no matter what you're paid on a job, it's still not enough to reward you adequately for the time and effort you put into earning those big bucks for your boss.

By going into a borrowed money business you overcome—instantly—a variety of knock-you-down problems like:

- Poor credit history
- No credit history
- Slow-pay history
- Judgment records in credit history
- Recent bankruptcy

- Too many inquiries on credit report
- Income too low to obtain a loan
- Self-employment unacceptable for loan approval
- And so on

I hear hundreds of different reasons for loan rejections given to BWBs. But go into a borrowed money business—such as real estate—and you remove almost every one of these reasons from the lender's arsenal. Let's see how *you* can get in on easy-approval low-cost financing for the real estate of your dreams.

START WITH VERY LITTLE—OR NO— MONEY OF YOUR OWN

Let's take—as we engineers say—a worst case scenario. You are *not* this worst case. But some of my other readers *are*. Let's see how the world's best borrowed money business— real estate—can make them millionaires—starting in their spare time on borrowed money.

This worst case friend of mine has these real-life problems:

- He recently went bankrupt because his credit card debts were too high
- He has worked for only 4 months on his latest job; prior to this job the longest term of employment with one firm was 2 years and 6 months
- He is separated from his wife and must pay a weekly separation allowance
- His savings balance in the bank is $437; his checking account contains $112.

Yet this BWB is ambitious. He wants to turn his life around by getting into his own real estate business. But, as you can see, his resources are limited. You might say he's almost at the poverty level—he's a worst case! What can this worst case BWB do to:

- Bring in some fast, steady income
- Build some assets to improve his balance sheet

- Start to overcome his recent poor credit history
- Get away from his tedious 9-to-5 job that pays peanuts

This BWB can get into income real estate using zero cash down. The property he chooses *must* have a monthly positive cash flow. Further, this worst case BWB must:

- Get property with owner financing, or
- Get property with an assumable long-term mortgage and zero cash down

Thus, by going into the best borrowed money business around, this worst case BWB can overcome most of his current financial problems. And if he runs his business carefully he can overcome *all* his financial problems while building wealth on his own.

So start with little, or no, money of your own. You gain in more ways than you might think. Let's look at some of these ways right now.

BORROWING IS EXPECTED IN REAL ESTATE

Many businesses operate on what's called self-financing. That is, the owner takes the money from his or her savings, or that of their relatives, to finance the business. Banks and other lenders don't get in on the scene until the owner has so much money he or she doesn't need financing!

Not so with real estate! Even in the toughest times for real estate, lenders *expect* you to borrow money to take over property. And even when real estate values are tumbling, it's almost unheard of to pay cash for properties. Why? Because cash is valuable. Experienced BWBs conserve their cash and borrow other people's money (**OPM**) to finance their deals.

As you know, I'm as close to you as your phone. Sometimes "smart" BWBs will call me, after being told that they need some collateral for a loan, and say:

> *If I had collateral I'd cash it in and get the money. Then I wouldn't need a loan of any kind. You must be crazy asking for collateral—don't you know if people had the collateral they wouldn't be asking for a loan?*

I try to tell these people, who are usually irate about being asked for collateral and who try to tell me I'm nuts, that:

> Smart wealth builders never touch their cash savings or other liquid collateral. Instead, they borrow what they need and make repayments from the income of the real estate they bought with the borrowed money. These BWBs know that once you withdraw your principal from a savings account it's almost impossible to replace it. But if you borrow and work to repay the loan, you end with both the asset you bought and the principal savings you originally had!

So do what others expect you to do—*borrow* the money you need to get started in real estate! Why? Because if you don't borrow, people may think you really don't know what you're doing. So they may treat you with less respect and awe than if you borrow. Crazy but true.

A reader recently phoned from the Pacific Northwest to tell me about his, and his wife's, experience in borrowing:

> *We had about $10,000 in cash when we started 2.5 years ago. Today our real estate holdings are worth $2.1 million. Yet we built all of this on borrowed money by using our parents to cosign on our first loan. Today we're specializing in golf courses and expect to open our first 18-hole course soon. We foresee a cash flow of $50,000 a month at the start. And all of this is being done on borrowed money.*

Here are two more recent letters—the first from Germany and the second from Canada—that show these methods work everywhere in the world:

> *"Thank you for your continuous support in making me a REMM (Real Estate Multi-Millionaire)."*

And:

> *"I worked for the government for 12 years but quit 2 years ago. I own my own home on 25 acres in the country. I have a 4-unit rental income property worth $185,000. My income, from this and my other businesses, is over $60,000 a year and I want to earn more!"*

Again—don't disappoint the seller, the broker, the attorney, the escrow agent, the recording clerk. *Borrow* the money you need for real estate!

YOU *CAN* BORROW THE MONEY FOR *ANY* REAL ESTATE YOU LIKE

This world of ours is great. Yet there are a lot of doubters, nonbelievers, can't doers, and so on, around. They'll tell you—without ever having owned a piece of real estate in their unsuccessful and unachieving lives— that you can't borrow for this or that kind of real estate. Why these people can't keep their flapping mouths shut I don't know.

The simple truth is: You *can* borrow money for *any* real estate *you* like. There's always some money—somewhere—available for any kind of property. Even for slum area properties there are rehab loans or grants you can tap, if this is the kind of property *you* like! So don't let any of these doomer and gloomers sway you from your goal. Listen to me: I *know* because I'm doing it, through the efforts of thousands of my loyal readers.

There are several simple keys to borrowing money for the real estate *you* like. These keys are:

1. Apply to a real estate lender for your real estate loan! While this may seem obvious, I'm amazed, again and again, at how little attention some BWBs pay to the type of loans a lender prefers. Put in other terms, don't apply to an auto finance company for a real estate loan.

2. Have a specific property for which you want to borrow. Lenders are busy and they don't have time to talk in general terms about a loan you *may* want *if* you find a suitable property!

3. Ask for an amount of money that's within the lender's guidelines. Thus, some lenders don't lend less than $500,000; others won't lend less than $100,000. Find out *before* you apply what loan limits a lender has.

Watching thousands of BWBs borrow millions of dollars for real estate, I *know* that these keys *do* work! And they *will* work for you, if you use your head when applying for *every* real estate loan.

To help BWBs get the real estate loans they seek, I keep a daily eye on lenders throughout the world. My staff and I collect data on lenders which we assemble into directories and a newsletter. The most helpful directories, listed in the appendix, are *Directory of 2,500 Active Real Estate Lenders, Guide to Business and Real Estate Loan Sources, Diversified Business and Real Estate Loan Sources,* and *Million Dollar Guide to Loan Sources.* The newsletter is *Money Watch Bulletin.* See the back of this book for data on these helpful publications.

MAKE EVERY APPLICATION
A WORK OF ART

In my lending business we receive thousands of applications every year. A high proportion of these applications are approved because our largest source of income is from the interest we earn on our loans. My board of directors is constantly urging me to find more borrowers for our funds. Why? Because we earn about 4 percent *more* on our loans than we do on investing the same money in a savings account. When you're talking of multimillions, as we are, the difference is real bucks!

When you apply for any kind of loan, the application you submit is *you*—in the loan officer's mind. Why is this? Because:

- Neatly prepared loan applications are easier to read and understand.
- A typewritten application is so much more appealing to a loan officer that it almost screams *Approved!*
- Handwritten loan applications are almost automatically rejected for all but the smallest real estate projects because they are the mark of an amateur.

So make *your* real estate loan application a work of art. Have it typed or prepared on computer. Make it neat, clean, clear, and accurate. You'll put yourself on the "yes" track from the moment the loan officer first sees your application.

I've often watched loan officers sorting through the loan applications in their *in* box. Many times I've watched as the loan officer chooses the typewritten applications to work on first, pushing the handwritten applications to the bottom of the pile. Don't let your application wind up there!

KEEP YOUR JOB WHEN FIRST APPLYING FOR LOANS

Having a steady job makes it easier for you to get your real estate loan approved. Why is this? Because:

1. Lenders like to have more than one source of income from which a loan might be repaid. Having your job makes the lender feel safer. And every lender wants to be as safe as he or she can be!

2. Being employed gives *you* greater credibility and respect. A lender *wants* to lend money to people having a good employment history and a steady income. *You* have both when you're still employed. Later, if you wish to go out on your own and leave your job, you'll have an excellent record of regular loan repayments and a growing list of important real estate assets.

3. Having two phone numbers (your job and your home) and having two addresses (your place of business and your home) makes your loan application look much more professional. You are much more likely to get an *Approved* stamp on your application than if you have only one phone and one address.

4. Being, or appearing to be, a "solid citizen" can carry more clout with lenders than you might think. Having approved thousands of loan applications myself, I speak from experience. Holding a job, especially with a known firm, gives the loan applicant, and the application submitted, a special attractiveness to all lenders. It may seem crazy—but it's true—I *know* from years of experience in the lending "trenches"!

Readers call and write me every day of the week to tell me about a new loan deal they've put through. Almost every one of these readers has a job or business that provides regular, dependable income. Again and again readers say, in awe:

> The fact that I have a steady job with a long employment history seemed to relax the lender. And the loan officer was very impressed with my wanting to get some real estate to make money in my spare time. I'm sure glad I kept my job, instead of tossing everything over to get started in real estate. I didn't believe you when you told me that holding onto my job would make things a lot easier. But you were right! Thanks for the suggestion.

HOW TO LINE UP LENDERS FOR
YOUR REAL ESTATE DEALS

Nothing succeeds like success. To succeed in building your real estate
empire, it's best to have two or more lenders vying for *your* loans. Can this
be done? It sure can! Here's how.

There are four simple, quick steps to get lenders lined up for your
deals. Here are these steps—and how *you* can take them:

1. Know who lends for real estate in your area, and elsewhere.
2. Qualify those lenders who might work with you.
3. Get friendly with lenders who may help you.
4. Develop a needs list for your preferred lenders.

Let's look at each of these steps to see how you'll use it in your
wealth building activities.

Know Who Lends for Real Estate

In this business, knowledge is power. Knowing who lends, and for
what purposes, can be the big difference between success and failure. So
you must get to know who's willing to lend for real estate in *your* area.
How do you do this? It's easy:

1. Look in your local papers for ads run by lenders seeking to make
   loans. Many of these ads appear in the Sunday edition.
2. Study your local Yellow Pages under "Loans," "Mortgages," and
   "Financial" entries.
3. Use any of the comprehensive real estate loan directories listed at the
   back of this book. Some give you thousands of lenders.
4. Read local real estate magazines; you'll often find lender ads in
   them.

Make a list of lenders you believe might work with you. This can be
a simple handwritten list featuring the name and phone number of your
prospective lenders. This list will become an important working tool for
you.

Here are two recent letters showing how BWBs use prospective lender knowhow in their wealth-building deals:

"I just got my loans. It took only three days to get $20,000. I used four $5,000 property improvement loans on a building I did not yet own. I took over a $200,000 38-unit apartment building and borrowed the down payment. The cash flow pays all the loans. By careful timing of the closing and prorations of rent and payments, I walk away with $3,000 cash and a building for my work!" CA

"I have purchased several homes over the last few years. But Friday I closed on a 12-unit apartment complex for no money down, a $225,000 value for $185,000. I assumed the 1st and 2nd mortgages and the owner gave a 3rd with interest only. I am on my way and I want to thank you." TX

Qualify the Lenders You Might Use

There are lenders *and* lenders! Some specialize in small loans; others won't look at any loan under $1 million. So you must:

1. Find out, from the lender, the guidelines used in making loans, including:

   a. Range of loan amounts—from low to high dollars

   b. Types of properties the lender prefers to loan on

   c. Typical loan term—from 5 years to 30 years

   d. Usual interest rate charged

   e. Any "equity kickers" required (a *kicker* is an extra offered the lender to make the loan—it could be extra points, a small portion of ownership of the property, etc.)

   f. Other unusual requirements the lender may have

2. Determine if you could qualify for any of the loans the lender makes. Do this by:

   a. Giving the lender a summary of your credit history

   b. Providing current data on your income and expenses

c. Listing specific information about the property you plan to finance with the lender's loan

In a matter of a few minutes you can easily qualify any lender you plan to use. Once a lender appears suitable for your real estate wealth building plans, add the name, address, phone number, and pertinent lending data to your list of qualified lenders. You'll soon have a lineup of lenders waiting to serve you. Note that all your contacts with a prospective lender can be by phone, mail, or in person.

Get Friendly with Your Lenders

You may not like meeting lenders. But let me tell you this: More deals go through based on knowing the borrower than with strangers. Let's face it: We all feel more comfortable with people we know. The same goes for lenders.

Getting friendly with your lender doesn't take much work. You can get to know a loan officer with a few simple phone calls. Or you can visit the loan officer in his or her office. And if you write well, you can set up a pen pal relationship via the mail. Of the three, the personal visit is probably the best way to become friendly with your lender.

You'll notice that most loan officers will admire your desire to go out on your own. In my experience, most loan officers are frustrated wealth builders. They'd like to do what you're planning to do. But they're so wedded to their monthly paycheck, and so-called security, that they can't break away.

If you notice that the loan officer looks at you with glowing eyes, use this admiration to get your loan. Remember: Friendship gets results!

Develop a Needs List for Your Lenders

You'll need all sorts of help from your lender. This help can cover items like:

- Preferred date of loan payment—that is, first, middle, or end of month
- Handling of real estate tax payments by the lender
- Automatic payment of your monthly mortgage principal and interest by deduction from another account you have at the financial institution

- Right to make direct principal payments to reduce your interest cost
- And so on

Presenting this needs list to your lender *before* you accept a loan can build your credibility with the lender and get you the loan sooner! Why? Because your needs request shows you've carefully thought through your responsibilities to the lender. You become—automatically—a desired borrower, even though you're making life easier for yourself.

So don't overlook your needs list. It will make your business life simpler while impressing your lenders!

Earlier we said knowledge is power. Here's a good example of combining knowledge and your needs list to get what you want from a lender:

Combine Knowledge and Needs

Ernest L needed money to buy, fix up, and get a long-term mortgage for an income property. These were his needs. He heard of a little-known EHA program called the 203(k) that meets these needs of buying, rehabbing, and getting permanent financing in one program. This is the *knowledge* part of the wealth building Ernest is doing. If the user of the 203(k) program occupies the property, only a 5 percent down payment is required. But if you're buying the property for investment purposes, the down payment required is 15 percent. In either case, this is a lower down payment than required by conventional lenders. In studying the 203(k) program, Ernest learned that he could also borrow 6 months of the needed mortgage payments to pay on his loan while the property was being rehabbed. Likewise, he could use some of the borrowed money to pay for any licenses or permits needed for rehabbing. This, again, is knowledge applied to needs. Today Ernest makes active use of the 203(k) program in his wealth building. To learn more about using this excellent program for your real estate needs, contact the local HUD office in your area.

HOW TO HAVE EVERY LOAN APPLICATION APPROVED

You can score 100 percent in your application process if you go about it in the right way. Thousands of BWBs who take my advice score big when they apply for a real estate loan. Others, who ignore that advice, often

strike out. I want *you* to be a home-run hitter—every time! Here's how—
just follow these simple rules:

1. Apply only where you're welcome.
2. Match your loan needs to the lender's guidelines.
3. Be sure your application has a good chance of approval.
4. Prepare a winning application.
5. Talk to your lender before you apply.
6. Use a participation mortgage to get easier approval.

Let's take a fast look at each of these steps to see how *you* can use it
in *your* borrowing activities. It will pay off in your getting more loan
approvals.

Apply Only Where You're Welcome

Earlier we showed you how to line up lenders for *your* financing
needs. You'll be welcome at these lenders because you—and they—meet
the criteria for your loans.

So don't throw all your work to the winds! Apply at those lenders
who are a good fit with your needs. If you can't find any such lenders in
your area I'll be glad to find suitable lenders for you at no cost of any kind,
if you're a two-year, or longer, subscriber to my newsletter *International
Wealth Success.* All you need do is supply me, in writing, the following:

*   Amount of money needed
*   Type of property being financed
*   Income and expense statements
*   Any limitation you may have on interest rate

With this information in hand I'm sure I can supply you with several names of lenders who'll welcome your application. So use your head—
go only where the welcome mat is out for you!

Match Your Loan Needs to the Lender's Guidelines

Build a file of lender guidelines. These cover loan amounts acceptable to the lender, types of properties preferred, tie-in with government

programs, interest rate charged, term of loan, down payment required, and so on. Be certain your project meets *all* the guideline requirements *before* you apply for the loan you need.

Ignoring the lender's guidelines, or hoping that the lender will overlook the guidelines for your loan leads only to rejection. Why risk turndown when—with a little work—you can make your loan conform with the guidelines? If you've chosen your lenders carefully, it should be easy to meet their guidelines.

Be Sure Your Application Has a Good Chance of Approval

One technique which many successful BWBs use to ensure approval of their loan application is:

- The BWB calls the lender on the phone *before* sending the loan application.
- Asking to speak with a loan officer, the BWB gives the loan officer the details of the loan—the type of property, amount needed, and term (duration) of the loan.
- Then the BWB asks: "Do you think this is the type of loan your organization is interested in making at this time?"

You'll get a quick "yes" or "no." If the response is "yes," then you have a good chance of loan approval. If the answer is "no," go on to the next lender on your list and ask the same question.

When it's so easy (and cheap) to learn if your application has a good chance of approval, it's foolish not to take the simple step of "checking it out." You now know how to do it—so check it out!

Prepare a Winning Application

To make money in real estate you *must* be businesslike! You can't fly by the seat of your pants. Why? Because there's too much at stake. People will ignore you if you act like an amateur.

And the surest sign of a professional is a carefully prepared loan application. *Your loan application must be typewritten!* There is *no* other way you'll get a loan for income real estate. Exhibit 8–1 shows a typical winning loan application.

Exhibit 8–1

Residential Loan Application

MORTGAGE APPLIED FOR	[XX] Conventional [ ] FHA [ ] VA	Amount $ 250,000	Interest Rate %	No. of Months	Monthly Payment Principal & Interest $	Escrow/Impounds (to be collected monthly) [XX] Taxes [XX] Hazard Ins [XX] Mtg. Ins [XX]

Prepayment Option — No penalty

Subject Property

Property Street Address 123 Main Street	City Any Town	County Central	State	Zip	No. Units 10

Legal Description (Attach description if necessary) — Attached — Year Built

Purpose of Loan [X] Purchase [ ] Construction-Permanent [ ] Construction [ ] Refinance [ ] Other (Explain)

Complete this line if Construction-Permanent or Construction Loan: Lot Value Data — Year Acquired $ — Original Cost $ — Present Value (a) $ — Cost of Imps. (b) $ — Total (a + b) $ — ENTER TOTAL AS PURCHASE PRICE IN DETAILS OF PURCHASE

Complete this line if a Refinance Loan: Year Acquired — Original Cost — Amt Existing Liens — Purpose of Refinance — Describe Improvements [ ] made [ ] to be made — Cost $

Title Will Be Held In What Name(s) — John Doe — Manner In Which Title Will Be Held — By lender

Source of Down Payment and Settlement Charges — Savings of buyer/borrower

This application is designed to be completed by the borrower(s) with the lender's assistance. The Co-Borrower Section and all other Co-Borrower questions must be completed and the appropriate box(es) checked if [ ] another person will be jointly obligated with the Borrower on the loan, or [ ] the Borrower is relying on income from alimony, child support or separate maintenance or on the income or assets of another person as a basis for repayment of the loan, or [ ] the Borrower is married and resides, or the property is located, in a community property state.

Borrower				Co-Borrower		
Name John Doe		Age 37	School Yrs 16	Name	Age	School Yrs
Present Address [XX] Own [ ] Rent No. Years 4				Present Address [ ] Own [ ] Rent No. Years		
Street 125 Main St				Street		
City/State/Zip Any Town				City/State/Zip		
Former address if less than 2 years at present address				Former address if less than 2 years at present address		
Street				Street		
City/State/Zip				City/State/Zip		
Years at former address [ ] Own [ ] Rent				Years at former address [ ] Own [ ] Rent		
Marital Status [XX] Married [ ] Separated [ ] Unmarried (incl single, divorced, widowed)	DEPENDENTS OTHER THAN LISTED BY CO-BORROWER NO / AGES			Marital Status [ ] Married [ ] Separated [ ] Unmarried (incl single, divorced, widowed)	DEPENDENTS OTHER THAN LISTED BY CO-BORROWER NO / AGES	
Name and Address of Employer ABC Manufacturing Co. 54 West St Any Town	Years employed in this line of work or profession? 12 years Years on this job 8 [ ] Self Employed*			Name and Address of Employer	Years employed in this line of work or profession? years Years on this job [ ] Self Employed*	
Position/Title Chief Engineer	Type of Business Manufacturing			Position/Title	Type of Business	
Social Security Number*** 0000-00-0000	Home Phone 123-4567	Business Phone 7654-321		Social Security Number***	Home Phone	Business Phone

Gross Monthly Income				Monthly Housing Expense**			Details of Purchase	
Item	Borrower	Co-Borrower	Total		PRESENT	PROPOSED	Do Not Complete If Refinance	
Base Empl. Income	$ 4,000	--	$ 4,000	Rent $			a. Purchase Price	$ 280,000
Overtime	--	--	--	First Mortgage (P&I)	1,200	$	b. Total Closing Costs (Est)	5,000
Bonuses	200	--	200	Other Financing (P&I)	--		c. Prepaid Escrows (Est)	2,000
Commissions	--	--	--	Hazard Insurance	100		d. Total (a + b + c)	$ 258,000
Dividends/Interest	1,000	--	1,000	Real Estate Taxes	200		e. Amount This Mortgage	(250,000)
Net Rental Income	2,000	--	2,000	Mortgage Insurance	10		f. Other Financing	(--)
Other† (Before completing, see notice under Describe Other Income below)	--	--	--	Homeowners Assn Dues	--		g. Other Equity	(--)
				Other:	--		h. Amount of Cash Deposit	(30,000)
				Total Monthly Pmt	$ 1,510	$	i. Closing Costs Paid by Seller	(6,000)
				Utilities	150		j. Cash Reqd For Closing (Est)	$ 2,000
Total	$ 7,200	$ --	$ 7,200	Total	$ 1,660	$		

Describe Other Income

	B—Borrower C—Co-Borrower	NOTICE: † Alimony, child support, or separate maintenance income need not be revealed if the Borrower or Co-Borrower does not choose to have it considered as a basis for repaying this loan.	Monthly Amount
B	None		$

If Employed In Current Position For Less Than Two Years Complete the Following

B/C	Previous Employer/School	City/State	Type of Business	Position/Title	Dates From/To	Monthly Income
						$

These Questions Apply To Both Borrower and Co-Borrower

If a "yes" answer is given to a question in this column, please explain on an attached sheet.	Borrower Yes or No	Co-Borrower Yes or No		Borrower Yes or No	Co-Borrower Yes or No
Are there any outstanding judgments against you?	No	--			
Have you been declared bankrupt within the past 7 years?	No	--			
Have you had property foreclosed upon or given title or deed in lieu thereof in the last 7 years?	No	--	Are you a U.S. citizen?	Yes	--
Are you a party to a law suit?	No	--	If "no," are you a resident alien?	--	--
Are you obligated to pay alimony, child support, or separate maintenance?	No	--	If "no," are you a non-resident alien?	--	--
Is any part of the down payment borrowed?	No	--	Explain Other Financing or Other Equity (if any) None		
Are you a co-maker or endorser on a note?	No	--			

*FHLMC/FNMA require business credit report, signed Federal Income Tax returns for last two years; and, if available, audited Profit and Loss Statement plus balance sheet for same period.
**All Present Monthly Housing Expenses of Borrower and Co-Borrower should be listed on a combined basis.
***Optional for FHLMC
FHLMC 65 Rev. 10/86

Fannie Mae Form 1003 Rev. 10/86

Forget *all* the excuses you can dream up about your typewriter being broken, your secretary on vacation, or your being on the road away from your office! None of these will work. If your application is hand-written it will be turned down without even being read. Hear me—I've approved thousands of loan applications for millions of dollars. They were *all* typed!

And your winning application will include all the other aspects we're discussing, such as meeting the lender's guidelines, and so on. It's truly easy to get the loan you need, if you follow my commonsense suggestions.

Talk to Your Lender Before You Apply

You can write your lender and ask for a loan application. But a better way to get an application is to talk to the lender *before* you apply for a loan. When you talk to a lender you build a relationship. Get the loan officer's name and use it when you send your application in.

When talking to the lender, give the loan officer general information about your project, such as the type of property, how large a loan you'll need, the outstanding positive features of the investment, and so on. You'll usually have an interested audience.

Ask the loan officer if there are any special aspects of the loan application that you should give special attention. You'll quickly learn that a winning application is one that uses the lender's special form—and *only* that form!

Lenders are a strange breed—they want you to use *only* their application form. Why? Because they know their form, they feel comfortable with it, and they're much more likely to approve a loan on their own form.

So get the message clearly. Talk before you apply. It pays in more approved loan applications for your real estate business.

Use a Participation Mortgage

With a *participation mortgage* you offer the lender a share of the income from the property, or a share of the profit on the resale of the property. The effect is to give the lender a higher return on the loan. Since the lender is in business to earn money, such an offer makes the loan more attractive to the lender. And you'll be much more likely to get a "yes" answer!

How much should you offer the lender? If you're offering a participation in the income from the property, consider 1 or 2 percent of the gross
income. Of course, if the income is very large, you might reduce the percentage you offer. Likewise, with a small income, you might increase the
percentage you offer. It all comes back to the number of dollars the lender
seeks and the amount of income you're willing to give up to get the loan.

With a percentage of the profit on the resale you can look at numbers in the 5 percent range. Again, though, you must relate the percentage
to the number of dollars potentially at stake. You'll vary the percentage to
make the dollar amount more interesting.

USE THE KNOWLEDGE-IS-POWER APPROACH

The more time you spend building *your* real estate fortune, the greater the
truth you'll see in that famous saying: *Knowledge is power.* Why is this?
For a number of good and proven reasons, namely:

- Lenders *do* respect—and treat better—smart borrowers.
- You can make every lender's job easier when you know more about
  correct borrowing procedures.
- Multiple loans *are* possible for you when lenders *want* to deal with
  you.
- You can use equity to take out tax-free cash to buy other income
  properties.
- Borrowing can help you build your real estate assets from a few
  thousand dollars to many millions.
- You *can* get the real estate funding *you* seek—if you keep trying.

Let's look at each of these reasons to see how *you* can use it in your
real estate wealth building. I'm sure you'll get plenty of good ideas you
can use immediately.

Lenders Respect Smart Borrowers

You'll be a *smart* borrower by the time you finish this book—I guarantee that! What's more, you'll see that being a smart borrower *does* get
you the results you seek. Being a smart borrower means that you:

- Apply at the *right* kinds of lenders, that is, lenders who make the kind of loan you're seeking
- Tailor your loan application for easy, quick reading and approval by having it neatly typed
- Apply for an amount which is within the range of money the lender lends
- Don't push the lender for a fast answer when the typical approval time is, say, 7 days
- Fax your typed application to the lender to shorten the approval time. But a "live signature" will be required before transfer of the loan funds to you

You're a smart borrower when you do all we list. And your smartness starts with knowledge. This knowledge comes from doing your homework, that is, getting information about "your" lender *before* you apply for any loan. A number of the loan directories listed in the appendix will put you in touch with lenders who might work with you.

Readers of my books and newsletters regularly borrow large sums to take over the real estate they like. Again and again these readers say or write:

Going to _____ Mortgage Company was the right step to take to get my loan for real estate. They liked my loan application so much they even said that it was the neatest and easiest to review they had ever seen. And the loan package I prepared with your help was the clincher. Sure, it took some work. But I did get the loan. That's all that counts in this business!

Probably the most important place where knowledge of borrowing pays *big* results is with foreign or overseas lenders. Such lenders are putting more money into real estate in the United States and Canada. If you're a smart borrower who knows his or her way around a loan application, be sure to check out foreign lenders for your large loans. Sources of foreign funds are given in a number of the real estate and business loan directories listed at the back of this book.

And if you don't feel smart about borrowing, give me a ring, if you're a subscriber of one of my newsletters or a buyer of any of my kits.

I'll be glad to help you get the loan you need—without charging you a penny. I'm as close to you as your telephone!

Make Every Lender's Job Easier

I wish you could sit with me for one day and listen to our loan officers as they approve loans. You'll often hear remarks like:

"The appraisal isn't here—why not?"

"What happened to the title papers?"

"I can't read the handwriting on this application—why wasn't it typed?"

Such remarks hurt the potential borrower. Why? Because they make the lender work harder. And with a pile of applications on your desk, it's easier to push such an application into the "Rejected" file than to ponder over missing documents and scrawled handwriting.

Your task then—if you want your loan application approved—is to make every lender's job easier. To do this, use the checklist in Exhibit 8–2. Run your eye down this list to be certain you've included all needed items for a real estate loan application *before* you submit any application to any lender!

At the start of your real estate investing, you won't need anything more than the loan application supplied by the lender, plus a short letter like that in Exhibit 8–3, on page 204. You can use the same wording as in the letter. Or you can vary it to suit your particular loan situation.

Borrowing is an art. You can learn this art by using the information in this book, plus listening carefully to lenders. You'll often learn more in a 10-minute talk with a lender than in a 4-year college course! So listen and learn, and put your learning to work to make the lender's job easier.

Multiple Loans Are Possible for You

Every real estate wealth builder I know, including myself, uses multiple loans (more than one loan at a time) during his or her wealth building. Multiple loans *are* available—even in the toughest of times. True, you *must* look longer, and harder, to get multiple loans when real estate is having a terrible time surviving. But BWBs are a hardy lot. So I see them come up with one multiple loan after another—even when everyone else in real estate seems to be crying the blues. With more than one loan *you* have great flexibility. Thus, *you* can:

- Use one loan for the down payment on a property
- Use a second loan for a long-term mortgage of 15 to 40 years
- Use a third loan to repair the property you bought using none of your own money
- Use a fourth loan to take cash out of the property tax free
- Use a fifth loan to "wrap" all the other loans

Exhibit 8–2

REAL ESTATE LOAN APPLICATION CHECKLIST*

	YES	NO
1. Does this lender seek, and make, real estate loans?	___	___
2. Is the loan amount sought within the lender's guidelines?	___	___
3. Is the loan application on the form the lender supplied?	___	___
4. Is the loan application typed throughout, except for the required signature?	___	___
5. Have you supplied data on your other sources of income and the value of your other property holdings?	___	___
6. If this is an income property, is the debt ratio coverage 1 .5 or higher?	___	___
7. Have you submitted a short business plan for the property with the loan application?	___	___
8. Have you included an appraisal, title search, and insurance coverage data with your loan application?	___	___
9. Have you signed the loan application in the space provided for your signature?	___	___
10. Can you supply a qualified cosigner for the loan if the lender requests one?	___	___

*You should have a "yes" answer for every one of these checklist items if you want quick approval of your loan application.

Exhibit 8–3

YOUR LETTERHEAD

Date

_____ Mortgage Company
123 Main St.
Anytown, USA 00000

Dear _____:

Enclosed is our completed application for a 30-year, $250,000 mortgage loan for the ABC Garden Apartments. We will be pleased to accept your current interest rate on such loans.

If you need further information about the property or the borrower, you can reach me during business hours at 123-4567.

Meanwhile, thank you for considering this loan application.

Very truly yours,

John/Mary Doe

I'm sure you can see the many advantages to you of multiple loans. Why use your own money for real estate when there are plenty of lenders fighting for the opportunity to lend you the money you need? What's more, multiple loans can put you into a profitable real estate business when you're cash poor, credit starved, and flat broke!

Though I haven't kept score, it's my feeling that those of my readers who've made it biggest in real estate started in a cash-poor, credit-starved, flat-broke condition. These readers are so driven by the desire to build their wealth that they overcome any obstacle in moments. *You* can do the same, especially if you use multiple loans to overcome your cash starvation! Let's see how you can get, and use, more than one loan for your real estate wealth building. Start by recognizing that:

1. Multiple loans *are* good for you, for the economy, and for real estate; they are *not* bad, as some people would have you believe.

2. Most properties can be bought with two loans—a down payment loan and a long-term mortgage. If the income from the property allows you to repay both loans and still have a positive cash flow, you have a good business!

3. The property you buy serves as the collateral for your long-term mortgage loan. So your credit rating, cash situation, and job history do not play an important part in the loan approval. What's important here is the income the property will provide and the resulting *debt coverage ratio.* If you must pay, let's say, $40,000 per year on the long-term mortgage (called the *annual debt service)* and the property has a total annual income of $94,000 with expenses of $30,000, then your debt coverage ratio will be $94,000 − $30,000 = $64,000 to repay debt; then, $64,000/$40,000 = 1.6, your debt coverage ratio. You should aim for a debt coverage ratio of at least 1.5, if you seek quick loan approval.

4. Borrowing the down payment will give you 100 percent financing. Your down payment loan will *not* be made by the same lender who makes your mortgage loan. Instead, you must apply at another lender. And you do *not* ask for a down payment loan—that's a no-no. You ask for a personal signature loan for a purpose that's acceptable to the lender. Once you get the loan you use the money for the stated purpose *and* the down payment. There's nothing wrong with overborrowing, if (a) you have full intentions of repaying the loan in a *timely* and *complete* manner and (b) you have sufficient income from the property to repay the loan according to the agreed terms. If you have suitable collateral, you can get a collateralized loan for your down payment. The same general terms likewise apply.

In my lending business we do two types of real estate lending helpful to BWBs. The first type is loans for long-term mortgages. The organization I head up has—at this writing— some 470 long-term mortgage loans for a total of some $70 million. The second type of loan* we make, through my firm International Wealth Success, is for real estate down payment.

_____

* Where permitted by state statute.

Why do we specialize in down payment loans in this second organization? Because:

- Getting a long-term mortgage for good property is relatively easy for most BWBs
- Coming up with the down payment, however, is hard for most BWBs, everywhere
- Our goal is to help BWBs everywhere, so we specialize in short-term (up to 7 years) down payment loans for BWBs wanting to get into the income real estate business

These down payment loans have been popular for years with our newsletter subscribers. Why? Because they answer a real need that's felt in every area of the world. And being able to borrow the down payment gives the BWB the multiple loans he or she seeks.

Become a hardworking, dedicated real estate wealth builder, and you can get multiple loans from thousands of real estate lenders. I talk to plenty of these lenders while building the lists in the lender directories I publish (listed in the appendix). These lenders say, again and again, we'll make multiple loans to any borrower who's taking over well-located income property having adequate debt coverage. Why don't you become my next reader to get multiple loans? I'm ready to help *you,* every day!

To prove the point of multiple loans, just read this excerpt from a recent letter:

> *"I got 100% financing from a local bank for my income real estate—even though the bank knew that the seller was taking back a 25% (of purchase price) mortgage."* OR

Get Your Tax-Free Cash from Equity

Equity is the part of a property that *you* own because you've made payments on the mortgage. Or it can be the part that you own which has increased in value while you went about your daily business. Let's see how this might work:

> You buy a property for $300,000, all on borrowed money. After a period of time your payments have reduced your debt on this property to $200,000. *You* now have an equity of $300,000 – $200,000

= \$100,000 in the property. You can borrow 75 percent of this equity, or 0.75 × \$100,000 = \$75,000 tax free. So you get \$75,000 cash to use as you wish—for another property, for current expenses, and so on.

Using the same property, if its market value rises to \$380,000 while you're reducing its debt to \$200,000, then your equity is \$380,000 − \$200,000 = \$180,000. On this equity you can borrow 0.75 × \$180,000 = \$135,000, tax free.

Most BWBs use their equity buildup at the start of their careers to buy more income properties. Once they reach their desired income level they use equity cash for property improvement purposes, or for personal needs. Either way, you're tapping a hidden asset that rises in value as you sleep. Could you ask for any better payoff in any business?

Borrow More to Build Your Real Estate Fortune

At the start you will use your equity cash to buy more properties, as we noted. You're using the borrowing approach to build your real estate fortune. This is the *best* way, in my view, to get rich today. You're doing it on OPM—other people's money.

Often, people are so cash poor when they start that the only way they can build their real estate fortune is on OPM. Sure, it does involve some risk. But there's risk in every business. Yet my experience, and that of others in real estate is:

> There's less risk for a BWB in real estate than in any other business because the inherent value of the property remains fairly constant, despite any mistakes a BWB might make. So you'll find many fewer failures in real estate than in any other business. And—being a borrowed money business—real estate puts none of the BWBs personal funds at risk.

So borrowing more is "in" —in real estate! You really can't go wrong if you borrow to buy more good income property. Even if the income from the property declines in bad times (as it most likely will), the income will rise again when good times return. This is proven each time we have a real estate slide followed by a recovery. Income from good property surges; values of these properties reach for the skies. So you can't go wrong!

To be able to borrow more for other income properties you want to buy, take these easy steps:

1. Run your current properties at a profit.
2. Keep accurate books showing your exact income and expenses.
3. Pay your taxes (real estate and income) on time and in full.
4. Keep all your insurance payments up to date.
5. Make each holding a "model property" that's so neat and clean and so profitable that anyone—including a lender— would be proud to own the holding.

When you follow these tips you'll have lenders vying with each other to put money into your hands. Then you can *select* the lender offering you the best terms for your loan. Why sweat and slave in your real estate business when—with a little planning—you can have a sweet deal all around?

Keep Trying to Get the Funding You Seek

Too many BWBs give up too soon looking for borrowed money. They come to me saying: "I've tried *everything* and nothing works! What should I do now?" To me, such statements are a sure sign of a loss of hope. Why? Because:

- I regularly see BWBs getting *all* the money they need.
- Giving up too soon is almost certain to cause failure.
- The more you try to get the loan you need, the greater the skill you develop in working with lenders.
- Almost any amount of work in applying for a loan is less than what you'd have to do to earn the same amount of money.
- The more you try to get a loan, the greater your chances of getting it!

Reader after reader reports to me via phone, fax, or letter that they got the loan they sought. And *you,* I'm certain, *can* get the money you seek. But I can guarantee you won't get the money you need if you give up your search for it.

Looking for money is 99 percent sweat and energy, 1 percent creativity. Once you set up your list of potential lenders, you just keep applying.

And if all these lenders say "no," just prepare another list of potential lenders and go after them.

My most memorable reader seeking a real estate loan is the person who applied at 356 banks over one summer. All said "No" for his $400,000 first mortgage loan. But bank No. 357 said "yes" and this BWB got his money. Though he wore out a pair of shoes during that summer he says: "The looking was well worth the results. Today banks chase me to take loans from them!"

To keep your enthusiasm high during your search, take these simple steps:

1. Keep a picture of the property you want to buy handy to remind yourself of the rewards of looking for funds.

2. Carry with you at all times a summary of the profits you'll earn from the property you buy with the loan.

3. Figure how much of the profits you'll divert into one or more of your hobbies or family fun activities.

There *is* money available for every kind of real estate you may want to buy. And you *can* get the money you need. All it takes is *looking* for the funds long enough.

And, as a 2-year subscriber to my newsletter, I promise you that if you call me I'll give you at least two—and perhaps more—lenders you can work with—after you give me full details of your project.

TEN KEY RULES FOR GETTING EVERY REAL ESTATE LOAN

You can score 100 percent in your loan search if you go about it in the right way. Here are 10 key rules that will help you score 100 percent, every time:

Rule 1: Prepare a good real estate business plan for the property you want to buy. Submit this business plan along with your loan application. Your lender will be ecstatic! (You can get two excellent real estate business plans from my firm; see M-1 and M-2 in the appendix to this book.)

Rule 2: Apply to a suitable *real estate lender.* Don't apply for a real estate loan at an auto lender. This seems so obvious. Yet BWBs send their real estate loan applications to—it seems to me—every type of lender *except* a real estate specialist! Don't you make that mistake; it only wastes your time.

Rule 3: Be certain the amount of money you seek is acceptable to the lenders you approach. Don't ask for $100,000 of a lender having a minimum loan of $1 million! You're sure to get a "no" answer. Know the lender's guidelines *before* you apply.

Rule 4: Never submit a handwritten application. Always submit typewritten loan applications and business plans. Get a reputation for a well-organized business by being well organized!

Rule 5: Don't "bug" your lender for a response. Give the lender time to study your application. Bugging the lender will only get you a fast "no"!

Rule 6: With income properties, be sure your debt cover ratio is 1.5 or higher. Lenders love higher ratios because it makes them feel safer. And every lender loves safety!

Rule 7: Supply information on all other income you have. Do this on the loan application. Why? Because, again, it makes your lender feel safer! And you know what we said about lenders and safety. How do I know this? Because I'm a lender—and have been for a number of very successful years. As they say, it takes one to know one.

Rule 8: Get the seller to take out a second mortgage for your down payment and you make the monthly payments on the loan from the property income. This gives you 100 percent financing without a credit check of any kind. And you can have your real estate attorney prepare a "reverse-flip" agreement whereby the seller will get credit for all the payments you've made, if you default on the loan. This offer will make any seller feel comfortable with taking out a second (or home equity loan) mortgage for *your* down payment!

Rule 9: Have a cosigner ready. With a cosigner on tap you 11 get your loan much faster. What's more, every lender will be favorable impressed by your readiness to supply a cosigner. Remember: *Every* lender worries about his or her money— they want to feel it's in safe hands. Be sure *your* hands are the safe ones!

Rule 10: Be ready to accept the lender's terms for interest rate, loan duration, points, and so on. When you're getting your first few loans you should, and *must,* be ready to accept the lender's terms. Once you own a number of properties you can then start negotiating with lenders for reduced interest rates and longer terms. But at the start you should not endanger your negotiations by demanding unacceptable terms from the lender. While this may seem like a coward's way out, it's better to be a rich coward than a poor hero!

Again, I'm here, ready to help you. Please call me on my business telephone (*not* my 800 number which is *only* for orders), and I'll try to answer every question you have. Over the years we've raised millions of dollars for BWBs and *never* asked for, nor accepted, one cent in fees or other charges of any kind. I *can* help you get the real estate money you need if you have a sensible project that's right for your stage of business development.

GETTING REAL ESTATE LOANS FOR VARIED PROJECTS

You do *not* use the same techniques to get real estate loans for different types of projects. Each project varies somewhat. Here are some proven and workable ideas for real estate that might interest you:

Commercial Projects

Such projects include stores, office buildings, and shopping centers. To get loans for such projects, you *must* have a business plan with projections of the project income for the next 5 years. An *anchor tenant* is the main, and usually largest, tenant in a shopping center, office building, and so on and may be required by your lender *before* a loan is made. So you'll often find that commercial money is readily available to you *if* you have a suitable anchor tenant. As a BWB you'll probably find it impossible to locate a major anchor tenant at the start. But you probably *can* locate an "anchor" tenant for a small property locally. From this start you can build to a larger property with a bigger anchor tenant. Eventually you'll be able to swing your bat with the big-league players. Other commercial properties *you* might like are hotels, motels, restaurants, and resorts. With each of these you *must* have your business plan for the lender. Without such a plan you'll have difficulty getting your loan.

When you combine your loan application with your business plan (which will include an appraisal of the property, details on the deed, a title search, and insurance specifics), the resulting overall document is called your *loan package*. Be sure to make *your* loan package a "work of art" because it will be *you* when the lender reviews your application. More loans with professionally prepared packages are accepted than those that are thrown together in a hurry without regard for quality of information or its appearance.

Industrial Projects

These include factories, manufacturing (both heavy and light) buildings, industrial parks, and research and development parks. Here, again, an anchor tenant is almost a must, if you are to get new financing. If you're assuming existing financing, you may not need an anchor tenant. And you *must* have a loan package which includes a business plan giving projections for the next 5 years. With these in hand, you should be able to get the funding you need because there are fewer loan applicants for industrial properties than for any other type.

Recreational Projects

Here you'll be buying properties such as marinas, summer camps, bowling alleys, private airports, amusement parks, theme parks, playing fields, and so on. The key feature of recreational property is deriving income from people at play of some kind. So you must organize your paying groups so they understand that while what they're doing is "play" to them; it's *business* to you! Since you have to pay for the property on which your tenants are playing, you *must* receive regular rent or lease payments. Without such income you may lose the property.

To get a loan approved for a recreational property you must have a business plan showing anticipated cash flows. And it will be wise to request sizable deposits from people who may give up their sport and get doing another sport or hobby. Since there are lenders who specialize in almost every type of recreational property, it's wise to deal with them. Why? Because they *understand* your borrowing needs!

Religious Projects

Here you have churches, synagogues, cemeteries, and similar facilities. Many BWBs who are acting as loan or financial brokers come to me to get help finding loans for religious projects. Over the years I've assembled the names and lending data for a number of lenders who specialize in religious projects. This data on religious project lenders is available free to 2-year, or longer, subscribers to my newsletter.

You can assemble data on religious lenders by referring to directories of lenders available in large public libraries. Most such lenders want full data on the type of congregation the religious project has. While some lenders specialize in one religious group, most lend to a wide range of religions. Your "business plan" for a religious project covers details on the congregation, weekly and annual contributions, and so on. While religious projects *are* different, you *can* get them funded if you keep applying to lenders who do religious lending.

Residential Projects

These cover apartment houses, garden apartments, town houses, single-family units and developments, retirement communities, and so on. A business plan is a must for any of these fundings. Your plan should include the expected income and expenses, data on the real estate, appraised value, and so on. While this work may seem like a chore, it's well worth your effort because loans on residential properties are the most popular with many lenders. So it's a lot easier for you to get the money you need for residential properties than for some other types. To make your dream come true, be sure to apply to lenders who count residential properties among the types they like to finance. Then you'll get a fast—and it is hoped—positive response!

Raw Land

Here you're buying land either to build on or to hold for a rise in value. When you plan to build on the land, called *developing* it, you'll find the money easier to get if you have a well-prepared *development plan*. This is your business plan for the land. And your plan should include the necessary real estate data mentioned earlier, plus the business details of expected profit and expenses. If you expect to hold land for a rise in value you will, in general, have to finance the purchase yourself. Why? Because lenders are unwilling to gamble on a rise in value of raw land to repay their loan. You can, of course, use funds from a personal loan or a credit card line of credit to buy raw land, if you wish. Just be *sure* you have the capacity to repay the loan in a timely and complete fashion!

I see thousands of BWBs getting the funding they need for real estate. You, too, *can* get the money you need. Just follow the tips in this chapter, starting right now!

SUCCESS STRATEGIES FOR BUILDING YOUR REAL ESTATE WEALTH IN GOOD TIMES AND BAD TIMES

1. Form a Real Estate Investment Trust—REIT (rhymes with "feet")—to raise oodles of cash for your real estate from private or public investors. To form a REIT you MUST have competent legal and accounting advice. But you can—and should—write the business plan (called a Declaration of Trust [DOT]) for your REIT. Why? Because only you know what you want to do with the money you raise for your REIT. And your author (Ty Hicks) will gladly show you how to write your REIT business plan, if you're a 5-year, or longer, subscriber to his IWS Newsletter, or you're a buyer of his REIT Kit. See the back of this book for more details. Remember this: The REIT is the way people raise public money to invest in real estate. And REITs are used to invest in every known type of real estate—from multi-family residences (apartment houses) to marinas, shopping malls, office buildings, raw land, etc. Mortgage REITs raise money to invest in mortgages—that is, a mortgage REIT doesn't own any property of its own. Instead, it funds mortgages in properties other people own. Your REIT can operate income-tax-free if it pays out 95 percent of its taxable earnings to its investors. These earnings are the income left after all expenses, including your salary and business expenses, have been paid.

2. *Take cash out of every property you own*—as soon as you can. Lenders like to see some "seasoning" of your property loans—usually one years on-time payments before they'll make you a new loan. So don't seek a new loan for at least 6 months after you buy a property. Once 6 months have passed, apply for (1) a property improvement loan, (2) a property equity loan, (3) a second mortgage loan, or (4) any other type of loan the property will support. If you're told to wait, do so. But be sure to tell the lender to hold your loan application on file. Why? Because when you apply again in the next 6 months the lender will feel impelled to grant you the loan you're requesting because you've waited so long for it! Remember—the longer you hold your properties, the greater their value because real estate grows in value as time passes. You'll use this value increase to collateralize your loan. When you get your loan money, invest it in new—profitable—real estate!

3. *Tap into the "sub-prime" (C and D credit) lending market*—even though yours may be "A" rated. Why do I suggest this? Because you'll delight the lenders with your stellar credit rating. And if your credit rating is less than "A" or "B" you'll be in "the right place at the right time" to get the loan you need. While your interest rate may be higher when you borrow from sub-prime lenders, your chances of getting the loan you need are much greater. So don't pass up a good chance to get the loan or loans you need. No one—especially a seller—will know, or care, where your money comes from. A seller's focus is only on closing a deal on time, at his/her price. So long as you have the money, they'll never ask you where it came from. As someone once said "Money is always in fashion!"

4. *Apply to my firm, IWS, Inc., for any advice on any down payment loan you might need.* On loans we can tell you about, the interest rate—we think—is low, just 6 percent simple. If you don't know the meaning of simple interest, I'll tell you what it is. *Simple interest is interest computed on just the money you owe.* Thus, if you borrow $10,000 for one year, your interest for the first month, during which you have the full $10,000, is $0.06 \times \$10,000/12$ months = $50.00. If, at the end of the first month, you repay $1,000 in principal, you will owe, at the end of the second month $10,000 – $1,000 = $9,000. The interest on this amount you owe for the second month will be $0.06 \times \$9,000/12$ months = $45.00. So you pay interest ONLY on the money you're using. With these business and real estate loans there are *no* points, *no* fees, *no* charges of any kind, except the simple interest which begins one month *after* you, as the borrower, receive your loan money. To help you understand borrowing and loan repayments better, we suggest you subscribe to the *International Wealth Success* newsletter. To do so, send $48 to IWS, Inc. PO Box 186, Merrick NY 11566-0186 and ask for your real estate loan application. It will be sent to you immediately.

IMPORTANT POINTERS TO KEEP IN MIND

- Real estate is the world's *best* borrowed money business—almost everyone borrows to finance his or her real estate investments.
- You *can* start in real estate on borrowed money—with little, or no, money of your own.
- Borrowing is *expected* in real estate. So don't disappoint anyone by paying cash for your investment real estate.
- Money *is* available for almost every piece of real estate you would like to buy. Look for the money and you'll find it.
- Make every loan application a work of art. Neatness *does* get more loan approvals than sloppiness.
- Keep your job when you're first starting in real estate because it will help you get the loans you need fast and easier.
- Line up the lenders you need for your deals. With proper planning you can have them begging you to accept loans!
- Get every loan application approved by using smart techniques to give the lender what he or she seeks.
- You *can* get multiple loans for real estate—if you plan your applications carefully.
- Get tax-free cash from your equity in your properties by borrowing money to invest in future properties.
- Follow the 10 key rules given in this chapter for getting every real estate loan you seek.
- Be sure to tailor your loan application and loan package to the type of project for which you're seeking money.

Using Real Estate to Get Rid of 9-to-5 Drudgery

Why be a drone slaving for someone else for popcorn wages when you can be king of your own hill? You *don't* have to be a wage slave all your life! There is a better, richer, easier way to earn a living. What is it? Real estate which gives *you* a regular income without demanding long hours of work. And it's real estate which you acquire without putting up any money of your own. You can even get rich in the worst of bad times—in your spare time!

REAL ESTATE IS A FREE-TIME BUSINESS

As some of my readers know, I'm an avid yachtsman. I sail my beautiful yacht on scenic Long Island Sound every spring, summer, and fall. When I go to the yacht club where we keep our boat I'm amazed to see, again and again, on weekdays that most of the people there using their boats are real estate investors. Why? They have the *free* time!

Organize your income real estate business right and you can have all the free time you want. You *can* work your own hours in real estate. All you need do is decide *which* hours *you* want to work!

To organize *your* real estate business for *your* time freedom, take these easy steps:

1. Decide what hours you want to work and be available to your tenants.
2. Display the times you're available in your office, in your rent notices, and in other communications with your tenants. You'll find

217

that tenants *will* comply with your work hours if they're told what times you're available.

3. Assign responsibility to your staff so they are your "front" when tenants call or visit. If you're not yet far enough along to have a staff, use a telephone answering machine or an electronic mailbox for messages from your tenants. You then call back at *your* convenience, not theirs.

4. Have your accountant handle the books for you so you're not slaving into the dead of night to do tax returns and other paperwork. Your accounting fees, remember, are fully deductible on your tax return as a cost of doing business. What's more, having your accountant do this work gives *you* more time for looking into future properties you may want to take over. There's *no* need for you to be a routine numbers cruncher!

5. Allow your tenants to fax you questions, complaints and any other communications they may have. Put your fax number on all notices and bills and invite your tenants to fax you. They'll love you for it.

Beyond these simple steps are personal considerations you must look at. Let's see what these are.

GET YOUR TIME PRIORITIES STRAIGHT— AT THE START

You want more free time. Right? Yes! But do you know what you'll do with that extra free time? I've seen people arrange for extra free time and then be lost because they didn't know what to do with the time. Don't let this happen to you. A number of uses for your free time are:

*   Relaxing with a hobby
*   Looking for other investment properties
*   Spending more time with your family
*   Taking vacations you've dreamed of
*   Serving some worthwhile charitable cause
*   Attending classes in a school or college
*   Studying on your own

Get to know yourself. Then you'll be better able to choose your free-time activities. You don't want to have "time on your hands" because you'll soon become restless. Better to be too busy than not busy enough!

Schedule your time if you want to be free of daily duties. Thus, one real estate BWB who frequently calls me to tell me of his progress toward becoming a real estate millionaire tells me:

> *I schedule one hour for each of three evenings a week to engage in my hobby—which is building model airplanes. Then I schedule one hour on the same evenings for reading your newsletter and books on real estate. Two hours on Saturday morning are scheduled for looking at new pro per-ties. I find this schedule highly productive and have built $800,000 in real estate assets starting with zero cash in just two years. It works!*

If vacations are your "thing"—as they are to lots of folks—schedule your time so you can get away from your business:

- Free of any worries
- Without being tied to a cellular phone
- Knowing that things will run right
- Expecting your tenants to respect your time

Again and again I see that your business associates and tenants *will* respect *your* schedule if you organize it carefully and publish it for all to see. Further, my experience in real estate shows me that:

- People *will* conform to your schedule
- People *will* call back later if they want help
- People recognize that all of us need some time off now and then

Setting a schedule early in your real estate career will allow you to get away from the 9-to-5 drudgery when you leave your current 9-to-5 job! You do *not* have to work 8 hours a day to become rich in real estate. Just a few hours, or less, will do. Using this approach you can quickly reach your income goal.

BUILD YOUR REAL ESTATE ASSETS TO ACHIEVE YOUR INCOME GOAL

We all need a certain annual income to live the life we enjoy. And for almost all of us, the annual income we need is different from that other people need. Thus, some people need a minimum of $50,000 a year to get by. Others seek $100,000 a year. Some friends of mine spend $100,000 a year just for their home mortgage, electric, fuel, and tax bills. So their need is in the $500,000-per-year range.

You *must* know what income level *you* need to kick your 9-to-5 pacifier job. To find out what level of income would be suitable for yourself and your family, fill out a simple form like that in Exhibit 9-I. It will quickly tell you the minimum income you need to maintain your present life-style. Multiply the result you get from Exhibit 9-1 by at least two to get a target income level for your real estate activities.

Exhibit 9-1

MY YEARLY INCOME NEEDS FOR TODAY AND THE FUTURE

	CURRENT COST	FUTURE COST
Housing	_____	_____
Electric	_____	_____
Fuel	_____	_____
Automobile(s)	_____	_____
Food	_____	_____
Clothing	_____	_____
Education	_____	_____
Club dues	_____	_____
Insurance	_____	_____
Taxes (federal and state)	_____	_____
Medical and dental	_____	_____
Credit card payments	_____	_____
Miscellaneous	_____	_____
Savings	_____	_____
Total	_____	_____

Once you have this target level you can evaluate your real estate buys in terms of how they will help you get the income you seek. Let's take a real-life example to show you what I mean.

Len S. is an ambitious real estate BWB. Married with two children he seeks a monthly income of $10,000 to meet his and his family needs. Offered three buildings for zero cash down, Len analyzed them thus for annual income and expenses:

	BUILDING "A"	BUILDING "B"	BUILDING "C"
Income	$98,000	$182,000	$569,000
Expenses*	74,000	161,000	452,000
Profit	24,000	21,000	117,000

*Including mortgage payments.

These three buildings would give him an annual income of $24,000 + $21,000 + $117,000 = $162,000. Looking at the detailed financials for each building, Len decided to pass up Building "B" because between buildings "A" and "C" he would have more than the $120,000 annual income, that is, $10,000 a month, he needs for himself and family. Based on this analysis, Len took over the two buildings. Once he became comfortable with his new holdings, Len quit his job as a bank vice president.

Note that in making his decision Len used a safety hedge to give him an income greater than his target. This brings us to the important Hicks rule for financial success:

Figure your financial needs accurately and carefully. Then multiply your "real" needs by at least two to give yourself a margin of safety so you overachieve your financial goal. You can never be too rich or too young in this world!

Having an excess income will cost you a few dollars in income taxes. But you'll still keep most of the money you earn. What's more, the dollars you pay in taxes are used for good purposes by the government.

Excess income can be used for lots of productive purposes. For example, you can:

- *Take a vacation* to recharge your mental batteries so you can work more creatively when you return.

- *Buy more property* to increase your income from real estate. Buying more property will help you build a real estate empire to make your future safer and more comfortable.

- *Improve your existing property* so you can increase its value while raising the rent for your current tenants, increasing your cash flow.

- *Build a retirement nest egg* using a pension for yourself and key employees. Contributions to your pension plan are tax deductible to your business. Invested with a carefully managed firm, your contributions can grow by a factor of 5 to 10 times in a few years. Your pension will become your life insurance policy which we hope no one will have to collect on. Then, when you retire, you can have a steady and stable income.

TAX STRATEGIES TO BUILD YOUR REAL ESTATE PROFITS

You'll never be able to get away from taxes in this business! Even though you may not have to pay taxes on your real estate income, you must know how taxes can impact your business. This brings us to the Hicks rule on taxes:

You must have a certified public accountant to do (or check) your books and tax returns. But you must not rely only on the accountant's opinion. You must know enough about taxes to be able to question, and check, the accountant's decisions and work. Because, after all, it is your money that pays the taxes, not the accountant's. You're certain to be more concerned about your money than the accountant is!

Getting to know the rules and guidelines of income taxes in the real estate field is both interesting and fun. To start I suggest you take these easy steps. I use them in my own real estate activities and they really pay off:

1. *Read the real estate section of several popular tax guides that are published annually.* The reason why I suggest that you read several tax guides is that some give you more real estate data than others. Also, some tax guides are easier to understand than others. You need not buy these guides. Instead, you can refer to them in your local public library.

2. *Seek out real estate tax shelters in the properties you buy.* Thus, I suggest that you form your own legitimate real estate tax shelter for yourself, using the tax guidelines you uncover in your research. Typical legitimate shelters that you should not overlook are:

   a. Depreciation of building, equipment, and improvements

   b. Real estate taxes paid to your city and state

   c. Interest on mortgage debts

   d. Maintenance expenses

   e. Investment tax credit, if it becomes available

   Legitimate tax havens are available in income properties. You must be sure to take full advantage of all the havens to which you are legally entitled. To do this, you must know as much as you can about real estate tax rules.

3. *Steer your selections to high tax-haven properties if you like such investments.* Today you get good tax benefits from:

   a. Low-income housing

   b. Rehabbing older buildings

   c. Historic preservation of important structures

   We don't have the space to describe the many advantages to you from such properties. But any good tax guide will show you how to compute the many savings available to you when you invest in such properties. The shelter you get can remove all your profit from any income tax for a number of years. This can be a strong incentive for choosing such properties as your investment vehicle!

4. *Get good tax advice from a CPA. You must*—as I said earlier—know real estate tax rules. But the final opinion must come from a CPA who knows the rules better than you do. While it will cost you a few dollars for a CPA's help, the cost is provable and tax deductible to your business. What's more, having a CPA do your books and tax returns will free you up for more leisure time!

5. *Have a qualified attorney on tap.* If you own income real estate you will have legal questions arise. It can't be avoided. But with a good attorney on tap you won't lose sleep over someone's complaint or threat. A wise attorney will outline your risks and tell you the probable outcome as soon as you outline the situation. Again, your attorney fees are provable and tax deductible to your business. So why worry and sweat when the business will take over the cost of all this?

You *can* get rid of your 9-to-5 slavery. Just use these tips, and those that follow, to cure yourself of the wage earners' addiction to a weekly or monthly paycheck.

USE PROPERTY SWAPS TO BUILD WEALTH

Once you buy an income property and operate it for a while, you have an equity buildup. That is, *you* own more of the property a month after you bought it than the day you took it over. Likewise, one year later, two years later, and so on. And this equity is valuable to *you!*

Your equity in an investment property is like cash. You can use your equity as the down payment on another more expensive property that gives you an income. But instead of putting down cash, you put down the equity in your first property in a swap or tax-deferred exchange.

Let's put this into focus. Suppose you have the following situation:

> You own a 4-unit building valued at $100,000. Your equity in this building is $90,000. You want to swap for a larger building with 10 percent down. Your equity will buy a building worth $90,000/0.10 = $900,000. So you look for a larger income property you can take over for $90,000 down, worth $900,000, or more.

Now equity swaps *are* complicated from a tax standpoint. So you *must* have complete and ongoing advice from an accountant and attorney, both of whom understand 1031 tax-deferred exchanges. The 1031 refers to the section of the IRS Code covering such exchanges. Without competent accounting and legal advice, your "exchange" could be classified as a "sale," and you would have to pay a tax on the profit.

Swaps are easy to do while you're fully employed because they really don't take much of your time. Your main job in a swap is:

- Find a suitable property to swap—it must be an income property of a type like the one you're swapping
- Talk to the seller to get him or her to agree to a swap Negotiate a suitable price for the swap
- Contact your accountant and attorney to handle the detailed paperwork for the swap
- Do the deal

You will have a tax-free exchange only when you trade *like* income or investment properties. You cannot swap your personal residence for an income property and enjoy the benefits of Section 1031. You *must* swap *like* properties. If you need further help, consult your accountant. You'll have to do this anyway. And it's never too early to start talking to him or her about such exchanges.

SIX KEY STEPS FOR KEEPING TAXES LOW

You are fully entitled to plan your real estate life so you're paying the lowest taxes possible. The law allows, and encourages, keeping income taxes low by careful planning. Six easy steps *you* can take to keep your income taxes low include:

1. *Know what deductions you're allowed by current tax law.* If you don't know what the law allows, you're almost certain to overlook some important deductions. While your accountant *should* know *all* the deductions to which you are legally entitled, it *is* possible that he or she might overlook an important deduction. Trust only yourself— check the work that others do for you! Remember: It's *your* money that's paying the taxes; guard it carefully.

2. *Use all the depreciation deductions to which you're legally entitled.* Thus, the building is depreciable at one rate, usually 27.5 years. But certain equipment in the building—like air-conditioning units— might be depreciable over a shorter life, say, 10 years. By using all the depreciation deductions to which you are legally entitled, you may be able to reduce your taxable income considerably, thereby saving on your taxes. Remember: Land is *not* depreciable. So before figuring the potential depreciation on a property, subtract the value of the land from the total value of the property. Section 167 of the IRS Code covers depreciation.

3. *Keep accurate, and complete, records at all times.* Save *all* receipts for items you buy for your properties. This means that you should save hardware store receipts for small items costing just a few dollars or less. Why? Because such receipts give you more legal deductions which can reduce your tax burden. Further, you're entitled, legally, to deduct such items on your tax return. So be sure your account books, which can be simple sheets of paper in a binder,

show *all* your property costs. If you overlook some legitimate costs, you'll be paying higher taxes. Why do this when, with a little planning, you can deduct *every* penny to which you're legally entitled?

4. *Be certain to participate actively in the management of your property.* This means you must be in on management decisions related to your property. Such decisions include choice of tenants, setting rental rates, approving the spending of funds for property improvements, authorizing repairs, and so on. Why is it important that *you* actively participate in running your property? For two good reasons: (a) You'll have better control of your financial future when you know what's going on with your properties, and (b) you can deduct any losses associated with the property when you actively participate in its management. Such losses can be used to offset other, nonreal estate income—such as that from your job. The overall result is to free your real estate profits from any income tax and to reduce the taxes on your other income. But you won't get these benefits unless you actively participate in the management of your property. So be sure you do!

5. *Buy—if you have a choice —properties offering tax advantages.* Thus, low-income housing, certified historic structures, and rehabbing of older buildings offer tax advantages beyond those for conventional income real estate. By investing in such properties you get better legal deductions for your real estate, increasing your profit. When combined with the regular depreciation and other allowances, your bottom line will be much bigger than with conventional real estate. So buy such properties if they appeal to you and you know you can earn a profit from them.

6. *Prepare, on a first-pass basis, your own tax return.* If you allow the accountant to prepare your return, I can almost guarantee that important business deductions will be overlooked. So do the return yourself. Then let the accountant fine-tune the return, based on better knowledge of tax laws and safe procedures in preparing a tax return. This way important deductions will not be overlooked. Your income taxes will be as low as possible because you will have taken all the deductions for your business to which you are legally entitled.

For almost all the real estate you buy for income purposes, the profit will be sheltered by depreciation. This means that the income from your real estate holdings will be tax free to you. You will—of course—

eventually pay tax on the profit from the sale of your income property. But that's in your future, and I'm sure you'll be savvy enough to deal with it at that time.

Remember: All capital improvements you make to a property while you own it become part of its cost when you sell. So keeping accurate records (as recommended) reduces your tax when you sell the property. And while you've owned the property you will have received a positive cash flow every month. Truly, real estate is a great business for getting *you* out of the 9-to-5 meat grinder!

KNOW THE JOY OF BEING YOUR OWN PERSON

I've been my own boss for years. And I love it. I answer to no one—except my customers. And they seldom give me a hard time. Why? Because they want what I have—money in the form of a loan, space in a building, or one of my helpful money publications. The result? They're all sweet to me!

You, too, can be your own boss. It's really not that hard to get started. All you need do is to:

1. Decide what kind of property you want to own to build an independent income.
2. Look for suitable income properties.
3. Analyze the income potential of a property you like.
4. Bid on the property of your choice, using zero cash, if at all possible.
5. Finance the property on borrowed money.
6. Build the desired level of income you seek to live the life-style *you* enjoy.
7. Quit your boring job to become your own boss. He, or she, I guarantee, will be the nicest boss you ever had!

Will it be scary taking that first step? Yes, it will be! But you have me at your side ready to advise and help. So you have a true friend at all times. If you begin to have doubts, give me a ring on the phone. I'll try to help in every way I can.

SUCCESS STRATEGIES FOR BUILDING YOUR REAL ESTATE WEALTH IN GOOD TIMES AND BAD TIMES

1. Look for older buildings in industrial areas of cities where prices are lower. See if these buildings can be converted to residential or commercial use. Such buildings can make you rich sooner than you think! Why? Because if you convert buildings early in the popularity "explosion" of an area you can quickly either raise rents to higher levels—say $3,000 per month, and up—for a two-bedroom residential unit. Or you can sell out at four to ten times your cost in just a year or two. "Catching a wave" of area popularity—such as SOHO or TRIBECA in New York City, or SOUTH BEACH in Miami, JACKSON HOLE, Wyoming—can make you a real estate multimillionaire in three years, or less. So keep your eye on developing sections in your area. It's both fun and highly profitable!

2. Buy properties when mortgage loan interest rates are low. Demand a fixed-interest-rate loan for a 15-, 20-, or 25-year term so your monthly payments are lower. Remember—the *lower* your monthly payments, the *higher* your monthly profits. So avoid variable-rate mortgage loans; they can snip away at your profits, reducing them every time your variable interest rate is raised—which could be as often as twice a year. Always keep in mind that the interest you pay on your income-property real estate loans is provable and tax-deductible. But higher interest-rate payments *do* reduce your profits while at the same time they do reduce your income taxes by giving you a higher interest deduction. In general, it's better to increase your profits than to lower your taxes! Why? Because increased profits are MIF—Money in Fist. Lower taxes have a much smaller effect on MIF than higher profits!

3. In bad times, use the lower labor and material costs available to you from workers and suppliers. Have work done when costs are lower and workers are glad to get the jobs you give them. You'll often find that the work done on your properties is finished faster and more efficiently— at lower cost. Why spend more money during good times when your work may be delayed and done shoddily? Pick the bad times to have your work done—you'll never regret it! So plan ahead for work you want, or must have, done. Where you have several properties you can plan the work for each on an extended schedule. Doing this will allow you to keep a number of your laborers and contractors busy over several months. They'll love you for giving them the work and the suppliers will have your materials at the job site on time!

4. Keep buying income properties until you have enough to rid yourself of your 9-to-5 (or other time) job. Thus, if you need $60,000 a year to replace your salaried job, buy enough properties to give you this, or a higher, annual cash flow after all expenses and mortgages are paid. And remember this: A $60,000 cash flow from your business will give you a lot more spendable dollars than the same income from a salary. Why? Because your real estate business cash flow will be all—or almost all—tax-sheltered. It is rare that you can shelter as much of your salary income. Why? Because on a salary you do not have legitimate depreciation deductions such as you do with real estate. Also, with your real estate income you have provable expenses for travel, repairs, advertising, legal consultations, accounting work, etc. On a salary almost none of these costs are deductible because you have no business to justify them!

IMPORTANT POINTERS TO KEEP IN MIND

- Real estate is a free-time business—you can take plenty of time off. All you need do is arrange your business schedule to suit your leisure needs.

- Organize your real estate business using four easy steps and you can have as much free time as you need.

- Tenants and business associates will respect your schedule. All you need do is tell them what your hours are.

- You can build your real estate assets to give you the income you seek. All you need do is analyze your needs and wants and get the income properties to satisfy them.

- Build excess income for yourself. It really gives you the financial freedom you seek!

- Become a real estate tax expert. It can put big dollars into your pocket, legally and profitably.

- Steer your real estate investments to tax-advantaged properties. You will benefit many ways, especially via your pocketbook.

- Explore, with competent legal and accounting advice, tax-deferred Section 1031 property swaps. It's a way to upgrade your real estate portfolio with little investment.

- Pay lots of attention to income taxes. Doing so will increase your take-home pay enormously.

- Be your own boss—you'll love it! Do it by becoming an ex-job-holder who's now a real estate tycoon with a barrel of money in the bank!

Offbeat Financing Methods to Speed Your Real Estate Fortune Building

You might think that in tough times that offbeat financing is "out the window." Not so!

In bleak, troubled, and somber times the person who creates an offbeat way to finance a property is often hailed as a genius. Why? Because people are looking for unique ways out of the business doldrums. Come up with a new and different way to fund good income properties and *you* can make *your* millions.

Why? Because financing *is* the key to all success in real estate! You can find the best properties, work the sharpest deals, and get the fastest closing times with little effort. But you don't have anything to put money into your bank until you get the financing.

Cash is king! You'll hear this in almost every real estate deal you work out. And cash comes from financing. Not from *your* pocket. So you must use offbeat financing methods to get the cash you need—especially if you're flat broke with less than $100 in the bank, as many of my readers are when they start on the road to real estate wealth with zero cash of their own.

Just remember this: Money is always fashionable. Money never goes out of style! Money is the universal solvent in real estate deals—not water.

MONEY *IS* AVAILABLE FOR THOSE WHO SEEK IT

Every day I see real estate BWBs who borrow the money they need for their deals. Most—like yourself—are just starting out. They have a job they hate. But they hold onto it knowing that with a job they have a better chance of getting their loan applications approved.

So if you learn nothing else from this book, stop for a moment and promise yourself, and me, that:

> *I won't quit my job for my real estate business until after my income from real estate reaches the level I've set as my goal—no matter how much I may hate my present job!*

As we said earlier, having a job will make it much easier for you to get a loan from any lender—conventional or non-conventional. So keep your job! It will help pay the bills until you're up and running in your own millionaire-making real estate business.

Money *is* available to you—if you look for it in the right places. So please don't call me on the phone and give me your long sob story that says: "Ty, I've tried *every* lender and they all said no. What can I do?"

You *haven't* tried *every* lender. That would be impossible—there are just too many lenders for any person to see them all! But that's good news. It means that there *are* plenty of lenders for *you*. For instance, in one of our lender directories, we list 2,500 *active* real estate lenders. With that many lenders around it's almost impossible for you not to find a suitable one!

When you apply at conventional lenders (banks, savings and loan associations, mortgage companies, etc.) you conform to their usual requirements, namely:

- A loan of 75 percent of the appraised value of the property
- Fixed principal and interest payments made to the lender on a monthly basis
- Private mortgage insurance that may be required by the lender on the loan

You may use offbeat methods with such lenders to enhance your chances of getting the loan you seek. Let's see what some of these methods are so you can use them in your next deal.

FUNDS COME FAST WHEN OFFBEAT METHODS ARE USED

Most real estate BWBs seek speed in their loan approval process. You can get speedier approvals using offbeat methods with conventional lenders. Thus, you can consider:

1. *Having the seller cosign for you on your loan application.* This improves your chances for approval because the seller will often have a stronger credit rating than you and more assets. Further, by cosigning, the seller gets the deal to go through faster so he or she receives the money from the sale sooner.

2. *Having the seller take out an equity loan on the property before the sale.* You give the seller a written agreement to repay the equity loan, which the seller uses as *your* down payment of the property. Your agreement will include a "reverse-flip" clause in which you agree that all the payments you made on the equity loan will revert to the seller in the event you default on the payment of the equity loan. This approach gets the seller the cash down payment, plus the sale while providing needed protection in the event you default. It also gets you the property!

3. *Taking in a partner to strengthen your credit with the lender.* Use the partner as a credit improver only. Or bring the partner into the business to share in the profits. Either way, you will be using an offbeat method to get the loan you seek. Many BWBs volunteer to do *all* the work in the partnership for just the improvement in the credit the partner brings. BWBs feel this is a wise offer because having the stronger credit allows them to get the property they seek. You can find such partners by advertising on local papers, real estate publications, or in newsletters such as my *International Wealth Success* (see the appendix for more information).

4. *Assuming the seller's debts to serve as a down payment.* This can get you the long-term financing needed to take over a property. Keep this in mind at all times: The seller will usually get much more money from the longer-term mortgage portion of the sale (the 75 percent referred to earlier) than from the down payment. So if you can substitute the payment of the seller's debts for a cash down payment, you can often get a property that you couldn't afford because you don't have the cash in hand. The seller comes

away from the deal with the cash from the long-term mortgage and freedom from debts. And in the closing the assumption of debt can be treated as cash. What's more, you can pay off the debt over a period of years. So you have plenty of time to finish the deal without taking any money out of your bank account. Let's look at a typical deal:

Price of property to you	$500,000
Mortgage @ 75 percent of price	375,000
Cash needed = $500,000 – 375,000 =	125,000
Seller's debts (auto, credit cards, property improvement, etc.)	100,000

You negotiate with the seller to take over the debts of $100,000 and give the seller a promissory note for the remaining $25,000 to be paid in 5 years. The seller, meanwhile, gets the $375,000 in cash from the mortgage, if the property is free and clear of debt. If the property still has some debt, the seller gets the $375,000 less whatever debt exists.

5. *Applying at lenders who are "hungry."* This is shown by their ads and other promotional materials seeking borrowers. Thus, some of the thousands of lenders I work with run ads saying:

   a. One-hour loan approval

   b. Home equity shopping stops here

   c. Credit no problem—first and second mortgage loans

   d. Think you can't get difficult deals financed? Think again . . .

   e. Turnaround and survival financing

   f. Overseas capital. Equity or debt for real estate

   g. Need capital? We loan money on stock . . .

   h. Take-out financing

   i. Borrow below prime rate! Commercial and industrial mortgages

   Ads such as these—and many others—will quickly tell you a lender is hungry for new loans. You should "jump in" and provide at least one new loan for this hungry lender. You do want to help the lender make money, don't you?

6. *Having seller refinance the property before the sale.* You then take over and make the payments on the refinanced loan. The seller has

the cash and *no* payments to make. Your attorney can draft papers covering the deal which will protect both you and the seller. This arrangement has the advantage of letting *you* get the property with *no* credit check, *no* income requirements, *no* collateral, and so on. Why? Because it's the seller who meets these requirements when he or she applies for the refinancing of the property.

7. *Buying on a contract of sale basis.* This occurs when the title stays in the seller's name until you have paid a certain stated amount, such as the down payment the seller asked for. Thus, let's say a seller seeks $25,000 down on an income property. You get the seller to agree to a contract of sale which states that you will pay $1,000 per month to the seller from the property income. When you have paid a total of $25,000 to the seller, plus interest, the seller will transfer title to the property to you. The contract must be written by an experienced real estate attorney to protect both you and the seller!

8. *Giving the seller a promissory note as your down payment.* Since the seller can take the note and have it discounted (that is, bought for about 65 percent of its face value), you can treat the note as cash at the closing on the property. You thereby meet the first mortgage lender's requirements of a cash down payment before the deal will be approved. If the seller wants the note secured, that is, backed up by hard collateral, consider using your home or other real estate for security. You can also use a bank account, actively traded stock, bonds, or a certificate of deposit as security for the promissory note. Just be sure not to pledge assets you might want to sell or pledge in other deals. Be sure to have an attorney prepare the note for you. Then you'll know it's properly written!

9. *Bringing the real estate agent into the deal to reduce, or eliminate, your cash down payment.* Suppose, for example, a seller wants $10,000 down on a $100,000 property. You know the seller will be paying a 6 percent commission, or $6,000, to the real estate agent. This means the seller expects to get $10,000 − $6,000 = $4,000 cash out of the sale. If you can get the real estate agent to take the commission over a period of time, say, 6 months or a year, you'll be reducing your cash down payment by $6,000 as of now. This could mean the difference between getting the property and losing it. And if you can get the seller to take a promissory note for the $4,000, you can reduce your outlay to zero cash!

There you have nine offbeat methods for getting real estate funds quickly. There are many other methods you can use. These nine will, I'm sure, suggest others for you.

Just remember one important fact when dealing with loan officers who work for conventional lenders:

> Almost every loan officer secretly harbors the desire to be a wheeler-dealer real estate entrepreneur. You can benefit from these secret urges by playing up to them during any loan negotiation. Do this by bringing the loan officer mentally into the deal. Watch as his or her eyes light up as they go through the details of the deal. Using this technique you can't fall to get your loan!

MAXIMIZE YOUR RESULTS FROM OFFBEAT FINANCING

There are many ways to get maximum results from offbeat financing. You can use these ways in any deal you like. To get best results from off-beat financing, consider using the following money sources for your deals:

- Nonbank real estate lenders—they have billions to loan for solid deals
- Private investment groups with plenty of money to loan but little time to do deals
- State and city rehab groups seeking hungry real estate wealth builders (like *you!*) willing to work hard
- Lenders who advertise "Brokers Protected," "Brokers Welcome," "Brokers Sought"
- Federal government welfare, urban development, and rehab agencies putting money out for real estate
- Credit card lines of credit you or your associates have that can be tapped for cash funds

Let's take a look at each of these sources of funds to see how *you* can use it to break out of your 9-to-5 chains. You'll welcome the relief they can bring you—quickly and easily.

Nonbank Real Estate Lenders

Such lenders have billions available to lend for good real estate deals. It's a shame not to allow such lenders to loan to you! But just what *are* nonbank real estate lenders? They are:

- Mortgage companies that have funds from various sources which are designated as money to be put into real estate mortgage loans— many such lenders will loan only on income property of some kind.

- Mortgage bankers who originate (offer), service (accept payments), and sell (to get cash back) mortgage loans of many types. Such lenders actively seek new loans because such placements give them a major source of their income. We deal with mortgage bankers throughout the country in helping BWBs get loans. A good mortgage banker can make getting a real estate mortgage a simple, quick, and easy procedure. And such lenders readily accept offbeat methods because they admire the go-getter in real estate.

- Mortgage brokers find real estate borrowers for various types of lenders. While your application must still be approved by the final lender, having a mortgage broker guide you in the preparation of your application can be a great help in getting the loan you seek. We have lists of mortgage brokers in every state in our *2,500 Active Real Estate Lenders* book.

Nonbank real estate lenders are easier to deal with than banks. Why? Because nonbank real estate lenders are basically businesspeople. As such, they understand you, and what you're trying to do. Banks often lack this understanding. Further, many bankers tend to feel they are superior to the working entrepreneur. So you won't get much understanding from some bankers.

To work with nonbank real estate lenders, you must offer them the best deal possible. Why is this? Because nonbank real estate lenders are risk takers. They'll lend when—and where—a bank won't lend. So you must seek, and offer, features that will attract nonbank lenders. Features of the loan you can consider offering include:

- Shorter term, that is, 15 years, instead of 25 or 30 years
- Higher interest rate, that is, 1/4 or 1/2 percentage point higher than current bank rates

- Fee in the form of points which is rolled into the loan so you don't have any out-of-pocket cost

- High debt-coverage ratio to make the lender feel more comfortable with the deal

The best example of nonbank lenders and the funding they provide are what people call *hard-money loans.* Such loans have these features:

- They are made to people with shaky, or no, credit.

- The term is short—10 or 15 years at most.

- Rates are high—typically 16 percent, or more.

But the loans *are* available! If the income from a property can repay a hard-money loan and leave you with a positive cash flow, a BWB may ask himself or herself: "Why not take this loan while I can?" I may never get a chance to get the money again.

A new feature of hard-money loans in difficult times is high points. Thus, I hear of lenders seeking to charge 10 points for their hard-money loan. Again, as a BWB, you must analyze if your property purchase can support such a charge.

Keep in mind, though, that few nonbank lenders are hard-money funders. Most nonbank lenders charge rates which equal those of local banks. Or if the rate is higher, it is only 1/8 or 1/4 percentage point over the bank rate. And some non-bank lenders will even charge a lower rate than local banks!

Private Investment Groups

There are lots of people in this great world of ours who have plenty of money but little time. What some of these people do is band together and put their money into a fund to invest in profitable deals. And some of the best of these deals is income real estate.

Such groups advertise in newspaper and magazines the availability of their money. Their classified ads might be worded like this:

REAL ESTATE LOANS AVAILABLE. $100,000 minimum; income properties only; competitive rates; call 123-4567 for full information.

Or

MORTGAGE MONEY FOR INCOME PROPERTIES. *Up to 90 percent of appraised value; terms to 30 years; rates competitive with other lenders. Call 1 23-4567 8 A.M. to 8 P.M. 7 days a week.*

To get the funding you need from private groups, you should prepare a loan package giving full details of the project. Without a loan package you can spend hours describing the project to members of the group and not get your loan. Why? Because it is difficult to follow project details without a written proposal, which is what a loan package is.

Your loan package can be short—three pages is all you really need for smaller projects. Multimillion-dollar projects will have a loan package that may run 20 pages. Even so, much of the data—like the appraisal—will come from other sources. So *you* need not spend time on it.

Some private investment groups are comprised of local medical doctors and dentists. They will often have monthly investment meetings where they review and evaluate proposed investments. Contacting the chairperson of such a group and providing a copy of your loan package can be a quick way to get money. Why?

Because the chairperson will present your proposal to the group. Thus, *you* do not have to do any selling. Instead, the chairperson does it for you. With a good loan package you can raise money quickly this way.

State and City Rehabilitation Agencies

Housing shortages abound—in good times and bad times. So you'll find that state and city rehab agencies are always looking for hungry BWBs who want to fix up buildings and make money while doing so. *You* can be one of these lucky BWBs and be paid *big* chunks of money for supervising the repair of buildings needing work to make them habitable for low-income people. To get in on this great bonanza of state and city rehab millions, take these easy steps:

1. Find out which agencies handle rehab funds in your area by calling (or writing) your state housing authority. You'll find a list of current phone numbers of housing authorities in your phone book. The state agency will be glad to give you the name and number of your city and county rehab authorities.

2. Ask your agency which way is best (and easiest) for you to get rehab money: (a) as the owner of property or (b) as a contractor who does work for property owners. In most states you'll find it easier to get money in the form of loans or grants (or both) if you own the property.

3. Acquire rehabable property by taking it over as a foreclosure (see Chapter 3) or in an auction.

4. Immediately apply for a rehab loan or grant. Do this by asking for, and getting, the free application from the agency. Fill out the application fully. Typewrite your responses—do not write them in longhand on the application! Be sure to have a *professional* estimate of your rehab costs *before* you fill out the cost section of your application. Then you won't have any disappointments over incorrect estimates.

5. Get your money and have the work done. Take pride in the quality of your work. Having superior work done means a lot for *your* future money supply. Why? Because if *you* have high-quality work done, the agency will come back to you—again and again—to put *more money* into your hands! Isn't that a great reason for doing the best work you can?

While rehabbing rundown properties may not be too appealing to you, it *can* provide you with barrels of cash:

1. With *no* credit check of any kind
2. Even though you've been bankrupt in the past one or more times
3. Despite a record of "slow pay" on your credit report
4. And even when you have "too many inquiries" on your credit report

So don't turn away from rehabbing! It can be *your* ticket to quick riches from offbeat financing.

Lenders Who Advertise

Hungry lenders, that is, those lenders who almost have to beg borrowers to accept their loans, will often advertise these ways:

- Brokers wanted
- Brokers protected
- Brokers sought

- Brokers welcome
- Mortgage loans available for brokered deals

What these broker mentions mean is one of several good messages for you, namely:

1. The lender needs help in finding borrowers. You can do the lender a favor by accepting his, or her, money for your good real estate deals.

2. You can act as a broker (*no* license required) for your own real estate deal(s). The lender will either pay you a commission for finding your own real estate loan or will reduce your interest cost for the loan.

3. The lender actively seeks new loans. He or she is expanding their lending business and seeks help in finding more borrowers. *You* can help the lender by providing a source of more loans, while helping your own real estate business. At the same time you'll be paid a commission on each loan you bring in—by the lender! You can also collect a commission from the borrower. But you *must* inform both the lender and the borrower that you're collecting a commission from each.

As part of my helping BWBs get positive cash flow income real estate, I monthly publish *The Money Watch Bulletin*. It gives BWBs 100 *active* lenders every month, with details about the loans they make. New subscribers (see the appendix) get a free list of "Brokers Wanted" lenders. This popular list helps a number of BWBs get the loans they need to take over highly profitable income property. So keep your eyes open for "Brokers Wanted" offbeat lenders. They could provide you with the loan, or loans, you need to get rich in real estate today!

Federal Government Agencies

As with the cities and states, the federal government has a number of agencies supplying financing for real estate. Many of these agencies are overlooked by BWBs seeking money for their deals.

The best place to start looking for money in the federal government is at HUD (Housing and Urban Development). You'll find the people there both helpful and willing to go the extra mile. You can easily find the nearest HUD office by looking in your local phone book under the U.S. government heading.

Visit your nearest HUD office, if you can. They have lots of free information on their services. What's more, HUD employees are willing to share their vast knowledge with you. In just 30 minutes you can learn enough in a HUD office to keep you in business for a lifetime!

Other government sources of real estate financing or guarantees include FHA (Federal Housing Administration), VA (Veteran's Administration), FmHA (Farmers Home Administration), and FNMA (Fannie Mae, or Federal National Mortgage Association). Again, you'll find them in your phone book.

If you don't want to (or can't) visit these government loan and guarantee sources, call on the telephone, or write. You'll find they'll be just as helpful as when you visit in person. Ask for what you want, and in most cases, you'll get exactly what you ask for. You'll find dozens of offbeat financing sources that will be happy to help you!

Use Credit Card Credit Lines

More real estate BWBs are tapping their credit card lines of credit than you might imagine. Almost every day I get at least one phone call from a BWB saying:

> *Boy, am I glad to talk to you! You say in your books that you answer the phone yourself on the first ring. To tell you the truth, I didn't believe you when I read that. Now I'm a believer!*
>
> *But the real reason I called is because I wanted to tell you that I just bought my second income property using my credit card line of credit for the down payment. I also used the line of credit to get my first income property. Though I didn't believe I could ever get income property this way, your methods really do work! I'm on my way, thanks to you, Ty, on zero cash.*

There are a number of features of credit card lines of credit that many people overlook. These features are:

1. You can get several cards, each with its own line of credit; this will increase your total credit line. Thus, with three credit cards, each of which has a $10,000 line of credit, your total credit line will be 3 ×

$10,000 = $30,000. Some people have as much as $1-million in their line of credit on their credit cards. Thus, 100 cards at $10,000 each = $1,000,000! And some cards have lines of credit as high as $35,000 per card. You'd need only 29 of such cards to give you your million-dollar line!

2. Banks and credit unions will push new credit cards on you if you keep applying for cards. A credit card you're offered is a lot easier to get than one you "beg" for!

3. Join some business organizations and you'll be offered "affinity" cards, that is, cards offered exclusively to a member of a clearly defined group. Each card will have its own credit line. The more credit lines you have, the larger the amount of money you can borrow. So your annual dues in the affinity group are well worth the price of having more than one line of credit!

4. When you have a business partner, you can use his, or her, line of credit to take over properties for zero cash of your own. Or you can combine the lines of credit of two or more partners to build up significant cash.

For most deals you'll use your line of credit for the property down payment. Your long-term mortgage (15 years, 20 years, 30 years, etc.) will be based on the appraised value of the property you buy. With the down payment easily available, there should be no problem getting the ideal income property you want! As one reader recently told me;

I used my credit card lines of credit to take over 10 income properties. They all show a positive cash flow. Each property pays off its line-of-credit loan, plus the long-term mortgage, while at the same time it puts cash into my pocket, every month!

DESIGN EVERY OFFBEAT LOAN APPLICATION TO BE A WINNER

You want to make money in real estate. So, too, do lenders who loan you money for *your* dreams. Lenders have dreams, too! These dreams? As a lender myself I *know* these dreams well. They are

1. To make a loan of the size the lender likes, that is, not too large and not too small for the lender's financial capacity
2. To have a borrower who qualifies in all respects, credit, collateral, consistency of repaying previous loans, and compatibility in terms of loan type
3. To deal with a borrower who doesn't give you any arguments over interest rate, term of loan, or other details
4. To have a borrower with whom you feel comfortable because the loan application is neatly, and completely, prepared and exudes a feeling of complete trust and acceptability of the borrower

Yes, we lenders *do* seek borrowers—especially "dream borrowers" who seem exactly right for us and our money. *You* can be the answer to your lender's dreams by taking these easy steps:

1. *Project a solid and dependable image.* Achieve this via your loan application by having it typed, filling in *all* the required answers, signing the application where indicated, and submitting it with a short cover letter on a printed letterhead.
2. *Accept the suggested interest rate.* Do this even if it's slightly higher than what you expected, if by so doing you get the loan from the offbeat financing source. Remember: A financing source is offbeat because it usually accepts greater risks than conventional bank lenders.
3. *Be cooperative with your lender.* Fights will never get you anywhere. They only lose you the loan or loans you need. So work *with* your lender, *not* against your lender! As has been said so many times by lender friends of mine, a polite, cooperative borrower is a joy to work with—we earn interest and the borrower gets the funds he or she needs—it's a perfect match!
4. *Always remember: Mortgage interest is provable and deductible on your business tax return.* So aim at *getting* the loan you seek. Don't lose a loan by arguing over rates, terms, or other details.

Your offbeat financing source may be the seller of the property. Here the seller "takes back" a second mortgage in place of cash. Or the seller might refinance the property before the sale, take the cash, and give you the loan payments to make. Either way, you get the financing you seek. As a reader wrote me:

Planning and hard work, coupled with determination, led to the acquisition of two single-family houses during April, with only $380 total down payment. The first property I acquired for 20 percent below market value and mortgaged out with $4,100. There are no payments on an assumable owner-held second deed of trust note for 13 months and the property nets $125 per month, The second property I acquired for 50 percent of market value from a distressed seller (divorced couple). Taking title subject to an existing 8 percent FHA loan and by obtaining a second mortgage enabled me to close the deal. The property is rented through the government Section 8 program, with $80 per month positive cash flow.

With a $380 investment I will net $2,460 in cash, giving me a 647 percent return on my investment the first year, excluding tax benefits and appreciation.

So you see, it *can*, and *is*, being done—using offbeat financing to mortgage out with money in fist (MW). This reader also used zero cash because his $380 investment was repaid by the $4,100 and the $2,460 in cash which he took out of the two properties. Can you ask for a better deal to get you out of the job rat race and into the wealth of your own business?

BECOME A "WALKING ENCYCLOPEDIA" OF OFFBEAT LENDERS

Knowledge is power! And in the borrowing business, knowledge of lenders is the greatest power you can have. Why? Because when you *know* lenders you:

- Apply to only those who make the kinds of loans you seek
- Ask for amounts within the lender's lending range
- Accept the lender's terms because you recognize that *getting* a loan is more important than "winning" an argument over 1/8 of a percentage point of interest and losing the loan

If you're like me, you'll want to become that walking encyclopedia of lenders so you know who's lending for what purposes—at all times. I'm a student of lenders because— being one myself—I want to *know* what other lenders are doing. When your bread depends on putting out good loans to stable people, you *must* know lenders and what they're doing.

And when your future financial freedom depends on getting loans for deals you'd like to finance, knowing lenders is just as important! To know lenders, take these easy steps:

1. Read good financial papers, newsletters, and books. Such publications can keep you up to date on what's happening in the money field.

2. Talk to lenders—on the phone or in person. Don't be afraid of any lender. They're human, just like you and me! The more lenders you talk to, the better the "feel" you get for the money business.

3. Read every loan application and agreement carefully to see what features a lender has for his or her loan programs. Getting to know these features will broaden your knowledge and skills to the point where you're better able to deal with any offbeat lender.

Remember: Knowledge is power in the borrowing business. Get that knowledge and you'll get lots more real estate loans of all kinds. Why be a "loan illiterate" when, with a little effort, you can become a loan expert? Especially when being a loan expert can pay off in such big dividends to yourself and your loved ones!

For example, people are always calling me, asking "Ty, where can I get 100 percent financing for my real estate deals?" Since I won't let myself be a "loan illiterate," I research lenders that do 100 percent financing. At the moment I have two such lenders. They work with larger real estate properties. Their names and loan details are available free to two-year, or longer, subscribers to my newsletter, *International Wealth Success,* described at the back of this book. So, knowledge *is* power—even with the most unique of all real estate lenders—those that do 100 percent financing!

TEN GUIDELINES FOR OFFBEAT
LOAN SOURCES AND APPROVALS

Knowing which lenders are offbeat *can* get you more loans than you might imagine. And following smart application procedures can up your batting average to nearly 1,000! Here are 10 timely tips for finding, and getting, offbeat loans:

1. *Collect ads that lenders run.* Paste them into your riches notebook under the heading of "financing." Having such ads on hand can get you loans when all other sources are unavailable to you.

2. *Look for "Brokers Welcome" ads in your local papers, national magazines, and professional real estate publications.* At my firm, IWS, Inc., we take special pride in assembling "Broker Welcome" ads from all over the world. Collections of these ads are available free as a bonus when a person buys one of our kits or subscribes to our *International Wealth Success* newsletter for 4 years or to our *Money Watch Bulletin* for 1 year. You can assemble your own list of such ads by keeping careful watch on the publications listed above.

3. *Ask lenders to recommend other lenders.* Thus, if you're talking to a bank about a loan and they turn you down, say "Who else do you recommend I try for this loan?" The bank, or other lender, may have several names to suggest to you. Write the names down immediately—don't trust your memory; you may forget a crucial name and lose an important loan!

4. *Explore government loan sources.* Almost every government offers real estate loans or guarantees for such loans. Many local governments (city, county, state) offer low-interest real estate loans for industrial and commercial buildings of various types. Watch your local papers for announcements of such loans. Attend local business and real estate meetings to get more information on these loans. You may find an offbeat source for loans that is right in your own town or city!

5. *Grab at "loan sale" offers by local lenders.* Such loan sales are made when lenders are hungry to make new loans. Thus, a shortage of loan applicants can turn a conventional lender into an offbeat lender. But you won't know this unless you grab at loan sale offers. Keep an eye on the real estate and business sections of your local paper to learn when such loan sales are being made.

6. *Seek "hard-money" lenders.* These are lenders who charge as much as 18 percent interest for their loans with 7 points on closing and only 50 percent loan-to-value (LTV) ratio (as opposed to the usual 75 percent LTV). And some of these lenders will seek another 10

percent of the loan amount when you refinance to get a lower interest rate. Despite all these charges and the high interest rate, you may be able to break even while getting title to the property. Having title makes it much easier for you to refinance the property and get a new loan at an affordable interest rate. The key here is: You *do* get to own an income property, as owner it *is* easier for you to get a new loan at a conventional rate, and your costs *are* deductible on your tax return—either currently (for interest) or when you sell (for points)!

7. *Work with wraparound lenders.* Some real estate lenders feature wraparound loans (called *wrap loans* for short). In a wrap loan you get enough money to pay for the equity the seller has in the property you want, plus the cash down payment required. *You* pay on the wrap loan and the wrap lender pays on the existing loan on the property. Wrap lenders are offbeat funders be-cause they structure deals in a way that a conventional lender would never consider. Watch for the word "Wraps" in lender ads. It means the lender is offbeat and will do wraps for you!

8. *Try refinance lenders.* Some lenders like "refi" deals—those in which they lend to refinance existing income property. Again, these are offbeat lenders. You can often work a deal with such lenders by getting the seller to refinance *before* the sale and you taking over the loan payments *after* the sale. The net effect is that the seller gets his or her money, you get the property, and the seller is free of any future payments because you make them. And the payments you make are the same as though you financed the property with a loan of your own. But the seller will usually be able to get the loan more quickly since the property is in his or her name and his credit rating may be stronger than yours. Further, if the seller can refinance for the total value of the property, you can get control of an income with zero cash down!

9. *Get the seller to give you a loan.* The seller does this by accepting from you a *purchase money mortgage* for the down payment, or part of the down payment. You either assume the existing mortgage on the property (if this is allowed by the mortgage agreement), or you obtain a new mortgage on your own. The purchase money mortgage (PM mortgage) is ideal for you because the seller normally won't charge points, won't charge loan fees, and will not have a prepayment penalty. So seek a PM mortgage whenever you can—it's tops in offbeat financing!

10. *Find, and use, "credit no problem" lenders.* Keep an open eye for lenders and you'll see those who advertise:

Bad credit—no problem

Bankruptcy OK

Slow pay acceptable

No credit check loans

No employment check

What these lenders are telling you is that they're offbeat. They're also saying—indirectly—our rates are higher because we take more risks. But if you fit one of the descriptions listed you'll probably be willing to pay a higher rate to get the loan you need. And even if you have good credit, with no record of bankruptcy, such lenders might be willing to work with you. And an offbeat lender may be so happy to get a fully qualified borrower like yourself that you may be offered a competitive interest rate and loan term. So don't ever overlook any offbeat lender—he or she may be your salvation for getting out of the paycheck jungle!

SUCCESS STRATEGIES FOR BUILDING YOUR REAL ESTATE WEALTH IN GOOD TIMES AND BAD TIMES

1. Save interest costs by using "conforming loans" (those loans that comply with all of a lender's criteria) instead of "non-conforming" loans which charge a higher rate of interest. Why? Because every dollar you save in mortgage interest goes directly into your pocket as increased profit. Thus, if you pay $100 per month less in mortgage interest, that $100 goes into profit at the end of the month. And since your depreciation on income properties legitimately tax-shelters this increased profit, you have a full $100 per month to use for buying additional properties or for improving your lifestyle. So take time to search out conforming mortgages that will lower your interest cost. Be certain that all your new conforming mortgages are at a fixed interest rate. Then you won't be subject to interest rate "Russian Roulette" which can send your interest costs soaring in times of unstable economic conditions.

2. Use actively traded stocks or bonds as collateral for zero-down income properties. A number of major brokerage houses have plans in which you can pledge stocks or bonds having a market value of 39 percent of the price of an income property for a zero-down deal. The brokerage house lends you the down payment, using your securities as collateral. You use the loan money as your down payment for the income real estate you want to take over. How can such a deal help you? In several ways: (a) You keep title to your securities—be they stocks or bonds, or both. (b) By holding title to your securities you are not subject to capital gains taxes, as you probably would be if you sold them to raise the cash for your down payment on the income real estate you're buying. (c) There is no credit investigation of you because your pledging of the securities eliminates the need for a credit report. (d) Your loan goes through much faster—in just hours because your securities pre-qualify you. (e) In a rising stock market your investment is secure and your securities will—in general—rise along with the stock market. You can even use this method with borrowed stocks or bonds. Such securities will give you the same advantages as those listed above. But you will have to pay a fee to the person or organization that lends you the securities. This is a one-time fee, and is typically 5 percent of the value of the securities loaned to you for your down payment loan. You will be subject to the same market fluctuation demands as when you pledge your own securities.

3. Get on the Internet to find useful information for building your wealth in real estate. There are many useful sites on the Internet which you can access free of charge from either your own home computer, a computer at your local public library, your computer at work, or by borrowing a friend's computer. Using these sites you can get data on the prices of recent property sales, listings of properties put on the market in the last few days, lenders seeking new real estate loans, etc. By going on the Internet you can save money and time in your search for income properties and the financing for them. Here are a number of commercial real estate Internet addresses which can help you build your wealth using data from cyberspace information: http://www.commercial.coldwellbanker.com; www.pikenet.com; www.rebny.com; www.biz.yahoo.com/news/realestate.html; www.realtyadvisor.com.

4. Improve "B"* class residential or office space, to the point where it rivals "A"-type space. Then you'll get some "A"-class tenants who are happy to pay your lower-level "B"-class rents to get space which is just as good as "A"-class space. You can raise the rent of your "B"-class space so you're being paid much more than other "B"-class space owners. For example, if "A"-class office space is renting at $50 per square foot per year, you can probably easily get $35.00 per square foot per year in your improved "B" building while other owners of similar, unimproved buildings are getting just $28.00 per square foot per year. Using this approach to marketing residential and office space can make you a millionaire!*

IMPORTANT POINTERS TO KEEP IN MIND

- Financing is the key to all success in real estate today.
- Money *is* available to those who seek it for real estate investment.
- Offbeat lenders (sometimes called nonconventional lenders) *can* be your source of money for income real estate.
- Offbeat methods in approaching a lender can get you needed money faster, with less hassle.
- "Hungry" lenders will make loans to you sooner, and with fewer hassles—watch for their ads in your local papers.
- There are a variety of offbeat lenders you might get money from. Work with as many of these as you can.
- Hard-money loans can put funds into your hands quickly.
- Government agencies of many kinds can be your source of offbeat real estate loans.
- Pay attention to "Brokers Protected" lenders—they love to make loans!
- Don't overlook your credit cards as quick sources of cash for loans you need for income properties.
- Design *every* offbeat loan application to be a winner.
- Get to know lenders nationwide—you never know when a new deal may pop up that one of "your" lenders may like.
- Use the 10 easy steps in this chapter to raise money from any offbeat lenders you find.

---

*"B"-class residential or office rental space is that in older buildings in less desirable parts of a city; "A"-class rental space is that in newer buildings in the most desirable area of a city or town.

Get Time On Your Side to Build Real Estate Wealth for Yourself

Gloomy times may pervade the real estate market when you decide to start building your fortune. Not to worry, as so many optimists say!

Why shouldn't *you* worry about getting started in such bad times? You should *not* worry because bad times in real estate are *good times* for beginners! The gloomier your seller is, the lower the price you can negotiate *now* to get time on your side.

Next to money, time is the second key to making your fortune in real estate today. You can't separate time from real estate. The two are linked, and always will be. Time is on *your* side when you're building riches in real estate!

To many people, time is an enemy. Why? Because as time goes on these people feel they are becoming less important. They're getting old, instead of getting better, as optimists are.

In real estate time is your friend! Time makes all real estate more valuable—if the property is properly cared for. So the passage of time *helps* you—instead of hurting you. Keep these important facts in mind at all times:

- Well-located real estate just gets better, that is, more valuable with age, or the passage of time.

- So the longer you hold property, the better, in general, will your profit be when you sell it, increasing your overall income from your real estate investments.

253

You can extend this basic characteristic of real estate to the oldest of properties in your area. Thus, some cities and states have historic properties funds. These funds make loans to owners of historic or landmark properties for preservation of the exterior and interior of the property.

One fund near me makes loans of $10,000 to $100,000 for exterior renovation "such as repairing or replacing crumbling wooden windows, restoring deteriorated brownstone or wood siding, or replacing a missing historic cornice." Even buildings in historic districts are eligible for such funding. Your building need not be a landmark itself to be eligible.

An advantage of historic funding is that you don't go through the usual credit check procedure. Instead, the loan is based on the property and on its importance to the area.

USE TIME TO GIVE YOU A BETTER CASH POSITION

As time passes, the properties you own rise in value. Thus, your equity or ownership position increases in value with the passage of time. And this equity can be converted into cash by means of an equity loan, called home equity loans or property equity loans.

The cash you take out via an equity loan is tax free to you. Why? Because the proceeds of a loan are *not* taxable. Let's look at a typical example of taking equity out of a property you own:

Price of property when you bought it	$650,000
Market value of property 5 years later, with 8.15 percent annual rise in value	961,000
Value increase in 5 years	311,000
Equity loan available to you at 75 percent of your equity in the property	233,000

Thus, in 5 years you can take out $233,000 from this property, free of current income taxes. (When you sell the property your loan proceeds which have not yet been repaid may be taxable income to you. See your accountant for an exact ruling on this matter.)

What happened here? Your holding of the property for 5 years increased your net worth by some $233,000! Time, as we said earlier, is on *your* side when you own well-located properties.

Today, with the "125 percent loan" you can take $1.25 \times \$311,000 = \$388,750$, or \$155,750 more out in your equity loan! Time led to the introduction of this new loan. As we said earlier: Time is on your side in real estate!

And the fact that you take an equity loan on a property does *not* stop its rise in value! The local market knows nothing about the loans on the property. A property's market value is determined by a number of factors, such as:

- Location
- Income
- Condition
- Value trends in the area

Obtaining a better cash position with an equity loan can help you in other ways. Thus, you can:

1. Operate more freely without financial pressures since you have cash on hand from the equity loan
2. Wait out minicycles in property values and be poised to sell at the best price when values rise again
3. Have time for conversions (to condo or co-op) if you see such deals as most profitable for yourself

There's nothing like cash on hand to make you relaxed and happy! An equity loan can give *you* that cash. And the interest (rent) you pay on this money is provable and tax deductible. So you have cash freedom with OPM (other people's money) and the cost of renting the OPM is deductible against income! Could you ask for a better deal? Remember: All these results come because time works *for* you in real estate, not against you.

"BUY TIME" BY USING YOUR ASSET BUILDUP

Most real estate BWBs aren't too sensitive to asset value increases. They buy a property, operate it, and take out their monthly positive cash flow. This keeps them happy.

Then, a few years later, someone says: "Hey, that property is worth big bucks! Did you ever stop to think what it's worth today?"

It's at this time that the typical BWB gets out pencil and paper and starts to figure current worth. A few minutes later the BWB's eyes are bugging. The rise in value is enormous! How could he (or she) have overlooked such an increase in one's holdings?

It's easy. As a BWB we get so involved in running our properties, giving good service to tenants, counting our monthly income, and looking for new projects that our current holdings—and their values—tend to be overlooked.

Yet values *do* rise—as all of real estate history shows. In the last 11 recessions real estate has *always* come back in terms of price. And recession-level prices eventually soared to new highs, once the economy recovered. When you're alert to these value rises, you can use them to buy time which can be turned into money. Thus:

1. Keep a constant eye on value increases. Plot the cash you'll take out of each property as its value rises.

2. Watch lender ads for equity loans. Sometimes they will offer special low rates when they're trying to put out more loans. If this low rate offer coincides with your money needs, grab the opportunity. Get the loan!

3. As your property rises in value you can develop new approaches to marketing your space for maximum rental income. And you can look ahead to the future sale of your property. Increasing its rental income means you can get more for the property when you sell it.

Buying time even gives you tax benefits. Why? Because the longer you hold a property, the larger your depreciation deductions. These deductions protect your cash income—giving *you* more money in fist!

So time really does serve the patient real estate investor. With your regular job income, you can wait out any real estate cycle. And you can do your waiting with confidence. Why? Because ever since real estate became a business, hundreds of years ago,

- Real estate values have always come back. Well-located property holds its value and increases in value with passage of time.

- Real estate cycles come and go. But after every cycle that depresses values, prices bounce back and rise above their earlier levels.

- Real estate investing takes patience. You *can* make a short-term profit on some properties. But the largest profits usually occur after long-term ownership of a property of some kind.

As an example of a short-term profit, here's a letter from a reader who, in my opinion, deserves a medal for his pursuit of the real estate dream:

> *I started buying rental houses a year and a half ago. I just turned 25 last month. Currently I have 29 rental houses which I bought during this year and a half. I live, eat, and breathe rental houses—I love it. I just "turned" my first house and made $8,000 in two months! I work for a lumber company full time. I want 100 rental houses in my hometown, which has 6,000 population. I have fantastic opportunities here. I will quit my job as soon as I get enough property to provide a monthly cash flow big enough to live on. I will make it within the next year. I enjoy teaching other people what I've learned. Currently I've helped my father-in-law buy his first house without any money down. And I've helped my sister buy two houses in two weeks!*

Not only has this reader started early in life to build his fortune, he also is conscious of the effect of time on his property and his income. And he knows that real estate can—and will—free him from his 9-to-5 grind at the lumber yard! Be alert, as he is, to the relationship between time and real estate income. Then you can plan your future freedom with certainty and precision!

ELEVEN WAYS TO MAKE TIME YOUR ALLY IN REAL ESTATE

Time is always. with us. None of us can escape time. Knowing this, your best strategy in real estate is to make time your ally, *not* your enemy! Here are 11 easy steps to take to make time your ally so you free yourself of time clock serfdom:

1. *Be patient.* Patience pays profits in real estate. You can hurt your financial future if you rush to turn properties too quickly. Count on your property going up in value and you'll seldom be wrong.

2. *Check out property value rises in your area.* This is easy to do. How? Speak to a local real estate broker and ask for records of prices on similar properties to the ones you own. If your area is typical, you'll see a 5 to 7 percent increase in property value *every* year!

3. *Keep track of your property values.* Have annual appraisals free of charge by a local real estate broker. Such appraisals aren't as accurate as MM appraisals (Member, Appraisal Institute), but they *do* keep you clued in to the change in value of your property. Most real estate brokers are happy to make such appraisals free because they believe they will have a better chance to serve you when you're ready to sell the property.

4. *Don't overimprove your property for the area.* Each area has a minimum price for properties and a maximum price. Be careful not to spend so much money improving your property that you increase its price above that of the maximum for your area. Why? Because when you're ready to sell, you may not be able to get the price you seek because it's too high above the going top price in the area. You will lose some of the improvement money you spent.

5. *Join neighborhood associations.* Keep in touch with proposed changes that may affect *your* property values. Further, you may meet other property owners seeking to sell their holdings. You may be able to work out a lucrative deal that will give you valuable properties for zero cash down. Such associations have built the wealth of many real estate BWBs. I'd like to see *you* do the same for yourself!

6. *Take cash out of the equity in your property.* The cash is tax free when you get it. (You may have to pay a tax on it when you sell the property.) Money in fist is a lot more valuable and powerful than equity that you can't spend. So watch your property equity and convert it to cash whenever you can. Remember: The interest is both provable and tax deductible!

7. *Keep your loan payments as small as possible.* The payments on your mortgages are called "debt service." Every penny you pay in debt service subtracts from your positive cash flow from the property. To raise your positive cash flow, lower your debt service. How? By getting longer-term loans. Thus, the monthly payment for principal and interest (P&I) on a $100,000. 5-year, 12 percent loan is $2,224.45 per month. For 25 years, the P&I on a $100,000 loan at 12 percent interest is $1,053.23 per month—less than half that for the 5-year loan. You'd have $2,224.45—$1,053.23 = $1,171.22 *more* per month cash flow if you took a 25-year loan instead of a 5-year loan! And the interest, as we said earlier, is both provable and tax deductible.

8. *Don't make deals that can box you in.* Real estate BWBs who've run into trouble in hard times are those having large payments to make on a specific date, such as interest for bondholders. Your monthly mortgage payments—by comparison—will be small. So if you avoid deals requiring large payments on a specified date you will, in general, survive even in the worst of times. So look for low monthly payments instead of delayed payments requiring large chunks of cash. Take this step and you'll survive even the worst downturn!

9. *Get lenders to help you.* Lenders are a strange lot! How do *I* know? I'm a lender myself. I should know the breed. Get a lender's understanding and sympathy, and you'll have one of the best friends in the world. Why? Because a lender who believes in *you* will go the extra mile. That is, such a lender will extend more credit to you when you need it, won't charge you when a payment is late, and so on. To get lenders to help you, use the many tips I give you in this book covering your application, attention to details, and so on. Work at the relationship with your lender, and you'll reap rewards far beyond your wildest dreams!

10. *Refinance whenever you can.* Money in fist is powerful. Money in land and buildings is not spendable. Cash is king! Get more cash in your business by refinancing your properties whenever you can. Sure, it will cost you to refinance. But having cash is worth the cost of refinancing. And that cost is—ultimately—tax deductible to you when you sell the property. So why not enjoy—and use—your cash *now,* instead of waiting years until you sell. To get cash today, refinance *now,* and whenever you can in the future!

11. *Help lenders make money while you grow rich.* Every lender is in business to make money. If you can help any lender do this, you'll make a friend for life. You can help lenders earn more by:

    a. Using their services for your first, second, and third mortgage loans

    b. Taking property improvement loans from the same lenders

    c. Helping the lender sell off any group of loans (called a *portfolio*) for which the lender would prefer cash, instead of monthly P&I payments

The last method is a separate business which is described shortly.

There you have 11 ways to make time *your* ally in real estate. Recognize here and now that if you're in a big rush to make huge sums of money, real estate probably isn't for you—unless you get into related fields such as portfolio brokering—such as that described shortly. Just remember: If you make time your ally in real estate you *can* get rich, very rich, but not overnight!

USE PORTFOLIO BROKERING TO SPEED REAL ESTATE WEALTH

Lenders often sell off their collection of real estate loans to bring in more cash. This cash, in turn, is loaned out to other borrowers. You can get in on this aspect of real estate by becoming a loan portfolio broker. By doing so, you'll put yourself into the world's best paper business!

In a paper business you don't own any machinery, buildings, truck fleets, and so on. You just use paper and stamps and—today—wires for telephones, computers and fax machines. Your major investment is your time and skill.

In loan portfolio brokering you bring a buyer and seller together to complete a sale. *You* do *not* do any selling. You just present the portfolio (which is a collection of loan applications and related papers) to the buyer. You step back and let the buyer and seller wheel and deal over the portfolio. When the deal is completed, you collect your fee. Typical portfolios are

- Residential mortgage loans for single-family homes
- Commercial mortgage loans on multifamily properties
- Industrial property mortgage loans

To show you what I mean about making money in big chunks quickly as a loan portfolio broker, here are a few actual examples of recent deals, along with the time required and the commission earned:

> On a $50 million bank portfolio sale the broker earned $31,250 on three phone calls, with the deal closing 4 weeks after the first call.
> An experienced broker earned $160,000 in fees on a $30 million portfolio of first and second mortgages. The deal closed 3 days after all papers were in proper order.

To make such deals, here's what *you* do—after you have enough knowledge and experience in the field:

1. You contact a lender and tell the person in charge that you can supply buyers for their real estate loans.

2. You tell the lender what papers are needed for each loan (these are the standard items in any loan file).

3. You have the loan papers delivered to the buyer (either by mail or by messenger).

4. You get any other papers that may be needed by the buyer to close the deal.

5. You collect your fee when the deal closes. Your fee for bringing the buyer and seller together is protected by your written agreement.

How can you "get up to speed" to do such deals in real estate? You take these easy steps:

1. *Study courses on the subject.* Such courses will give you the needed background information. (See the back of this book for Kevin Clark's "Portfolio Brokering Kit," which is one example of such a course.)

2. *Associate with people in the business.* Get to know these people by asking around your bank who buys paper locally. You can learn a lot during a half-hour conversation with someone in the business.

Yes, there are many ways for you to make big money in real estate. And loan portfolio brokering is one of the best. Why? Because you can get started for just a few dollars. All you need is a few sheets of paper and a phone! Why not try—right now?

SUCCESS STRATEGIES FOR BUILDING YOUR REAL ESTATE WEALTH IN GOOD TIMES AND BAD TIMES

1. Use the "sandwich lease" for vacation rentals. See Chapter 12 for a full discussion of the sandwich lease. In good times vacation rental charges soar. Here are a few *actual* examples as of the writing of this book: (a) In Southampton NY a 5-bedroom, 6.5 bath oceanfront home having a pool rents for $150,000 for the month of August—just one month! (b) On Cape Cod a 4-bedroom, 3-bath New England style beachfront home rents for $3,500 per week during July and August; (c) In New Jersey, a 5-bedroom, 5.5-bath beachfront home rents for up to $25,000 per week during July and August. What you do is rent one or more of these desirable homes for a week, or month, depending on your analysis of the market. Then you sublet at a higher price, giving you the "sandwich lease." Vacation homes are better candidates for sandwich leases because (a) There is no "standard rate" to compare them with, such as in office or residential leases; (b) People are willing to pay high prices to ensure their rental for a given week, month, or season; (c) High rental charges are expected for scarce vacation rentals; hence people grab what they can get and write the check. Thus, if you rent a home from the owner for $25,000 for one month, there's a good chance you can sublet it for $30,000 or $35,000 for the same month. Result? You pick up $5,000 to $10,000 for just signing a few pieces of paper! No license of any kind is required for this business. All you really need is a car to drive to see the homes you want to rent. And once you start subletting 10 or 12 properties a summer in the North and the same number in the winter in the South, you'll have a chauffeured limo drive you around! Time is on your side in this business because warm-weather seasons are short and people feel compelled to grab the first nice rental—regardless of the price. The inventory of suitable sublet homes is declining, while prices for weekly and monthly rentals are rising. So why don't you grab a piece of this time-forced rental market? You'll never regret it!

   2. Act legally as a broker with written Power of Attorney author-ity. You can legally act as a Real Estate Broker when the seller of a property gives you written, signed Power of Attorney to sell one of his or her properties. Note that you can use this exemption from the Broker Law for only *one property at a time.* And you can use this exemption only until the property is sold, after which the exemption ends. But this exemption can be a powerful tool when you have an inside track on a buyer of a specific type of property. You bring buyer and seller together, along with their legal advisors and complete the deal. Your commission will be the usual 6 percent of the purchase price—the standard commission paid to Real Estate Brokers. True, as a broker you do not own any real estate. But you do earn hefty commissions acting as a Broker. And you can invest some of your commissions in income properties you own for current income and future appreciation. The time you spend acting as a Broker will save you in acquiring income property because you'll learn what properties are available, who loans on such properties, what the fair going price is, and how to negotiate a profitable deal for yourself. You'll never go wrong acting as a Real Estate Broker with Power of Attorney because you'll learn quickly and become a competent real estate BWB!

3. *Get the most financing you can for every property.* Why? Because as time passes you'll be paying off with cheaper dollars than today's dollars. Thus, as time passes you'll raise rents, bringing in more cash. But if you have a fixed-rate mortgage your monthly payments will stay the same. So you'll have more dollars in your pocket, and your bank, at the end of each month. Getting a long-term mortgage for the maximum term reduces your monthly payment and gets time on your side. And if you can negotiate 100% financing of a property you've worked the best deal possible. Why? Because all the money in the property is OPM—Other People's Money. None of your money is at risk. And with a good cash flow you pay off the loan(s) on the property while having a reliable monthly positive cash flow. You can't ask for a better deal—especially when your income-producing asset (the property) is financed by others and you get all the income, plus the tax shelter provided by the depreciation.

4. *Take control of desirable properties as soon as you can.* Why? Because every day you hold a property it rises in value. So the longer you control a property, the higher its value will go. Time comes to your aid in real estate, pushing up property values—especially in established areas where construction has slowed or stopped altogether. In areas with widespread new construction, be careful not to take control of properties you plan to flip. Why? Because with lots of new construction, existing properties do not rise in value quickly. Instead, such properties often stay at their original price, or may decline slightly in value while new construction continues. Only when new construction ceases do existing properties start to rise in value. So, to get time on your side, seek control of properties only where the lack of new construction makes values rise quickly!

IMPORTANT POINTERS TO KEEP IN MIND

- Time is the second most important key to making money in real estate. Financing, of course, is the most important key.
- Time is always on your side in real estate. Properties will rise in value with the passage of time.
- Well-located real estate, like some people, just becomes more valuable with age or the passage of time.

- There are a number of funds around the country which make both large and small loans for the preservation of older properties. You can latch on to some of this money if you own older properties.
- Use of time in real estate can give you a much better cash position.
- Use of an equity loan permits you to take cash out of a property. Why let money sit idle when you can put it to work to earn more money!
- A property's market value is determined by a number of factors, including location, income, condition, and value trends in the area.
- Taking cash out of a property helps you survive cycles in real estate without a major impact on your finances.
- You can "buy time" by using your asset buildup in real estate. Do this by being alert to the increase in your property's value.
- Real estate values always come back! So don't give up if you have a short period of declining values.
- Patience pays profits in real estate!
- Don't overimprove a property for its area. Bring it to a high level of attractiveness, but stop there.
- Be active in neighborhood associations. You'll often learn many valuable details of making money locally. You may even find an anxious motivated seller who'll give you a bargain on desirable property.
- Keep your loan payments as small as possible. The smaller your loan payment, the larger your positive cash flow from the property.
- Never make a deal that can box you in. Avoid large, specific payments at a future date.
- Get lenders to help you. Many like to do so.
- Refinance whenever you can. It will keep your payments low.
- Devise other ways to make money from real estate. Loan portfolio brokering is a quick way to large profits in real estate today.

Successful
Real Estate Techniques
to Expand Your Fortune

Many people are "professional" pessimists. Nothing—even the most beautiful sunrise or sunset over a spanking new rental building—is good for them. So you'll hear such people bad-mouthing real estate whenever they can.

Don't let such conveyors of doom and gloom get *you* down! Why? Because, as I write this, a national report says that one of the richest persons in the world is a real estate operator. He owns buildings and land that are valued in the multibillions!

While I'll be happy making you a multimillionaire, I do want you to know that there are larger goals open to you. The important point here, of course, is that you *can* become extremely wealthy in real estate today. You just have to use smart-money techniques to expand your fortune, day after day! Let's see how *you* can build great wealth in real estate today.

UNUSUAL REAL ESTATE TECHNIQUES YOU CAN USE

There's more to real estate wealth than just collecting rents once a month. (But I must say that rent collection is very satisfying!) Unusual real estate techniques allow you to expand your income while working with the same property. Thus, you might:

- Convert space to needed uses in your local area
- Have profit-making machines installed on your property

- Earn maximum interest on your rent security deposits
- Rent facilities to sublet to others
- Subdivide buildings and land to produce income
- Swap land or buildings for improved financial results
- Provide real estate services of various types
- Run a rehab business—if you like such work
- Operate a real estate management firm
- Get your real estate license to reduce commission costs
- Explore other, local opportunities

To show you how, and where, you can apply each method, we'll take a fast look at how they're being used today. You'll get a number of good ideas you can use in your area.

Convert Space to Needed Uses

Each area of the country has unique space needs. If you can spot the needs for your area, you can generate extra income. Typical of unique space needs are:

- Storage for personal belongings
- Meeting rooms and conference centers
- Entertainment facilities
- Parks or fields for recreational uses

If you own buildings or land you can consider converting them to these or similar uses. When you meet local space needs you'll find that:

- You rent up quickly, that is, people rush to rent the facilities you offer
- Past rents do not influence your rent because the service you're offering is different from others currently available
- People will be more likely to work with you since you're a local person and you speak the "same language" that is, local dialect

The key to making more money from converted space is spotting the needs of your area. You can do this by:

- Talking to local real estate people and asking them what facilities people are looking for

- Watching your local papers and magazines for clues as to what needs businesses and people are expressing

- Reading national real estate publications so you latch onto trends in the marketplace while trying to translate them into your local market

Thus, a good friend of mine converted a bowling alley he owned into a ministorage warehouse. Why? Because local people had a stronger need for small rented storage spaces than they did for rolling a ball down a waxed alleyway! So far, five years after the conversion, his gamble is paying off. His income from the miniwarehouse is far in excess of the income from the bowling alley. Besides which, he sleeps at night. Why? Because his warehouse is automated—he doesn't have to be around to serve his customers' needs.

Another group I know of converted several rotting steamship piers into a successful sports complex. They got local financing and the state helped them at the start with a reduced rental on the piers.

Today the piers feature a huge swimming pool, rock climbing wall, an enormous indoor running track, a boxing ring, a children's summer camp, two ice skating rinks, a large party space, a marina, volleyball court, a golf driving range, bowling alley, restaurants, and TV production studios.

Three years after startup, this attractive real estate complex is profitable. The operators converted dilapidated space into a productive facility serving local needed uses.

To show you how smart they are, these operators did not install any tennis courts because there were plenty in the area served. Instead, they installed sports facilities the local area needs. Result? Outstanding success!

Have Profit-Making Machines Installed

If you own an income property of some kind, it may be attractive to other wealth builders as a profit source. Thus:

- Washing machines and dryers are important profit makers in apartment houses, motels, and hotels.

- Storage lockers can generate income in garages, industrial plants, and recreational facilities of various types.

- Telephones can be big profit makers where people pass through your store, restaurant, and so on.
- Electronic games can be big winners for you in hotels, motels, stores, and so on.

You need contribute nothing to have such profit generators installed, other than the space needed. The cost of the equipment, its installation, and maintenance will be paid by the vendor offering it to you. And you'll be paid a percentage of the income from each item installed.

Among my real estate friends the largest income generated is from electronic video games. Why? Because kids love to play these games. So you'll find they have deep pockets—kept filled by their parents—when it comes to video games.

Don't take the first offer that comes along for installing equipment in your real estate! Get competitive bids. You may be able to double or triple your monthly take from the equipment that's installed free of charge. And try to get the vendor to pay the electrical charges for the equipment. Or have the vendor make a monthly electric charge payment if the equipment can't be metered separately.

Earn Maximum Interest on Rent Deposits

With multioccupancy real estate you'll have rent security deposits for one, or more, month's rent from each tenant. You're allowed to earn interest on these deposits. Some banks pay higher rates than others. And if you put some, or all, of the money in a certificate of deposit (CD), you'll earn a higher rate than in a savings account.

Since interest is regarded as income on your tax return, why not earn the highest interest possible? Such interest will be another income source for you. And it will build your total positive cash flow. So search around for the highest interest you can earn. It will mean more money in *your* pocket! You might as well get the highest return possible.

Rent Facilities to Sublet to Others

One of the smartest moves you can make in real estate is to earn money on other people's property. You do this by:

1. Deciding what type of property is in short supply

2. Finding such property for rent at a reasonable rate

3. Checking to see if you can rent the property at a higher rate than you're paying

4. Searching out potential tenants for the property

5. Taking an option on the property rental

6. Signing a lease with your potential tenant, based on your option for the property

7. Tying up the property by exercising your option

Some real estate BWBs are able to lease, and then sublet, thousands of square feet of desirable space. You—too—can do the same if there's a demand for such space in your area.

You never, of course, own the property you sublet. So you don't share in the appreciation of the property as time passes. But you *do* have a positive cash flow each month. Let's look at an example of leasing, and then subletting, office space:

> You *lease* 10,000-sq.-ft. of office space at $20.00 per sq. ft. per year, for a total cost of $200,000 per year, paid on a monthly basis
>
> You *sublet* this same space for $28.00 per sq. ft. per year on a *net* basis, that is, the tenant pays *all* expenses associated with the space, such as maintenance, increased taxes, and so on.
>
> You earn an income of $28.00 per sq. ft. – $20.00/sq. ft. = $8.00/sq. ft. for 10,000 sq. ft., or $80,000 per year. This is your positive cash flow.

What are your risks? There are a few. These include the following:

1. Your rent for the space may be raised after a few years.

2. The firm leasing the space from you may have business problems and be unable to pay its rent.

3. Your tenant may move sooner than expected, leaving you to chase him or her for the unpaid rent.

But if you choose your tenants carefully, it should be easy to make the subletting work. Plenty of BWB real estate operators do. I'm sure you can, too. Just examine all options carefully before signing on the dotted line!

Subdivide Buildings and Land

Many times people won't want to rent what you offer. But they would be happy to rent a portion of your offering. What can you do—especially in a slow market?

You can subdivide, that is, offer a portion of your building or land for rent. This way you *do* generate a cash income. And, if you plan carefully, you can rent the other portion of the building or land to another tenant.

Your outcome can be exactly what *you* want—a larger income for the same space. Why? Because when you subdivide:

- You can usually charge your tenant a higher rent than due based on the percentage of space rented.
- So your cash flow from, say, half of a building will be 60 percent of what you'd get for the entire building. Result? Your cash flow is 10 percent higher than you planned!

With careful planning you can rent the second half of the building for 60 percent of the whole rental. Your overall result will be a 20 percent rise in your cash flow, without any increase in costs!

Remember: When you subdivide at the tenant's request, the needed alterations, if any, are paid for by the tenant! So your increased cash flow has *no* strings attached to it.

Swap Land or Buildings for Better Results

You can swap (exchange) buildings or land to improve your cash income. While swaps may seem tough to do, they really aren't. All you need is a person seeking the type of property you have who owns a property you'd like to take over.

Be certain to have an attorney to help you with your swap. A good attorney can point out tax advantages to you with the right swap deal. To benefit most from swaps, take time to look around for the best deal. Don't rush into a swap without full advice from a competent attorney!

Provide Real Estate Services for Others

There are numerous services you can provide to others in real estate. By providing these services *you* can earn extra income while you broaden your skills and increase your knowledge. Typical services you can consider providing include:

- Offering loan brokerage—more commonly called *financial brokerage*—for people seeking real estate loans, including yourself
- Setting up shared appreciation deals for people who don't have enough liquid cash to buy the property they want
- Finding good real estate deals for people with cash who don't have the time—or know-how—to find the best deal
- Arranging swaps or barter deals for people with property
- Arranging seller financing for people seeking to buy property without a lot of cash
- Finding buyers of purchase money mortgages to allow the holders to cash out of the paper they're holding
- Showing real estate BWBs how to take over property for low, or zero, cash down, while paying only 60 percent, or less, of market value
- Guiding BWBs through a "reverse flip" where the buyer uses the seller's credit and assets to get cash to take over a property
- Showing—for a fee—B WBs how to use a contract of sale to take over property for zero cash
- Arranging options-to-buy for real estate BWBs who want to speculate in selling property they don't own but which they control for just a few dollars, which can be refundable
- Formulating lease-with-option-to-purchase deals for BWBs you advise who are short of funds and who need guidance on zero cash investments for themselves
- Starting limited partnerships, with the help of an experienced attorney, for experienced real estate investors seeking high returns with little involvement in the day-to-day operation of real estate holdings, collecting their funds—usually from $5,000 to $100,000 per investor and putting them in safe interest-bearing accounts for future investment
- Providing rehab guidance for people who want to engage in the fix-up business; you will be paid a fee for small jobs; on large projects you will be paid a fee plus a sweetener in the form of a small percentage of the profit when the property is sold

Most of these services do not require a real estate or other license. But if you do run into services requiring a license, consider working with an experienced real estate attorney. An attorney can handle real estate transactions of all types under his or her legal license. You then become a helper to the attorney, putting deals together for eventual funding or training of the people in the deal.

A number of these services are covered by courses and kits listed in the appendix. It is wise to get the training you need when you start offering any of these services.

Run a Rehab Business—If You Like It

Rehabs are the hope of the future rental market. Why? Because new construction is so expensive that only wealthy people can live in new luxury buildings. But rehabs—being already in place, and of sound construction—can rent for much less than luxury buildings. So the rehab appeals to the low- and middle-income renter.

Analyze any real estate market anywhere, and you'll find that there are a lot more low- and middle-income renters. This means that rehabbed units are aimed at the largest segment of the market. Result? You can have people "breaking down the doors" to rent one of your rehabbed units.

But to run a rehab business you must have certain personality traits. These are

- A willingness to deal with rundown property
- An ability to work with contractors
- An eye for future value despite poor appearances today

If you don't have these traits, I suggest you try other ways to make money in real estate. One of the best ways is what I call the "reverse rehab." What is it? It's this:

A reverse rehab is the purchase—at a large reduction off the list price— of a new, modern unit suitable for renting to others at a positive cash flow. Financing—often at 90 percent of the purchase price—is already in place, making it easy to close the deal. In some cases, closing costs will be paid by the seller, thereby further reducing your cost.

Where can *you* find such reverse rehabs? They're all around you in times of slow real estate sales. Thus, you will typically find condo units being auctioned during times of sluggish sales. During these auctions:

- Units are sold to the highest bidder, regardless of price.

- Investor financing of 90 percent is offered by the seller; this means you don't have to search for money.

- Deals can be closed quickly because the entire auction is designed to "move" units into the hands of investors or owners.

- Savings can be significant for you.

- *No* repairs of any kind need be made—these are *new* units with all fixtures and equipment guaranteed.

- Many buildings in which units are auctioned offer a sauna, swimming pool, exercise room, and so on.

- Buy a reverse rehab and your only task will be finding a suitable tenant.

What kind of savings can you get when you buy at an auction? Here are some real numbers from a recent auction in a large-city area:

UNIT TYPE	ORIGINAL PRICE	AUCTION PRICE	SAVINGS
Studio	$203,600	$116,390	$ 87,210
1 Bedroom	308,200	158,620	149,580
2 Bedroom	377,300	182,310	194,990
3 Bedroom	550,800	339,900	210,900

These units are in an excellent building. Construction is superb throughout. Marble floors in the bathrooms, polished brass fixtures, and wood parquet floors are just a few of the features of the units.
So if fixing up (rehabbing) older buildings turns you off, consider doing a reverse rehab. It can put big bucks in your pocket after you get several units giving you a positive cash flow. Thus, if you buy at auction 5 units which give you $400 per month cash flow per unit, your net income will be 5 × $400 = $2,000 per month—while the units are paying for themselves. Double this to 10 units and you're in the $4,000 per month positive cash flow—all in your spare time!

Operate a Real Estate Management Firm

Plenty of owners of income property would like to go fishing, skiing, or sailing instead of managing their properties. They *like* their business but enjoy leisure more than working. So they look to a real estate management firm to run their properties for them. Services they receive include:

- Collection of rents every month
- Direction of maintenance and repair activities for the property
- Finding new tenants by advertising for them
- Handling tenant requests and/or complaints
- Working out lease agreements with tenants

Now don't be frightened by this list. Most of the duties are easy to perform. Further, you'll be paid between 5 and 10 percent of the rent collections as your fee for performing these duties. Any repair costs are paid for by the owner—you just get someone in to do the work.

You'll have a steady, dependable cash flow when you manage property. And *no* license of any kind is needed to run such a firm. But the big advantage to you is:

> You learn what it takes to run a profitable real estate business. You'll get a "college education" in rental property in just a few months. Your learning will be paid for without you having to invest one penny!

How can *you* set up a management company? That's easy. You just take these simple steps:

1. Choose a name for your firm—it could be ABC Management, XYZ Property Associates, and so on.

2. Register your business with your county clerk; at the start you can operate as a sole proprietor or as a partnership. Later, when your income grows, you may want to incorporate. Just be sure to consult an attorney as to the best form for your business.

3. Advertise your services to local property owners. Use the Yellow Pages. real estate publications, and nearby newspapers.

Once you get a few clients for whom you do a good job, your reputation will be spread by word of mouth. Soon you'll have more requests for work than you can handle.

Get Your Real Estate License

None of the money-making tips we've given you so far requires you to have a real estate license. It is *not* necessary to have any kind of license to buy, hold, or sell any type of property for your own income purposes. But if you handle transactions for others, you may be required to hold a real estate salesperson's or broker's license.

Getting a license is easy. You just buy one of the exam review books and read it over. Most of the information in such books is useful to you in two ways:

1. As background information for your own investing
2. As data for passing your license exam

One big advantage of having your own real estate license is that you can save on sales commissions. Thus, if you handle the sale of a building you buy, the commission the seller pays—usually 6 percent of the sales price—will be paid to *you*. This, in effect, reduces *your* price by 6 percent! So having the license *can* put money into your pocket.

If license exams turn you off, you can take another approach. Go into partnership with a local attorney who knows real estate. An attorney does not have to have a real estate license to conduct such transactions. As his or her partner, you operate under the attorney's license, without any examination.

Another way of doing this if you prefer not to have a partner is to hire an attorney to conduct transactions for you. Again, you won't need a license because the attorney's legal license permits such transactions. The result of all this is to help *you* earn more money from nonownership real estate deals!

Explore Other Income Sources

Real estate is interesting to almost anyone. So if you're a pro who knows how to make money from real estate, you can help others do the same, while *you* earn money for yourself. Thus, as a real estate pro you can:

- Conduct seminars for groups interested in earning money from real estate
- Give one-on-one guidance to BWBs seeking to earn their fortune in real estate

- Consult for investment clubs needing help on real estate investments
- Write articles or instructions for real estate BWBs needing guidance

There are dozens of other ways you can make money in this great business of real estate—in both good times and bad times. Just look around you to see what services are needed. Then offer that service—for a good fee!

Build Wealth with Combined Incomes

If you follow the suggestions we give you here, you'll have three— or more—incomes. These are your:

- Job income
- Rental real estate income
- Other real estate income

With these three incomes you should be able to build your wealth quickly.

To build your wealth quickly, take these easy steps:

1. *Control costs.* Don't allow your expenses to get out of hand; the results can eat up your profits.
2. *Conserve cash.* Don't go on a spending spree just because you have a strong cash flow. Cash is king; so keep it in safe, insured investments that won't decline in value!
3. *Get good financial advice.* Use an accountant and an attorney to guide your money decisions.

Combine your incomes and your future will be bright. Keep a careful eye on what you spend, and where. Know your income and expenses and you can build a million-dollar fortune much sooner than you think!

As you know by now, real estate BWBs contact me about their successes—and their problems. A few successes reported to me include these:

> *I grossed $3,000 the first week in our new business in which we supply listings of commercial real estate that are available in specific cities and states. We get $300 per listing and can't seem to satisfy the demand for them. Of course, I can do much better in this business, once I settle in.*

Another real estate BWB who acts as a financial broker for entrepreneurs seeking funding for their deals says:

> *I just closed a $2.7 million real estate loan deal. My commission was 1 percent, or $27,000. Sure, I worked hard for a short while. But the results are worth it! I advertise in newspapers around the country and have an 800 number. It pays off for real estate and good business loan deals.*

And a third real estate BWB—one who looked long and hard for a loan for her property—says:

> *The loan was accomplished here in southern California very easily with the help of your newsletter. The names and companies requesting our loan package from our ad were terrific and an added plus benefit for future use.*

So you see, you *can* make big money in nonrental real estate deals. And with your regular job income, and your rental income, you *can* build financial freedom in this great business! And I'm here to help *you* every step of the way.

LITTLE-KNOWN WAYS TO MAXIMIZE YOUR REAL ESTATE INCOME

There are dozens of ways to keep more of *your* cash flow dollar in real estate. Let's look at a few. They'll suggest other ways you can build your riches faster in real estate today.

Work with Market Share Seekers

Many lenders, when seeking to increase their share of the market in a given area of the country, will offer generous loan deals to you. These deals might include:

- Low interest rates
- Long terms for repayment
- Balloon deals where you pay interest only for years, thereby reducing your monthly loan payment

- Folding any point charges into the loan so you don't have to put down any cash

When you see offers like these, grab them! Why? Because you'll get benefits that you couldn't obtain, even if you begged for them. Market share seekers will do almost anything legitimate to get your loan business to build their conquest of an area. As the man said: "Grab it while it's hot!"

Capitalize Borrowed Money and Earn More

If you can borrow money, you're in a position of power. Why? Because you can take that borrowed money and put it to work at a higher rate of return than it's costing you. You then operate on what we bankers call the "spread"—the difference between your-cost of money and what you're earning on it. Let's look at a typical situation:

> You borrow money, we'll say, at 12 percent simple interest. You can invest this money in safe second trust deeds on good homes at 14 percent. Your spread is 14% − 12% = 2%. This 2 percent is automatic income which doesn't require any time, or effort, on your part. And if you could get 16 percent on second trust deeds (as is entirely possible), you could increase your spread to 4 percent, again an automatic income for *you!*

You can, of course, invest your borrowed money in other, safe deals. The key fact to keep in mind when capitalizing borrowed money is this:

> Do not invest in an instrument or security that can go down in value while you hold it. If you do, you may find that your spread income is eaten up by your loss in value. Invest only in items that will hold their value for the duration of your investment.

Get More After-Tax Spendable Income

You can have the largest income in the world. But if taxes take away all of it, you might as well not work. The key to getting rich is MIF— money in fist—*after* you pay your taxes.

To increase your after-tax income, increase your legitimate tax deductions from your gross income. Deductions which the law allows for real estate include:

- Depreciation of buildings and equipment (*not* land)
- Real estate taxes you pay
- Maintenance costs on buildings and equipment
- Labor costs (including *your* salary)
- Interest on all loans on the property
- Miscellaneous costs—lighting, cleaning, trash removal, and so on

Keep accurate records of *all* these costs. Then you'll be better able to take all the deductions to which you're legally entitled. This will increase your after-tax cash income. With more money in your fist, you can buy other properties, start another business, or otherwise profit from your business.

So keep in mind at *all* times: Your key to success is arranging your business accounts so you maximize your after-tax take-home pay. Hire a good accountant to advise you on your tax matters. But be sure to review the accountant's work. It's *your* money that's at stake!

Make Money from Real Estate in Good and Bad Times

Good times make it easy to earn big bucks in real estate. Bad times offer beautiful bargains that can make *you* rich.

So keep tuned to the market. When real estate values come crashing down, shift into a buying mode and:

- Bargain aggressively to get the lowest price possible
- Get seller financing on every deal you can
- Take over attractive foreclosures for zero cash down
- Be brave when all around you are running scared—your courage will pay off in dream deals

Real estate *always* comes back! So the property you buy at a bargain today *will* be worth more tomorrow. Sure, you may have to wait until the next day. But your value *will* be there—if the property is in a decent condition and is located in a stable area. And your property *will* rise in value as time passes.

Real estate bought at depressed prices will sell at higher prices— later. You can count on that, just as surely as you do the rise of the sun tomorrow morning. So be brave! It can put big bucks into *your* pocket or purse. Like these readers who say:

> *Last year I bought and sold two houses (foreclosures). This netted me $30,000. Now I've launched my next project.*

> *And*

> *Thank you for running my ad in your newsletter. I had more responses to it than I could possibly use. I've found a lender who's willing to finance my shopping center, and I'm on my way to a very good start in the money brokering business.*

There you have the real-life experiences of brave people! You, too, can do the same. Just set your goals and work toward them.

SUCCESS STRATEGIES FOR BUILDING YOUR REAL ESTATE WEALTH IN GOOD TIMES AND BAD TIMES

1. Look for auction-offered buildings you can often buy for as little as $1.00 per building which you can convert to big income producers. Thus, one couple bought a complete school building (K–12, kindergarten through 12th grade) for just $1.00. They renovated the building and soon had it fully rented to a number of reliable tenants. Their profit on the building is enormous because they have no mortgage payments to make! You can find such auction buildings listed in your local large-city newspapers and in the *Commerce Business Daily* available in any large public library. Keep looking for such auctions. Sometimes it will take you longer to find such properties than you'd like. Just be patient; they will show up—eventually. And when you find such properties, be a "bottom-fisher"—that is, a person who offers the lowest price possible. The most the seller can say is "No." And you can always raise your bid to a higher price!

2. Seek unusual deals for the real estate you own. Thus, one owner was offered $90-million for the air rights over his corner property on a main street in a large city. He would still own the land and his building and could earn $12-million per year from renting the building out to suitable tenants. There are many other unusual deals you can work out—

such as using the basement of a building for a transient garage, leasing roof space to satellite and communications companies, allowing advertising signs or paintings to be mounted on your building, etc. By keeping an eye open for such opportunities, you can improve your real estate income enormously while still retaining full ownership of the property.

3. Use the "sandwich" lease to increase your non-ownership profits. With a "sandwich" lease you rent all, or a portion, of a property. For example, you might rent for one year a full floor in an office building for $25,000 per year. You then sublet the entire floor to an organization needing the space for $32,000 per year. The person subletting the floor from you rents it out to several different tenants, receiving a total income of $35,000 per year. The "sandwich" consists of the building owner, you, and the person subletting from you. You're in the middle of the sandwich. But you receive $32,000 a year for space that costs you $25,000 per year. Thus, your profit from your sandwich lease is $32,000 – $25,000 = $7,000. Put together ten such deals with the same profit per floor and your income is $10 \times \$7,000 = \$70,000$ per year for just "shuffling paper"—that is, writing up deals and getting them signed. While your life is simpler because you don't have the responsibility of building ownership, you miss out on the appreciation in the price of the building as time passes. You can get in on some of the appreciation by raising rents each year. But the gains seldom equal the rise in price of a building with the passage of time. Further, you do not have any depreciation to shelter your income. But a sandwich lease is a successful real estate technique that can make you rich!

4. Cold-call your way to real estate mortgage success. If you prefer not to own real estate but want to make money in mortgages, consider cold-calling your way to wealth. Here's how it works: (a) Associate yourself with a local mortgage company that makes home-equity, second-mortgage, and refinance loans. (b) Work out an agreement wherein you'll be paid 1 percent (or more if you can get it) on each new loan of the above types you find. (c) Start cold-calling home owners in your area, asking them if they're interested in one of the three types of loans listed above (or any other types of mortgages your lender may handle). If a person is interested, get the needed data from them and send it on to your lender. (d) Collect your fee when the loan goes through. *Wealth Tip:* Some BWBs who do cold-calling work with older telephone books for their area. Why? Because the older phone books have the names and numbers of people who've owned their home for a number of years and are more likely to be candidates for one of the types of loans listed above!

IMPORTANT POINTERS TO KEEP IN MIND

- You can use unusual real estate techniques to expand your fortune and get richer. Some of these strategies are converting space to needed uses, installing profit-making machines on your property, swapping land and buildings, and providing real estate services of various types.
- Reverse rehabbing is an excellent way to make rental income without the hassle of fixing up neglected properties.
- Operating a real estate management firm can give you a "college education" in rental management in just months while earning a nice spare-time income and learning the numbers of income property.
- Combined income—from several real estate sources—can make *you* rich; just be sure to control costs, conserve cash, and get good financial advice.
- By working with market share seeking lenders, you can often get loans when others are turned down. Go where money is seeking borrowers!
- Work to get more after-tax spendable income from your business. It *will* make *you* rich!

How to Hit the Real Estate Jackpot Anywhere, Any Time

As you have read, I have my own lending business for business and real estate loans. And I'm also director and on the board of a large eastern lending organization with nationwide real estate loans.

At this writing, when real estate is hurting in some areas, our large lending organization has some $70 million in residential mortgage loans—a total of about 470 loans. Yet, when things are supposedly very bad, *only* 4 of nearly 500 loans are slightly behind in payments. Not one is in default!

What does this tell you—and me? It tells us that real estate is the best bet for *you* for a secure business future while you still hold your present job or run your current business. Let's look a little closer.

REAL ESTATE IS YOUR BEST BET FOR FUTURE WEALTH

There's no business that can offer *you* the many advantages of real estate, including:

- Tax-favored income protection
- Control of an income asset with no upfront investment
- Cash flow increases due to good management
- Shrewd mortgage payoff techniques that can save you a bundle
- Tax-free swaps that produce greater income
- Guaranteed monthly income with Section 8 tenants

- Cheap financing of income real estate with smart approaches to lenders
- Bargain-basement prices for high-value properties in times of real estate downturns
- Distressed properties and foreclosures that can make you rich sooner than you think
- Chance to be an Independent Loan Originator (ILO) to earn money from home in your spare time helping people get residential loans for homes they want to buy

Let's take a fast look at each of these benefits for you to see how *you* can prosper from it.

Tax-Favored Income Protection

In every income property you're allowed to depreciate the building and its internal fixtures to recover your investment over a period of time. The effect is to give *you* a "paper" deduction which puts cash into your pocket!

By working with a competent accountant and a smart attorney, you can take full advantage of all the deductions to which you are legally entitled. Doing so will increase your after-tax income significantly. And spendable income is, remember, the reason why you're in business!

The depreciation tax rules are simple. You're allowed a certain "life" for your building and a shorter life for the machinery, furniture, and other equipment in it. Your overall benefit is a protection of some, or all, of the cash flow from your property. You have an expense—depreciation—for which you do not lay out any money today. Yet this "expense" reduces your taxable income. So you end the month, and each year, with more MW. Could anything be sweeter?

But before you run off on a depreciation binge, take these easy steps:

1. Get good advice from a competent CPA who knows real estate tax rules.
2. Keep an experienced attorney at the other end of your phone line to answer any legal questions that may arise.
3. *Understand* depreciation rules yourself—they're not difficult and knowing them can give you the ability to check on the work of your accountant and attorney. (Remember: It's *your* money they're working with. You want to be sure they know what they're doing!)

Control an Income Asset with Zero Cash

There *are* zero cash properties available! But you *must* look for them. They will *not* seek you out. Zero cash properties often have these characteristics:

1. An assumable mortgage which you can take over with *no* credit investigation or check of any kind

2. Owner financing of the down payment so you don't have to put up any cash at all

3. A strong need for a quick sale—such as a divorce, a death in the family, a sudden change in a neighborhood, and so on

4. A liking of *you* by the seller because you appear to be a reliable and "safe" buyer who will repay the debts you've taken on

Getting, and controlling, an income asset with no cash of your own is the ultimate business coup. And if you can do it again and again, as many of my readers have, you can grow rich in your spare time while you hold onto the job you hate!

The main point to keep in mind in this: *You must look for zero cash properties. They won't—at the start—seek you out!*

You Can Increase Cash Flow with Good Management

An income property—by definition—gives *you* income! But sometimes the income is less than what you'd like. How can *you* raise the cash flow from a property you've taken over? There's just one answer: *good management.*

With good management you take advantage of every technique available to you, including:

- Establishing precise cost controls

- Increasing rents regularly

- Developing sources of extra income

- Doing work yourself to save labor charges

- Hiring part-time workers to do work you can't do

- Avoiding every fixed expense you can
- Being "on top of" your business 24 hours a day

You don't need a college degree to be a good income property manager! All you need is some common sense. And by using your head you can build a monthly rental income exceeding $10,000 per month in a short time.

Running dozens of income properties that make money every month is simple if you:

- Plan your expenses, that is, create a monthly expense budget
- Plan your income, that is, prepare a monthly income budget

Do your expense budget first. Why? Because it's smart to know—early on—what your costs will be. Then do your income budget.

Having your budgets allows you to look ahead at upcoming expenses. Knowing what you'll have to pay next month allows you to plan how you'll make your payments.

Doing budgets is a chore! But having your income and expense budgets is the key to success in property management. And the good news about budgets is:

> Once you've prepared your monthly expense and income budgets for a year, it's easy to update your budgets for the following year because the numbers normally won't change much from one year to the next. So all you really need do is prepare your budgets once and they're good for as long as you own the property!

Increased cash flow puts more money into *your* pocket—where it belongs! Good, easy, simple management will do just that for you. So start now.

Shrewd Mortgage Payoff Techniques Save Big Bucks

When you buy a property your mortgage will usually be paid off on what's called *monthly principal and interest* (P&I). This means you make 12 monthly payments a year. Each payment reduces the principal (the amount you borrowed) and pays the interest for the month.

At the start of your mortgage payments, most of each payment goes to pay interest on your loan. Only a small amount of the payment reduces the principal or the amount of money you borrowed.

If you come into excess cash from your property, you can reduce your interest cost by using some of your cash to pay off principal. Here's how it works:

> Let's say you're paying $2,200 per month on your income property mortgage. You receive $20,000 cash from the sale of another property. Deciding to use $11,000 of this to pay down your mortgage, you say to yourself: "Gee, I can make five payments at once because 5 × $2,200 = $11,000." But in those five payments will be a large interest sum. Instead, you decide to pay the $11,000 to reduce your principal directly, with no money being applied to the interest. So you write on your check: "For principal payment only" and send it to your lender. Your principal (what you borrowed) is reduced. So, too, is your interest cost. Your next P&I payment will have less deducted for interest and more applied to principal reduction.

Try to eliminate any early repayment penalty clause from your mortgage. This will save you money if you want to repay your mortgage earlier than its completion date.

Work at getting big chunks of cash into your business so you can repay your mortgage by reducing the principal. Doing this can save you many thousands of dollars in interest. And each dollar you save can go directly into your pocket to be used for whatever purpose *you* choose!

There's nothing complex about paying off any mortgage. The simple rule that should govern all your borrowing is: *Pay off a loan early and you'll reduce your interest cost.*

Look for Tax-Free Swaps

You can exchange like properties used in your business or trade or held for investment purposes tax free. Section 1031 of the Internal Revenue Code allows you to make these tax-free swaps.

Look for increased income from *every* swap you consider. Don't go into a swap unless it gives you more MIF. And have an accountant and attorney on hand to advise you every step of the way.

Swaps are best made *after* you've had some experience with property ownership. It is better to start accumulating positive cash flow properties for several years before you begin to make swaps. Why? Because your experience with the properties you own will improve your ability to judge potential swap properties.

Get a Guaranteed Monthly Income

You can be paid directly by the federal or your state government for rental residential property you provide for low-income families. Such payments will provide *you* with a guaranteed monthly income because you will receive your rent for as long as a tenant chooses to stay in your property. You can get rents from both state and Section 8 federal programs.

Since the Section 8 housing program is an evolving activity, check with your local Housing and Urban Development (HUD) office for the latest benefits for you. You'll find HUD listed at the back of your phone book under the "U.S. Government" heading.

Your rental income will be larger if you can provide 2-and 3-bedroom apartments for your Section 8 tenants. So when you're considering buying a new property, evaluate its potential income based on higher Section 8 rental payments. Then your cash flow will be larger from the property.

While some BWBs might turn away from Section 8 tenants saying: "I don't want those kind of people in my building," studies show that these tenants are:

- Careful of the apartment they occupy
- Likely to stay for years
- Ready to do work in their apartment if you supply materials (such as paint, wall coverings, spackle, etc.)

So don't turn away from Section 8! It could be your big cash cow that provides the bulk of your income.

SEEK—AND FIND—CHEAP FINANCING

Lenders *do* have "fire sales" when they push out loans at reduced rates. In my two lending organizations we frequently go on "loan sales," that is, marketing campaigns in which we seek new borrowers for our loans. *You* could keep me happy by applying for mortgage loans for well-kept, nicely located real estate anywhere in the United States. All I ask is that you be a reader of my newsletter so you understand my views of lending.

Why do we go on loan sales? Because:

- It's a tough, competitive world out there, with hundreds (even thousands at times) of lenders vying to get *your* loan business.

- It isn't easy to find sincere, serious, qualified borrowers; we lenders need borrowers as much as borrowers (maybe more) need our money.

- My success dreams (and those of many other lenders) are of borrowers who are well qualified who come into my office and ask for our biggest loan ($100,000 for IWS where allowed by statute, and $1 million for my other lending organization), take it, and send us a monthly repayment check on the first of every month.

Unless you're in the lending business as I am, you have no idea of how hard we work to find suitable borrowers. I plead with my staff to do more aggressive marketing of our services to potential borrowers. Sometimes this works; most of the time it doesn't.

So if you know any qualified real estate borrowers (including yourself), be sure to recommend them to me. See the appendix for more data.

The main point to keep in mind is that cheap financing for real estate *is* available. But *you* must look for it. Cheap financing won't look for you!

Bargain-Basement Prices Can Be Yours

I keep my boat on the north shore of Long Island. During a recent real estate downturn houses in that area that people paid $2.4 million for sold for $900,000. Yet their true value with 6 waterfront acres having sweeping views of Long Island Sound and the bay is around $2.5 million. And someday they'll be worth $3.0 million.

Why do such places sell for under a million during a downturn? For a number of reasons, which. you should look for when seeking bargain-basement prices:

- The seller lost his or her job.
- The seller's fortune was killed by a stock market crash.
- The seller's business was torpedoed by a recession.
- The seller has marital problems and wants out.
- The seller took on too many debts and can't make mortgage payments on the property.

Note that *none* of these problems relates to the real estate. The problems relate to the seller's life. And they cause the seller to offer the property at a bargain price. *You* can rescue the seller by taking the property over at a price that relieves the seller of his or her payment burdens.

But, as with cheap financing, you *must* search out such properties. They won't come looking for you! To find these bargain-basement offerings, take these easy steps:

1. Look in your local papers every weekend.
2. Watch for key words indicating the seller is anxious—phrases such as "price negotiable," "make offer," "seller has two mortgages," "estate sale," and so on.
3. Inspect the property; make a low-ball offer; don't give up when the seller laughs at you.
4. Keep looking—you will find a suitable property if you look long enough.

The bargains available to you during hard times prove that you *can* make big money in both good times and bad times. How? By buying in hard times and waiting for values to rise in good times—when you sell. Meanwhile, of course, the property will give you a positive cash flow *every* month!

Distressed Properties Can Make You Rich

You learned about these properties in an earlier chapter. What I want to emphasize here is that distressed properties offer you a quick path to riches in real estate today. These properties have the advantages of:

- Ready availability
- Wide price range—from low to high
- Minimum cash up front
- Easy paperwork
- Plenty of room for expansion

You *must* look for distressed properties. Just keep an eye on your local paper and you're almost certain to see an ad for an auction sale. Get over to it and learn. You'll quickly become a local expert while building *your* fortune in distressed properties!

CASH IS KING IN YOUR WORLD

Cash is your ticket to freedom! And *your* cash in real estate will come from the cash flow of your business. Remember this at all times in your business:

> A dollar in hand is worth far more than any promises of future cash flow or payments. Since it's much harder to build up cash reserves than it is to spend them, borrow needed cash today and pay it off with future income of inflation-depleted dollars. But above all, conserve your cash—every day!

Take every step you can to build your cash flow income and reduce your cash flow outgo by reducing costs. You won't get rich in real estate if you neglect your income and costs. You *must* control these two elements of your business. Earlier chapters give you the methods. This chapter points the critical importance to *you* of controlling your cash flow—every day!

To help you cope better with the cash flow challenge, here are a number of ideas for you:

10 Key Cash Flow Techniques

1. *Insist, and get, on-time payment of all rents and other fees due you.* Every day a payment is delayed is a loss of income to you! So don't tolerate late payments of any kind.

2. *Penalize any late payments made to you.* Levy a hefty charge for late payments, bounced checks, and so on. Charge $25, or $50, for any late payment or bad check. The word will soon get around to your tenants that they must pay on time or be penalized.

3. *Earn all you can from cash you have on hand.* Deposit funds for even overnight earnings. Why? Because *every* penny you earn from your cash adds to your income! So get smart—don't ignore potential income. It helps pay the bills!

4. *Raise rents regularly so you keep up with inflation.* Too many BWBs are satisfied with just a modest income from their real estate. Don't you be one of these! Get *every* penny of income you can from every property—starting right now.

5. *Develop other income sources to increase your cash flow.* Look into sources such as parking space rental, laundry machines for tenants, baby-sitting services, telephone answering, package receipt services, and so on. Every penny of extra income adds to your overall wealth!

6. *Borrow against cash reserves instead of taking cash out of savings.* Why? Because you're much more likely to repay a loan than you are to replace cash you spent. Further, your true interest cost is the difference between the loan interest rate and your savings interest rate. Thus, if you're paying 10 percent interest on a loan and earning 7 percent on your savings, your true interest cost is $10\% - 7\% = 3\%$. That's a low and tax-deductible cost to pay for conserving that scarcest of all items—cash!

7. *Keep costs low at all times.* Watch for sales by suppliers of maintenance items—paint, caulking, light bulbs, and so on. You will often save as much as 30 percent when you buy during annual sales by local suppliers. Hire parttime workers as independent contractors. Why? Their costs are often lower and their service better than full-time salaried workers. Watch your costs at *all* times—it will save you a bundle, increasing *your* cash flow!

8. *Get your family into the business.* They'll often work for less. Further, family members are less likely to steal from you. And if times get tough, family members will help you get through by cutting their wage demands, working longer hours without overtime pay, and so on.

9. *Refinance your mortgage(s) where the savings on your monthly payments are enough to justify the points you must pay.* In general, if you reduce your interest cost by two percentage points, or more, the monthly savings in interest will justify the points (usually 1.5 or 2) you pay to refinance your mortgage.

10. *Take advantage of all real estate tax abatements offered in your area.* And if no tax abatements are offered, explore ways to have your real estate taxes reduced. You can often get big savings by just presenting your case to local town or county officials.

When you combine strong cash flow (which gives you MIF) with leverage (getting a lot of value for little—or no—money), you have the strongest way to become rich ever invented by anyone! Now that you know how to produce strong cash flow, let's look at using leverage to build your millions.

LEVERAGE DO'S AND DON'TS
FOR WEALTH BUILDERS

You can get more value from leverage in bad times than in good times. Why? Because in bad times there are more bargains seeking investors like yourself. And these bargains can give you big savings:

> A 3-story townhouse owned by a celebrity was put on the market at $8 million in bad times. The seller refused an offer of $5.5 million for the townhouse soon after it went on the market. Some three years after being put on the market the townhouse sold for $3 million.

To get the most from leverage in good times and bad times, follow these simple rules:

1. *Seek value at low cost.* You'll profit every time because value always stays with a property, despite changes in the economy.
2. *Convert troubled properties into money machines.* Do this by emphasizing their benefits to tenants in all your advertising and promotion efforts.
3. *Buy at rock-bottom prices during poor times.* This gives you the chance to skyrocket your money for a major killing at the time you sell.
4. *Develop bonus income from your property.* That way you pocket more cash while you own it and sell for a higher profit when you decide to unload your holding in it.
5. *Put as little cash into a deal as you can.* For maximum leverage, borrow the down payment cash. Then your leverage is infinite!
6. *Always buy for value and upgrade for sale.* This is the way to sizable wealth for you. Remember: There is *no* substitute for value in real estate! Value grows out of location, quality of construction, income potential, and future trends in the area (improvement or decline).

To show you how you can cash in on value during tough times, look at what a friend of mine is doing during the tough times prevailing at this writing:

> Tom T., a friend, set up a venture fund limited partnership to raise $3 million from 30 investors ($100,000 each) to buy condominium apartments at distress prices. The partnership will hold the condos until their price rises enough to allow them to be sold off at a profit. Meanwhile,

the condos will be rented to tenants at $1,900 to $2,500 per month to offset expenses and give the partners a modest return on their investment. Each investor will receive about a 5 percent return while the apartments are rented. When a condo is sold, the profit could be much larger.

So Tom gets the advantage of venture funds which do not have to be repaid. Meanwhile, he can run his condo empire on OPM and share in a big profit when the units are sold. His leverage is enormous!

Ten key factors controlling the value of any real estate are:

1. Location
2. Construction quality
3. Operating cost
4. Labor requirements
5. Size of units
6. Income
7. Neighborhood trends
8. Property condition
9. Rent level versus competition
10. Plumbing/wiring age

Use this list as a guide when choosing properties for your investments. The key thought in every purchase is: *Get maximum value for minimum dollars!* Readers who use these guidelines call or write to say:

> *I have eight rental units, thanks to the information I got from reading your real estate books. Now I have an owner who says he will finance property for a person having experience in managing rental units.*

> *And*

> *I was homeless, without even an auto, but I managed to buy 69 income units with zero cash down. I was so poor I had to take a bus to my first closing. Yet I've never been to a bank for these deals—they're all owner financed. My income is $37,000 a year from real estate. And I'm getting ready to buy a plumbing company doing $480,000 a year.*

I'm no longer homeless. And it took just a year to go from homeless to a very nice income with a brilliant future!

HOW TO GET RICH IN REAL ESTATE ANYWHERE, ANY TIME

Real estate has been with us since the days of the cavemen! And it will never go away—people will always need a nice place to live, a factory, land for development, and so on. So you might say: Real estate is forever, because it is.

Know what makes real estate attractive to renters and buyers and you can get richer than you ever thought possible. General elements making real estate attractive to people include:

- Location
- Closeness to transportation
- Shopping nearby
- Spacious units
- Cleanliness
- Freedom from crime
- Construction quality
- Affordability
- Neighborhood stability

Seek these elements in every property you buy. You will *not* go wrong when you seek these elements—and others—in *every* property you buy.

AVOID THE NIGHTMARE OF BUYING THE WRONG PROPERTY

Let's face it—real estate is partly an emotional business. I know that when a BWB asks me to lend him or her money on a beautiful piece of property that the appearance of the real estate often entices me to take greater risks than my lender's mind will allow. So even I'm affected by the emotional aspects of real estate! But I'm supposed to be a "tough" lender (I'm really not) who sees only the numbers of the deal.

Buying the wrong real estate for you can be a mistake. You really won't be penalized for life. But you may have a few years of tight money. That's why it's important that *every* piece of real estate *you* buy be a good "fit" for you.

To ensure a good fit, take these easy steps:

- Know what kind of real estate *you* like.
- Spend time getting to know the ins and outs of your kind of real estate.
- Visualize owning the real estate you like; go through the ownership in your mind.
- Avoid buying any real estate until you've visited proper. ties, talked to owners, and done "dry runs" in your head.

Buying the wrong real estate is *not* a death sentence for your career. But why make a mistake when it's so easy to get the *right* property?

SMART TECHNIQUES FOR GETTING JACKPOT PROPERTIES

Real estate BWBs who plan their future hit the jackpot every day. And *you* can do the same. All it takes is sensible use of proven techniques. Here are a number of such techniques you use—starting this instant:

- *Look for real estate workouts.* These are deals in which a lender extends the maturity date of a loan to reduce the monthly principal and interest payments to avoid foreclosure. Workouts offer you big opportunities to get trophy projects at prices way below market value. Where can *you* find such deals? Watch the real estate sections of both local and national papers. You'll often spot good deals there.
- *Watch for turnarounds.* These are deals in which a rundown property is fixed up and commands much higher rents or selling price. You can often buy a turnaround for a bargain price—especially if the seller has "rehab fatigue," that is, he or she is weary of fixing up and wants a quick out. *You* can be the one to provide that out at a big saving to yourself!
- *Attend local property auctions.* They're fun and educational! You'll learn plenty about local property at such auctions. What's more, you'll

meet many local real estate movers and shakers. These people, when they see how sincere you are, will likely steer you to many profitable deals. And your only cost is the gas or carfare to get to the auction!

- *Explore tax foreclosure certificates in your area.* This is one way to acquire good properties or make money from them without ever owning the real estate. These certificates can be bought from local tax authorities for properties on which owners have not paid their property taxes. Once you own one of these low-cost certificates, you have the right to wheel and deal to sell the property to others, take it over, or otherwise make money from it. It's another way to move in on jackpot properties with small cash outlays that can make *you* rich—soon!

- *Check the availability of government financing for real estate that meets the needs of a changing population, namely senior living and long-term care facilities.* The government offers a variety of programs, including credit enhancement (making you a stronger borrower) via insurance on properties serving senior citizens. Programs worth getting free information on include the U.S. Department of Housing and Urban Development (HUD) 221 (d)(3) (Rehabilitation); 221 (d)(4) (Senior Multi-Family Housing); and 232 (Nursing Home and Board and Care). There's a booming market developing in the senior living and long-term care industries because the population of the U.S. is aging. This produces a strong demand for such properties. *You* can cash in on this demand by using the offered financing and/or guarantees available. Check HUD in your local telephone book.

- *Review tax-exempt financing available to start up, acquire, or expand senior living communities.* Tax-exempt financing for senior facilities is available from both national and local sources. You can make some of this financing yours to build your wealth if you concentrate on senior living start-ups, acquisition, or expansion. There is such a great need for such facilities that there is enormous pressure on agencies to get money out where it will produce clean, well-kept accommodations for seniors. Jump on the senior bandwagon and I guarantee you won't be disappointed! Check your local government for details.

- *Watch your local newspaper for bargains.* Sellers often try local ads after all else fails. That's when *you* can come to the rescue and take an ideal property off their hands for little or no cash out of your pocket.

- *Network with property owners in your area.* Share information on your plans and goals. Doing this will often put a "bug" in the seller's mind. So, when it's time to sell, the seller will think of you. And you may be the first to be offered the property on an "insider" basis. You can work out a suitable deal long before the vultures begin circling the prey, namely, that desirable property. Networking will not only get you sales—it will also give you lots of useful inside information about local properties.

- *Follow-up offers in your local owners association.* This is another source of jackpot properties. You will often be given a chance to buy a property long before the general public knows about it. If a seller is weary of a property and wants to get out quickly, you're in a great position to offer a responsible and safe deal. A seller will often reduce the sales price to a person he or she thinks is sure to take good care of the property and run it profitably. It's better for any seller to get a few dollars less in a sale, knowing the buyer well, than to get a few more dollars from an unpredictable stranger. That's why it's important for you to join, and be active in, your local owners' association. The membership cost is small, compared to the many benefits you obtain.

- *See future uses for low-priced properties.* The United States Postal Service rents buildings for post offices, distribution centers, and maintenance facilities from private real estate firms and owners. The Service leases such properties for long terms—often 20 years. And their lease is as good as gold. Taking over properties which potentially are open to such leases can put you into an extremely comfortable financial position!

- *Arrange for a deferred down payment on a property if you don't have cash to put down.* Thus, if you defer a down payment for 120 days after the closing on a property, you may be able to get a second mortgage, property improvement loan, or a rent subsidy payment that will allow you to pay off the deferred down payment. You "buy" time when you defer the down payment while you take control of the property. And once the property is yours you can start to wheel and deal to get the loan for the down payment money. But with the property in your name, you work from a position of power. You don't have to beg for a loan!

- *Have current lenders subordinate their loans on the property.* This way, you can put a new loan on it. Often, it is easier to get a new first mortgage for a property than any other type of loan. Why? Because lenders are familiar and comfortable with first mortgages. So they're happy to lend on firsts because the paperwork and terms are familiar to them. By asking for a first mortgage, instead of a second or third, you zero in on the lender's "comfort zone."

- *Seek assumable loans on properties you want to buy.* Such a loan allows *you* to take over a desirable property with *no* credit check by a lender. This means that if your credit is shaky, you can get control of properties and start rebuilding your credit rating, all on your own. Meanwhile, of course, you'll have a nice positive cash flow from your properties. This will allow you to get a secured credit card. Having this, you can make purchases, repay quickly, and establish a solid new credit history. Within a year you should have an unsecured credit card with a sizable line of credit. And all of this grows out of taking over properties having an assumable mortgage!

- *Use an option to control a property while you seek to sell it to generate enough cash to buy it.* An option is a low-cost way to control a property for 60, 90, or 120 days while you seek to sell it to someone else. For as little as $100 you can control a property worth multi-thousands. You lose your option money if you don't sell the property during the time limit. But the amount is so small that the gamble is worth it. And, if you're short of cash, or the amount asked for an option is more than you have on hand at the moment, try offering a promissory note for the option. You'll still have to pay if you can't sell the property. But your cash outlay is delayed.

- *Have seller take out a second mortgage for the down payment and you assume the payments with a "reverse flip."* That is, the property reverts to the seller if you fail to make all the payments due. And *every* payment you made is credited to the seller, as though he or she made them. The advantage of this approach is that the seller gets the down payment (or even more, if desired) he or she seeks, *you* get control of the property, and the positive cash flow that is generated provides income for you and your employees.

- *Lease with an option to buy.* Here you rent a property with an option to buy it at some future date. The term of a lease option is much longer than with a straight option. Thus, the usual lease option will run one year, or longer. Some such options run for three years—depending on the view of the seller. While your lease option is running, you can rent out the property and derive a positive cash flow from it. Meanwhile, of course, the property is rising in value as time passes. With a long lease option you can position yourself to sell the property for the high-est price possible.

Do these methods work? They most certainly *do!* How do I know? From the letters and phone calls that come in from readers almost every day of the year. Like these:

I will be acquiring two properties this week for a low down payment of $100 because of the ad I placed in the IWS Newsletter. Last month I bought two older doubles for zero cash down. The newsletter and your books have been a big help. I can now start working for myself and stop working for other people.

And

We are very active in. the Canadian real estate market and have just gained control of another property (via option with no expiration date) valued at $5,850,000—again with NO money down.

And

I built a real estate fortune on your ideas, Ty, starting by borrowing $27,000, using your idea of multiple loans. Today I have a booming real estate business and I estimate my net worth as $3,500,000—built in just 5 years in my spare time on borrowed money—without putting up a cent of my own money. Thank you for giving me the idea.

And

Ty—we're off and running. Borrowed $400,000 as follows:

Equity loan	*$100,000*
Land acquisition loan	*231,000*
Signature loan	*69,000*
Total	*$400,000*

You said it could be done! Cost of property was $390,000. All monies borrowed from savings and loan which has our home mortgage. The same bank is giving us construction money, too. When we found the right bank they sold us on our project! Thank you very much for your assistance.

The message in all these notes and calls from readers is: You, too, can get rich in real estate—in good times and bad times. You just have to set your goals and then take the right steps to make them come true!

SUCCESS STRATEGIES FOR BUILDING YOUR REAL ESTATE WEALTH IN GOOD TIMES AND BAD TIMES

1. Don't overlook parking lot and parking garages as your source of real estate wealth. With enormous proliferation of autos, SUVs, vans, and similar vehicles, parking space is at a premium in every large city. For example, one parking garage operator in a large eastern city charges $1,000 a month for *one* parking space for *one* car! And do you know what? He has a waiting list of auto owners wanting his $1,000-per-month parking spaces! Another multi-family building owner having an underground parking garage leases it to an operator for $1-million a year! He gets some $83,333.33 per month for just making the space available. He never parks a car, never deals with an irate customer wanting his/her car in a hurry! When you own or operate a parking garage or parking lot you receive an income from your "tenants"—i.e. your short-term (a day or less) parkers. You may also have monthly parkers who pay you every 30 days—anywhere from $100 to $1,000 a month. And while these people are paying you to use your owned or leased space, the value of your owned building and land are rising. When you're ready to sell owned parking property you're almost certain to make a profit on it!

2. Look for industry-specialist lenders. Thus, there are lenders who specialize in real estate loans for companies in various businesses—such as printing, marinas, airports, textiles, auto factories, gas stations, etc. Such lenders often have lower lending requirements because they know the inside details of the specialized business. As such, they can see opportunities more clearly than a lender who knows nothing about the business and turns down a loan application for just this reason. Look in industry publications (magazines, newspapers, and website) for *Money Available* ads run by specialist lenders. You'll be delighted with the reception you're given—they'll make you feel you're doing them a favor by borrowing their money for specialized real estate use!

3. Look for 100 percent financing lenders. There *really* are such lenders operating today. My staff researches constantly for 100 percent financing lenders. And I share this information with subscribers to my *International Wealth Success* newsletter. The reason I do this is because my subscribers—by their act of sending me money to subscribe for two years or longer—show they're serious about earning big money in real estate. People who are not subscribers call me and want an analysis of a real estate project on the telephone, along with full data on three or four lenders who will do the deal quickly at a low interest rate, even though the borrower has bad credit. Such a request is foolish because (a) I can't analyze a deal without the numbers on a piece of paper in front of me; (b) We never give a final response on the phone—its always done in writing; (c) You can't get big real estate loans when you have bad credit unless you have the help of a cosigner, comaker, or guarantor; (d) You haven't shown me your deep sincerity by taking a step to better yourself by getting more information—such as from my newsletter, real estate magazines, or real estate books.

4. Build a list of aggressive lenders—who tell you they're aggressive by their ad which say things such as: "Bad Credit, No Problem"; "Bankruptcy, OK—No Problem"; "Quick CASH, Regardless of Your Credit Rating!"; "No Credit Check, No Documentation"; etc. Such words show that the lender is aggressively pushing loans out into the marketplace to increase their income. You can help them achieve their goals by taking out as many loans as you need. This will make the lender(s) happy and delight you also because the loan(s) you get will help you build your fortune while increasing the lenders interest income. Work with local aggressive lenders at the start when the properties you're buying usually are smaller. When you move on to larger properties—say 50 units and up—you can work with distant lenders who make bigger loans. Some lenders will telegraph their aggressiveness with the message "Brokers Protected," or "Brokers Welcome." These messages mean that the lender is trying to expand its world by working with brokers who will find borrowers for the lender. Why don't you help both a broker and a lender and become a big borrower to build your real estate riches? You'll be helping the world while helping yourself!

IMPORTANT POINTERS TO KEEP IN MIND

- Real estate is your best bet for future wealth, especially if you want to do spare-time work while you hold your regular job.
- Real estate offers *you* many advantages, including tax favored income protection, control of an income asset with no upfront investment, cheap financing, and bargain-basement opportunities.
- Zero cash properties *are* available—if you look for them.
- You can save big bucks with shrewd mortgage payoff methods.
- Tax-free swaps and a guaranteed monthly income *are* possible if you seek them out in the sources given in this chapter.
- Leverage can make *you* rich—if approached carefully.
- Watch for the general elements which make real estate attractive, including location, transportation nearness, availability of shopping, spacious units, cleanliness, freedom from crime, and quality.
- Jackpot properties *are* available to *you,* but you must seek them out using the many opportunities open to you.

Your Riches Timetable for Great Real Estate Wealth

The worst of times are often seen as the best of times by ambitious BWBs. This is so true in real estate that smart BWBs buy in bad times because they see such days as giving them the best (lowest-price) bargains.

Thousands of fortunes are built by BWBs who start their business when property prices are abnormally low. You—too—can start building *your* fortune if you use a simple timetable.

Some BWBs try to bumble along without a timetable for their future wealth. While such an approach may work for some, it causes much lost time and energy for most folks. I don't want *you* to lose one moment in building your wealth and financial freedom. So I strongly recommend that you create a timetable for yourself—starting right now!

TIMETABLE YOURSELF OUT OF THE 9-TO-5 RAT RACE

A timetable—which is a plan with dates—focuses your thoughts and energies. It frees you from a number of worries, allowing you to concentrate on bringing in that beautiful four-letter commodity—*cash!*

Now don't be frightened by the word timetable. Making one up for your future wealth can be fun. And having your plan in the form of a timetable can give you a great feeling of freedom. Why? Because you know that your planning work is done. Now all you have to do is find the properties you want, take them over, and start depositing the steady stream of cash that flows your way! Let's see how *you* can use a timetable to give you the freedom and success you seek.

Elements of Any Good Timetable

Every good timetable gives *you* key facts about your wealth plan. The timetable tells:

- *What* you will do on your path to wealth
- *When* you will complete certain steps in your plan
- *How* you will achieve your desired results

While you can carry a timetable around in your head, as some people do, I strongly suggest that you *write out* your timetable. Why? Because when you write out a timetable you:

- Fix your plans in your mind
- See ways in which your plan can be improved
- Give yourself a strong push toward success
- Direct your energies toward specific goals, instead of wandering idly from one impulse to another

While you may not yet know the exact *what, when,* and *how* of your timetable when you sit down to write it out, the thinking you do *will* help you come up with specific answers for these three questions for *you!* Let's look more closely at how *you* can prepare *your* wealth timetable.

If you don't like paper and ink, you can use your computer spreadsheet program to prepare your timetable. This will save you time and energy. And if you have a laptop computer you can put your timetable on your hard drive and carry it with you whenever you're traveling around on your real estate business. Then it will be easy to make new entries on the spot as conditions change.

How to Plan Your Release from Your Daily Grind

You, we'll say, have a regular job you've held for some time. But you want *out* of the job as quickly as possible, while you develop another income for yourself and loved ones. And this other income, you've decided, must come from real estate. So the *what* of your timetable is:

Develop an alternate source of income from real estate that will exceed my present job income. I will develop this alternate income from the cash flow provided to me by the ownership of _____ real estate. (Fill in the blank after writing out this *what* on a page in your riches notebook; use the guidelines in Chapter 2 to select the type of real estate *you* want to use to build *your* wealth.)

Decide on the *when* of your timetable by using the probable cash flow from your acquired properties to replace the lost income from your job—after you leave it. But play it safe here! How? By planning on bringing in at least $1.50 for every $1.00 you give up on your job. Why? Because by seeking a larger cash flow from your alternate income you'll protect yourself against downturns or other temporary reverses in the real estate market. You'll be able to weather any storm.

So the *when* of your timetable might look like this:

Build an income of $1.50 per $1.00 of my regular income starting July 1 of this year. The positive cash flow to me, after *all* expenses, should reach half of my current job salary after 18 months of investing in income real estate. In 48 months my real estate income should be 1.5 times my regular job income, at which time I can quit my job!

Now we come to the *how* of your timetable. Each of you will probably pick a different *how*. Why? Because conditions vary from one area to another. So the *how* will also vary, depending on the real estate situation in *your* area.

But for purposes of illustration, let's take a typical *how* and see how it will be worked out. Our BWB decides that he or she will build their real estate riches:

1. Borrow the down payment for income property from suitable lenders
2. Buy the income properties chosen using the borrowed money for the down payment
3. Choose only positive cash flow properties
4. Expand my holdings by using the acquired properties as collateral for more loans to buy other income properties

The lenders you choose can come from many sources. Thus, you might seek—as a 2-year subscriber to my newsletter—money from my firm, you might ask the seller to help you by getting a loan which you repay in a reverse flip, you might ask a tenant in the building to put up the cash for the down payment, or you might use any of the many other methods given earlier in this book. The main point is that you do *not* put any of your own money into the deal.

> One reader took over a $15.8 million office building with zero cash down by having the major tenant in the building put up the cash for the down payment. The reader will repay this money to the tenant over a period of years. There's a total annual cash flow of $1.2 million to the reader from this property. After paying all costs, including mortgages, he still has a hefty positive cash flow of over $100,000 per year from the property. This reader got into real estate after he was injured on his job as a painter and wallpaper specialist. A back injury prevented him from lifting anything heavy. So he switched to investing in real estate and has a booming business which grew from nothing to a profitable empire in just two years. He has other properties besides this one.

You can do the same! It just takes some planning with your simple timetable. Without such a guide your efforts are likely to be much less productive. Just be sure that the financial goals you select for yourself are in keeping with the ones you chose earlier in this book. Consistent effort will deliver the results *you* seek.

When you relate your time and money goals in your timetable, you release a powerful creative force within yourself. This force pushes you into doing the important things for *your* success.

Exhibit 14–1 shows a typical BWB's timetable. You can prepare your own timetable using this one as a guide.

PUT YOUR TIMETABLE TO WORK FOR YOUR FUTURE WEALTH AND FREEDOM

Real estate is such a great business that almost any creative person can become wealthy in it. Here are a few techniques that will work almost anywhere for *you:*

- *Real estate does "come back."* Every downturn in real estate history is followed by an upturn that's stronger than the trend before the falloff. Downturns give *you* a Exhibit 14–1 rare opportunity to buy income property at wholesale prices. Never run scared during a downturn—it's the best time to be daring and aggressive!

Exhibit 14–1

TYPICAL BWB'S RICHES TIMETABLE

STEP NO	WHEN I WILL COMPLETE THIS STEP	WHAT I WILL DO	HOW I WILL COMPLETE THIS STEP
1	By end of month 1	Find interested lenders	By calling and writing suitable lenders
2	By end of month 3	Find suitable income property with positive cash flow	By looking at local and national real estate ads every week; contacting brokers
3	By end of month 4	Buy the chosen income property	By borrowing any needed down payment; getting long-term mortgage for balance
4	By end of month 5	Choose second income property to buy	By using all available information sources
5	By end of month 6	Buy second income property	By using other people's money to buy
6	By end of month 7	Check organization and income earned	By reviewing business with an accountant
7	By end of month 8	Buy income property no. 3	By using 100 percent financing for the purchase
8	By end of month 12	Buy two more suitable income properties	By using 100 percent financing with earlier properties as collateral
9	By end of month 13	Review real estate income; compare with job income and the $1.50 per $1.00 goal	By comparing actual income with desired income; take steps to increase actual income, if necessary
10	By end of month 24	Continue buying suitable income properties	By using 100 percent financing in all possible purchases

- *You can find the lenders you need.* All you must do is look for them, using the techniques given you in this book. I know of lenders who allow you to have a second mortgage on a property for the down payment. This means *you* can get 100+ percent financing for a property when you use such lenders. How'd I find these lenders? I *looked* for them! All it took was a few phone calls and I had their information (called *lending parameters*) detailing how much they would lend under what circumstances. I'll be glad to share such data with you if you're a 2-year, or longer, subscriber to my IWS newsletter.

- *You can develop fee income to smooth out a decline in real estate income during bad times.* Thus, as noted earlier, one reader put together a $2.7 million real estate loan and earned a $27,000, or 1 percent, commission for his work. This amount of income would help if there were a downturn in his real estate income from rental sources. *You,* too, can do the same! I have dozens of lenders who'd be delighted to pay you a hefty commission for bringing them good real estate loans of all kinds.

- *Use a "broker of record" in your real estate corporation to engage in commission generating activities to smooth out your income.* Remember this: You do *not* need any kind of real estate license to invest in income properties, speculation properties, construction projects, and so on. But a broker of record *does* allow you to engage in fee generating projects completely legally.

- *Apply at "Brokers Protected" lenders when all other lenders turn you down.* Why? Because brokers protected lenders are usually looking for borrowers. So they'll welcome you, instead of rejecting you! Go where you're welcome. You'll even be able to beat your timetable by getting money sooner than you planned!

- *Self-liquidating loans are possible from domestic lenders.* But I've never heard of one that went through with an overseas lender. Now my experience may be limited to only a few million readers, so I could be wrong! In my research for lenders of all kinds I've uncovered some who make self-liquidating loans, that is, loans that pay themselves off over a period of time. But *all* these lenders are in the United States. This type of loan can be a powerful source of money for you in your search for real estate wealth to free yourself from the servitude of a weekly paycheck.

- *Combine your hobby with real estate by investing in properties in tune with your interests.* Thus, boating enthusiasts—like myself— often invest in marinas. Ownership of such a property can be rewarding both financially and recreationally. Golf enthusiasts often consider investing in a golf course. Since there are a number of lenders specializing in golf courses (as there are in marinas), funds *can* be obtained faster than you think. What's more, when you invest in property that "turns you on" you do a better job. As a result, your investment prospers quickly. This can help you beat your timetable while you remove yourself from your daily chores for a cranky boss.

- *Know your cost and income per square foot for all properties you handle.* Why? Because this is the only objective way for comparing two or more properties. Knowing your square foot numbers allows you to make quick estimates of prices and incomes. Since such estimates can eventually put money into *your* bank, it's important that you know how—and when—to compare costs! Do it by the square foot method—everybody understands it!

- *Look for "cramdown" values to save money.* A cram-down occurs when a court reduces the value of a loan on a property—usually during a bankruptcy proceeding. In a Chapter 13 bankruptcy, a judge will reduce the loan on a home to the current market value of the house. This means you can "pick up" the property at a bargain price. Doing so gives you a good example of how *you* can make money from real estate in good times and bad times. The cramdown property you buy in bad times is almost certain to rise in value in good times. You can then sell it at a good profit. Meanwhile, you will rent the property to pay expenses plus a positive cash flow to you, while you're holding it for resale.

- *Keep an eye on the absorption and overhang of rental property.* When space is rented, it is "absorbed" in rental agent terms. If a property is being absorbed quickly in your area, you have an active rental market. You can raise rents on vacant space and increase your cash flow from space you have available. But if there's an *overhang* in your area, more property is being vacated than is being rented. When this happens, consider reducing rents for new tenants to induce them to rent your property instead of that next door. This way you'll reach your timetable goals faster!

- *Be alert to population trends when buying real estate.* With an aging population (some 90 million people over 65 by the middle of the next century), there's a booming market in retirement housing and similar facilities for seniors. While you don't have to go out and start building retirement homes, you can get ready for the boom by adapting your present holdings to this age group—if it will make money for *you!* But if you see another group developing in your area, such as young marrieds, you should also go after it. Why? Because catering to emerging markets can put extra cash in *your* bank every month.

- *Explore new uses for older buildings.* With many neighborhoods in decline in large cities, BWBs are making big bucks finding new uses for older buildings they grab for just pennies on the dollar. Many older buildings are better built than newer ones. Sure, these buildings often need rehabbing. But if you enjoy doing, or supervising, such work, older buildings can make *you* a fortune!

- *Keep up to date on tax changes for real estate.* New tax laws change the structure of some real estate deals. By keeping up to date on the changes which occur every few years, you can increase the money you raise for your real estate deals. Thus, some people think that real estate limited partnerships are out because of tax law changes. This is *not* true! Limited partnerships for affordable rental housing for low-income people are alive and booming. Why? Because such partnerships offer *tax credits* of up to $8,250 per year (at this writing) for investors. This credit offsets, dollar for dollar, federal tax on other income the investor may have. So it's a powerful incentive for putting money into a limited partnership you use to raise funds for *your* real estate investments. Having limited partners eliminates your having to borrow money. Instead, your investors put up money with no credit check, *no* collateral (other than the property to be bought at a later date), *no* job history requirement for you. Truly, the limited partnership *is* the way to go when you're seeking real estate money without borrowing.

- *Be alert for profit opportunities in your timetable.* One real estate investor bought a building from a cash-hungry seller for $14 million. Six years later he sold the building *back* to the same seller for a $43 million profit! That's an average of $7 million a year profit from just one building. How did he do it? By being alert to the opportunities available in the real estate market.

- *Be sure to take any equity you can out of a property when you need cash for your next property.* Do *not* take equity cash out of a property (with a home equity or second mortgage loan) to buy personal items like a TV auto, clothes, and so on. Take equity out *only* to meet, or improve on, your investment timetable. Then you'll be operating your real estate investments at the most efficient pace.

- *Get a lender who'll make you a bridge loan to allow you to buy a new property while you have an older one up for sale.* The sale of your older property repays the bridge loan which was the down payment on your new property! Having a bridge lender on tap can allow you to meet your timetable deadlines easily, without stress or strain!

- *Bring in foreign lenders and/or investors when your real estate deals go big time.* You won't get foreign lenders or investors interested in a small 10- or 20-unit building. But they will be happy to look at a new office structure, a shopping plaza, and so on. Show foreign lenders and investors only trophy projects. Then you'll have a much better chance of getting the money you seek!

- *If you don't like people, consider ministorage real estate.* These small self-storage warehouses are booming around the world. With 24-hour access, all you need is a person with a set of keys on duty. *You* never see your tenants. So you don't have to deal with people! You make money to free you from your payroll blues but do it in a way that makes you happy. Meanwhile, the land on which your ministorage building sits will rise in value as time passes. So you'll get more for the land when you sell—meaning that your total income from the investment is greater than just your cash flow!

- *Take a balloon loan whenever you can.* It can help you meet your timetable dates sooner. On a balloon loan (also called a *standing mortgage)* you pay interest only on a loan for a stated number of years— often 3 to 10 years. With a balloon loan you can hold a property while you take a strong cash flow from it every month. Meanwhile, you're making much smaller monthly payments because you're paying only the interest on the loan, instead of principal and interest. While you hold the property it will rise in value. Then, when the time for repayment of the balloon loan approaches, you can either sell the property at a nice profit and pay off the balloon loan or refinance the balloon loan (possibly at a lower rate), and continue collecting your monthly cash flow. Where can *you* get your next balloon loan? Try any conventional real estate lender—many will make the balloon loan you seek!

- *If you lease space in your property to tenants, be sure to index your rent to the rate of inflation.* This way, if inflation increases you'll collect more in the rents you receive. Since inflation has been with us since the invention of money, it's foolish to ignore it in your rentals. Keying your rents to inflation will increase your income as time passes—I guarantee this to you!

- *Consider converting your real estate holdings to some form of a security in which you sell off part of your ownership for cash in hand in big chunks of money.* You can convert your holdings to a real estate investment trust (REIT), a finite-life real estate investment trust (FREIT), a limited partnership (LP), or a master limited partnership (MLP). To use any of these vehicles you *must* have qualified legal and accounting advice. So take steps to form a strong relationship with qualified legal and accounting personnel. Then get them to help you. You may even beat your timetable dates when you turn your holdings into securities!

- *Keep close to lenders—it can pay off in better deals.* People who know that my two organizations make real estate loans keep in touch by calling me every few weeks. They tell me about their new deals and what they expect to earn from each. This is useful information for me because I can use the principles involved (what the BWB is doing, and how) to guide other BWBs who need help. I *never* reveal the name, location, or specifics about the deals people report on. But the *methods* these BWBs are using to put together successful deals *are* important to other, upcoming BWBs. So I emphasize the methods—just as I have throughout this book.

- *Learn all you can about real estate.* Knowledge is power! The more you know about real estate, about lenders who can help you, and about ways to build *your* wealth, the faster you'll free yourself from the shackles of a hated job. To increase your know-how, keep reading and learning. It can take you out of the poorhouse and put you into a castle of *your* choice. In the appendix to this book I give you many valuable books, newsletters, and kits on making money in real estate. Use these sources to improve your know-how. The money you spend on education will be repaid many times over. Knowledge—as you know—*is* power! Using their timetable and knowledge of real estate, many BWBs build large cash flows from their properties. They even develop bonus income from other income generators on their properties—like parking facilities, recreation rooms, washing machines and dryers, and so on. You, too, *can* do the same.

As you know, my readers regard me as their friend. Why? Because I *am* a friend to every reader—including *you!* I hope you can write me someday to tell me of *your* success, as these readers have:

> *Thanks. Things are working out just as you said. No cash down is possible. I bought 25 acres of prime land without one penny of mine. I completed a joint venture where I obtained the land with no down payment and payable to the seller only when the planned construction of resort cottages is completed and sold.*

And

> *It has been several months now since our luncheon meeting in Manhattan when I ordered your "Real Estate Loan Getters Service." The information from this material enabled me to obtain financing for three different properties. The first was for 95 percent financing of a duplex in my hometown. The second was for 100 percent financing of raw land. The third is a single-family home on which I was able to obtain 105 percent financing which will net me 700 percent after closing costs and points. I have signed a lease which will net me a small positive cash flow with the tenant responsible for all repair and maintenance. I am on my way to building wealth, and I thank you for a great part of this.*

And

> *I'm writing after reading your book How to Borrow Your Way to Real Estate Riches. I've been to various real estate seminars and through many courses, but your book taught me more than all of them combined—especially the depth you went into on preparing a winning loan application package to borrow from any lender. I recently bought a really nice villa, using one of your no-money-down techniques (a lease option). I did this even though I went through a Chapter 7 bankruptcy!*

And

I bought several of your books and subscribe to your newsletter. I currently own 20 pieces of income property and am interested in forming a real estate investment trust. I have been very successful in buying properties at a good price and upgrading their value in a short time. I have followed several of the suggestions in your books and have thereby increased my net worth greatly. Thank you.

And

I spoke to some mortgage banks (as you suggested) and they can lend me $400,000 on this property.

And

I subscribed to the IWS Newsletter in November and bought my first income property with no money down the same month. I got an investor's loan from a local S&L, and the seller paid all closing costs and took back a second mortgage for the balance of the purchase price. This duplex gives me about $100 per month profit after the two mortgage payments and all expenses. Not bad for no cash investment of my own. Now this same property owner wants to sell me four other properties under the same terms. I'm on my way to building my wealth in real estate.

SUCCESS STRATEGIES FOR BUILDING YOUR REAL ESTATE WEALTH IN GOOD TIMES AND BAD TIMES

1. Use the cram-down features of foreclosures to reduce payoff time for low-cost properties you buy. In many foreclosure sales any second or third mortgages that exist on the foreclosed property are crammed down—that is settled for one dollar each, or the property value obtained at the auction. Either way, such junior mortgages are wiped out as far as you're concerned. The effect on you? It shortens your payoff time for the foreclosure property you buy at auction. Thus, if a property has a $25,000 third mortgage on it and a $50,000 second mortgage and you buy the property at auction for $30,000, the two junior mortgages which equal $25,000 + $50,000 = $75,000, are crammed down to $30,000, the amount you pay for the property. It will take a lot less time for you to pay off a $30,000 mortgage than it will to pay off a $105,000 mortgage (= $30,000 + $25,000 + $50,000). Thus, you can say that if you want to save time in building your real estate fortune that your plans should include the use of foreclosures to acquire multiple properties quickly, at low cost!

2. Become the "perfect buyer" for motivated sellers to keep your wealth timetable on track. Let's face it. Convincing a seller to cut you a zero-cash deal, give you a "reverse flip" sale, or take out an equity loan for his/her down payment isn't easy! You have to sell yourself and your ideas to a suspicious, doubting, non-trusting seller who may have been burned in earlier deals. And this isn't easy, especially if the seller has other buyers in view. To buy the property you want and make a reluctant seller choose you over other buyers, take these easy steps: (a) Prepare a short business plan—one to two pages—showing how you'll improve the property; (b) Write a short "position paper" in the form of a letter to the seller telling him/her how much you're interested in the property, what you'll do to serve the tenants well, and where you plan to make improvements to bring the building back to its former glory; (c) Give full data on your former real estate experience (if any) and your real estate education—such as self-study of books like this one. If you have earlier real estate experience, give details on how you improved a property's income, condition, and salability. While all of this may seem a chore to you, the amount of money and time you can save is enormous, if the work gets you a zero-down deal.

3. Build a list of specialty lenders—such as those for senior housing, marinas, golf courses, motels, etc.—for the types of properties you plan to invest in. Having such a list handy will save you time and help you keep to your timetable when you find a property that interests you. To build such a list, read suitable real estate publications. Thus, my *Money Watch Bulletin* newsletter gives you 100 active business and real estate lenders each month. We often feature specialty lenders, giving 20 or more such lenders who are actively seeking to make loans *now*. Building your list of specialty lenders will also keep you focused on the types of real estate projects you've selected to build great wealth for yourself in this wonderful business. And—good friend—focus is what pays profits in any business!

4. Keep this book's message in front of you at all times and you'll be successful in real estate in good times and bad times. The message for your success is this: (a) Real estate *can* make you *rich* in good times and bad times; (b) Zero-cash real estate—where you take over property using borrowed money—is the best way to start in this business today; (c) Foreclosure properties are a powerful way to start on little cash; (d) You can mortgage out—get money at the closing—if you arrange financing right; (e) To build your real estate wealth quickly, buy two properties a month with no down payment on either; (f) Use top-line management—steady cash flow—to ensure your financial success in real estate today; (g) Start building your real estate fortune while still holding your regular job; don't leave your job until you're sure your real estate income can support you and your loved ones; (h) Borrow to buy real estate—everyone borrows in real estate; (i) Use your real estate income to get rid of your 9-to-5 (or other time frame) drudgery; (j) Look for—and find—offbeat financing methods to speed your real estate wealth building; (k) Use time to build your real estate wealth—time does work for you in real estate; (l) Put little-known ways to work to build your real estate fortune; (m) Let smart methods help you build your real estate wealth faster; (n) Prepare—and follow—a wealth-building timetable for your real estate fortune!

IMPORTANT POINTERS TO KEEP IN MIND

* A simple timetable can take *you* out of the daily job rat race and put you into a safe, secure, and profitable real estate business of your own where you're the boss.
* A good timetable tells *you* the *what, when,* and *how* of your real estate wealth building.
* You *can* build riches in real estate—like many others have—during both good times and bad times—by following the plans you lay out in your timetable.
* Remember, at all times, that real estate *does* come back! It has in every downturn in history. You can count on it. So prepare your timetable to reflect the rise in the future value of your properties!
* You *can* find the lenders you need! If all others say no, you can always try your friend, Ty Hicks. He may be able to help you.
* Keep close to lenders. They can be the best friends you'll ever have because they can help you when you need assistance.

- Learn *all* you can about real estate. Keep reading and studying good books and courses. Their cost is peanuts compared to the riches you can earn from just one *good* idea!

- If you have questions you can't get answered on the phone by other people, you can always call your author, Ty Hicks, and I'll be glad to help—if you're a 2-year, or longer, subscriber to either of my newsletters. And if my phone answer isn't good enough, we can always meet for lunch in Manhattan—and I'll answer your questions *and* pay for your lunch! My business phone number is 516-766-5850; my business fax number is 516-766-5919.

Appendix

Helpful Real Estate Money Books, Kits, and Newsletters

"Knowledge is power" is so true in real estate that every successful BWB I know (and I know thousands) reads several good books each year. And these same BWBs often subscribe to newsletters serving the field.

Since I know you, too, want to be a successful BWB, called an SWB, here are a number of excellent real estate books, kits, and newsletters. These publications will help broaden your knowledge of the great field of real estate. And they *will* put money into *your* pocket. Why? Because, as we said, before, *knowledge is power!*

Our first list is a partial compilation of some of the many excellent real estate and business management books available from Prentice Hall—probably the largest publisher of real estate and management books in the United States, if not the world. So I recommend these excellent real estate and management books to you. They will surely help you build *your* fortune in real estate, starting today!

REAL ESTATE INVESTMENT AND MANAGEMENT BOOKS

Albrecht, Mike, *Computerizing Your Business,* 192 pages.

Bartlett, William, *Mortgage-Backed Securities,* 528 pages.

Blankenship, F., *Prentice Hall Real Estate Investor's Encyclopedia,* 556 pages.

Blankenship, F., *Semenow's Questions and Answers on Real Estate,* 720 pages.

Cummings, Jack, *Real Estate Finance and Investment Manual,* 480 pages.

Ferris, Kenneth, et. al., *Understanding Financial Statements,* 320 pages.

Fuchs, Sheldon, *Complete Building Equipment Maintenance Desk Book,* 656 pages.

Fuller, George, *The Negotiator's Handbook,* 304 pages.

Handmaker, Stuart A., *Choosing a Legal Structure for Your Business,* 192 pages.

Hetrick, Patrick and Outlaw, Larry, *North Carolina Real Estate for Brokers and Salesmen,* 944 pages.

Hiam, Alexander, *The Vest-Pocket CEO,* 480 pages.

Hicks, Tyler, *How to Make One Million Dollars in Real Estate in Three Years Starting with No Cash,* 276 pages.

Hopkins, Tom, *How to Master the Art of Listing and Selling Real Estate,* 416 pages.

Hornwood, S. and Hollingsworth, I. L., *The Number One Real Estate Investment No One Talks About,* 254 pages.

Jackson, et. al., *Day-to-Day Business Accounting,* 192 pages.

Lorenz-Fife, Iris, *Financing Your Business,* 192 pages.

Loscalzo, William, *Cash-Flow Forecasting,* 192 pages.

Meyer, Harold and Sievert, Scott, *Credit and Collection Letters that Get Results,* 272 pages.

Oncken, William, *Managing Management Time,* 260 pages.

Prentice Hall Editorial Staff, *The Prentice Hall Small Business Survival Guide,* 480 pages.

Rye, David E., *The Vest-Pocket Entrepreneur,* 448 pages.

Shim, Jae and Siegel, Joel, *Budgeting Basics and Beyond,* 464 pages.

Tanzer, Milt, *Real Estate Investments and How to Make Them,* 352 pages.

Thomas, Paul I., *The Contractor's Field Guide,* 608 pages.

Tylczak, Lynn, *The Prentice Hall Credit and Collection Handbook,* 352 pages.

Winston, Arthur, *Complete Guide to Credit and Collection Law,* 720 pages.

Zuckerman, Howard, *Real Estate Development Workbook and Manual,* 768 pages.

REAL ESTATE SUCCESS KITS, BOOKS, REPORTS, AND NEWSLETTERS

The following are available from International Wealth Success, Inc. (IWS, Inc.), PO Box 186, Merrick, NY 11566-0186:

SUCCESS KITS

Fast Financing of Your Real Estate Fortune Success Kit shows you how to raise money for real estate deals. You can move ahead faster if you can finance your real estate quickly and easily. This is not the same kit as the R. E. Riches Kit listed above. Instead, the Fast Financing Kit concentrates on getting the money you need for your real estate deals. This kit gives you more than 2,500 sources of real estate money all over the United States. It also shows you how to find deals which return big income to you but are easier to finance than you might think! $99.50. 7 Speed-Read books, 523 pp., 8½" × 11" for most.

Financial Broker/Finder/Business Broker/Consultant Success Kit shows you how to start your private business as a Financial Broker! Finder/Business Broker/Consultant! As a financial broker you find money for firms seeking capital and you are paid a fee. As a finder you are paid a fee for finding things (real estate, raw materials, money, etc.) for people and firms. As a business broker you help in the buying or selling of a business—again for a fee. See how to collect big fees. Kit includes typical agreements you can use, plus four colorful membership cards (each 8" × 10"). $99.50. 12 Speed-Read books, 485 pp., 8½" × 11", four membership cards.

Foreclosures and Other Distressed Properties Kit shows you—with 6 audio cassette tapes and a comprehensive manual—how and where to find, and buy, foreclosed and other distressed properties of all types. Gives names, addresses and other data about agencies offering foreclosed properties—often at a bargain price. Presents forms giving examples of actual foreclosure documents and paperwork. $59.95. 150+ pp., 6 cassette audio tapes.

Hard Money Commercial Real Estate Loan Kit shows you how to raise hard money for commercial real estate—such as industrial and medical buildings, mixed-use properties, mobile home parks, apartment complexes, townhouse developments, residential sub-divisions, shopping malls and strip centers, hotels and motels, golf courses, nursing homes, offices, etc. Five-hour videotape and manual with comprehensive loan data and forms present useful guidance on how to do hard-money deals today. Covers financing from $300,000 to $20-million+; close in 1 to 3 weeks; nationwide lending; brokers protected; minimal documentation required; short form appraisals accepted; flexible loan structures. $150. 150+ pp., 8½" × 11"; 5-hour videotape and manual.

How to Build Your Real Estate Fortune Today in a Real Estate Investment Trust Kit shows you how to start a REIT to finance any type of real estate you want to invest in and earn money from. Gives you the exact steps to take to raise money for your real estate from either private or public sources. Today REITs raise millions for almost every type of real estate used by human beings—multi-family residential (apartment houses), factories, marinas, hotels, motels, shopping malls, nursing homes, hospitals, etc. REITs can own these types of properties, lend on them (issue mortgages), or make a combination of these investments. $100; 150+ pp., 8½" × 11".

Loans by Mail Kit shows you how and where to get business, real estate, and personal loans for yourself and others by mail. Lists hundred of lenders who loan by mail. No need to appear in person—just fill out the loan application and send it in by mail. Many of these lenders give unsecured signature loans to qualified applicants. Use this kit to get a loan by mail yourself. Or become a loan broker and use the kit to get started. Unsecured signature loans by mail can go as high as $50,000 and this kit lists such lenders. $100; 150 pp., 8½" × 11".

Loans by Phone Kit shows you how and where to get business, real estate, and personal loans by telephone. With just 32 words and 15 seconds of time you can determine if a lender is interested in the loan you seek for yourself or for someone who is your client—if you're working as a loan broker or finder. This kit gives you hundreds of telephone lenders. About half have 800 phone numbers, meaning that your call is free of long-distance charges. Necessary agreement forms are also included. $100; 150+ pp.; 8½" × 11".

Mega Money Methods covers the raising of large amounts of money—multimillions and up—for business and real estate projects of all types. Shows how to prepare loan packages for very large loans, where to get financing for such loans, what fees to charge after the loan is obtained, plus much more. Using this kit, the BWB should be able to prepare effective loan requests for large amounts of money for suitable projects. The kit also gives the user a list of offshore lenders for big projects. $100; 200 pp., 8½" × 11".

Real-Estate Loan Getters Service Kit shows the user how to get real estate loans for either a client or the user. Lists hundreds of active real estate lenders seeking first and junior mortgage loans for a variety of property types. Loan amounts range from a few thousand dollars to many millions, depending on the property, its location, and value. Presents typical application and agreement forms for use in securing real estate loans. No license is required to obtain such loans for oneself or others. $100; 150+ pp.; 8½" × 11".

Real Estate Riches Success Kit shows you how to make big money in real estate as an income property owner, a mortgage broker, mortgage banker, real estate investment trust operator, mortgage money broker, raw land speculator, and industrial property owner. This is a general kit, covering all these aspects of real estate, plus many, many more. Includes many financing sources for your real estate fortune. But this big kit also covers how to buy real estate for the lowest price (down payments of no cash can sometimes be set up), and how to run your real estate for biggest profits. $99.50. 6 Speed-Read books, 466 pp. 8½" × 11".

Starting Millionaire Success Kit shows you how to get started in a number of businesses which might make you a millionaire sooner than you think! Businesses covered in this kit include mail order, real estate, export/import, limited partnerships, and so on. Kit includes four colorful membership cards (each 8" × 10"). These are not the same ones as in the financial broker kit. $99.50. 12 Speed-Read books, 361 pp., 8½" × 11", four membership cards.

Zero Cash Success Techniques Kit shows you how to get started in your own going business or real estate venture with no cash! Sound impossible? It really is possible—as thousands of folks have shown. This big kit, which includes a special book by Ty Hicks on *Zero Cash Takeovers of Business and Real Estate,* also includes a 58-minute cassette tape by Ty on "Small Business Financing." On this tape, Ty talks to you! See how you can get started in your own business without cash and with few credit checks. $99.50. 7 Speed-Read books, 876 pp., 8½" × 11" for most, 58-minute cassette tape.

REAL ESTATE BOOKS

Comprehensive Loan Sources for Business and Real Estate. Gives hundreds of lender's names, addresses, and lending requirements for many different types of business and real estate loans. Does *not* duplicate *Diversified Loan Sources.* 136 pp., 8½" × 11" $25.00.

Directory of 2,500 Active Real-Estate Lenders. Lists 2,500 names and addresses of direct lenders or sources of information on possible lenders for real estate. $25; 197 pp.

Diversified Loan Sources for Business and Real Estate. Gives hundreds of lender's names, addresses, and lending guidelines for business and real estate loans of many types. 136 pp., 8½" × 11" $25.00.

Guide to Business and Real Estate Loan Sources. Lists hundreds of business and real-estate lenders, giving their lending data in very brief form. $25; 201 pp.

How Anyone Can Prosper and Get Wealthy Trading Country Land by Frank Moss. Shows how to acquire wealth and have fun doing it in country land. Covers supply and demand, starting your own home-operated spare-time moneymaking business buying and selling woodland, estimating value, time/distance analysis, financing, buy/sell strategies, zero-cash deals, plus much more. $21.50. 100+ pp., 8½" × 11".

How to Be a Second Mortgage Loan Broker by Richard Brisky gives complete details on how to set up your office, find clients, find lenders, negotiate with clients and lenders, what fees to charge, how to comply with any licensing laws in the area of your business, what files to keep, plus much more. Using this book, a person can get started in this lucrative aspect of today's real estate market. $25.00. 90+ pp., 8½" × 11".

How to Create Your Own Real-Estate Fortune by Jens Nielsen. Covers investment opportunities in real estate, leveraging, depreciation, remodeling your deal, buy-and lease-back, understanding your financing. $17.50; 117 pp.

How to Finance Real Estate Investments by Roger Johnson. Covers basics, the lending environment, value, maximum financing, rental unit groups, buying mobile-home parks, and conversions. $21.50; 265 pp.

How to Find Hidden Wealth in Local Real Estate by R. H. Jorgensen. Covers financial tips, self-education, how to analyze property for renovation, the successful renovator is a "cheapskate," property management, and getting the rents paid. $17.50; 133 pp.

Ideas for Finding Business and Real Estate Capital Today. Covers raising public money, real estate financing, borrowing methods, government loan sources, and venture money. $24.50; 62 pp.

Rapid Real Estate and Business Loan-Getting Methods by Tyler Hicks, gives innovative techniques to get loans, ways in which real estate can make you rich, declaring your independence from the "9-to-5 grind," new steps to getting venture capital, smart-money ways to get loans, plus many other methods for getting the business financing you seek. $25.00. 90+ pp., 8½" × 11".

Real-Estate Second Mortgages by Ty Hicks. Covers second mortgages, how a second mortgage finder works, naming the business, registering the firm, running ads, expanding the business, and limited partnerships. $17.50; 100 pp.

Supplement to How to Borrow Your Way to Real Estate Riches. Using government sources compiled by Ty Hicks, lists numerous mortgage loans and guarantees, loan purposes, amounts, terms, financing charge, types of structures financed, loan-value ratio, special factors. $15; 87 pp.

REAL ESTATE REPORTS

Here are seven reports on various aspects of real estate finance. Each report is 8½" × 11" and presents essential information on getting money for the real estate transaction detailed in the report.

Neighborhood and Convenience Shopping Center Loan Package, M-1. Example of a typical successful real estate loan package. $10, 40 pp.

Downtown Office Building Loan Package, M-2. Example of a successful loan package for a typical office building. $10; 16 pp.

Single-Family Home Foreclosure Business Plan, M-3. Shows how money could be raised to buy single-family home foreclosures and rent them out or re-sell them for a profit. $10; 16 pp.

Single-Family Home Income Property Business Plan, M-4. Shows how money could be made by owning a string of single-family homes that are rented to tenants at a profit. $10; 7 pp.

High-Rise Apartment Building Loan Package and Business Plan, M-5. Presents a comprehensive loan package and business plan for the financing and operation of a multi-family apartment building. $10; 12 pp.

Refinancing Proposal for a Multi-Family Apartment House, M-6. Shows how a large apartment house can be refinanced to enhance its competitive position in its marketplace. $10; 61 pp.

FHA Multifamily Building Loan Package and Business Plan, M-7. Shows a typical loan package and business plan that complies with agency requirements. $10; 14 pp.

NEWSLETTERS

International Wealth Success, Ty Hicks's monthly newsletter published 12 times a year. This 16-page newsletter covers loan and grant sources, real estate opportunities, business opportunities, import-export, mail order, and a variety of other topics on making money in your own business. Every subscriber can run one free classified advertisement of 40 words, or less, each month, covering business or real estate needs or opportunities. The newsletter has a worldwide circulation, giving readers and advertisers very broad coverage. Started in Jan., 1967, the newsletter has been published continuously since that date. $24.00 per year; 16 pp. plus additional inserts; 8½" × 11".

Money Watch Bulletin, a monthly coverage of 100 or more active lenders for real estate and business purposes. The newsletter gives the lender's name, address, telephone number, lending guidelines, loan ranges, and other helpful information. All lender names were obtained within the last week; the data is therefore right up to date. Lender's names and addresses are also provided on self-stick labels on an occasional basis. Also covers venture capital and grants. $95.00; 20 pp.; 8½" × 11".

Index

Shopping centers:
 desirable/undesirable features for
  BWBS, 36
 linking goals to, 38–39
Silent partner, bringing in, 142
Small Business Administration (SBA),
  finding foreclosure properties
  through, 60, 64
Smart borrowers, lenders' respect for,
  200–202
Space, converting to needed uses,
  266–267
Spread, 278
Standing loan, 104–105
Starting Millionaire Success Kit, 324
State city rehabilitation agencies, obtain-
  ing financing from, 236, 239–240
Storage lockers, installing, 313
Strip malls:
 desirable/undesirable features for
  BWBS, 36
 linking goals to, 37–38
Subdividing buildings/land, 270
Subletting, 268–269
Success kits:
 *Fast Financing of Your Real Estate
  Fortune Success Kit*, 323
 *Financial Broker/Finder/Business
  Broker Consultant Success Kit*,
  323
 Loans by Mail Kit, 323
 Loans by Phone Kit, 323
 Mega Money Methods, 324
 Real Estate Loan Getters Service Kit,
  324
 Real Estate Riches Success Kit, 324
 Starting Millionaire Success Kit, 324
 Zero Cash Success Techniques Kit, 324
Success strategies, 23–25, 52–53, 85–89,
  114–116, 143–144, 162–163,
  181–183, 214–216, 228–229,
  249–251, 261–263, 280–281,
  301–302, 316–318
Suitable properties:
 making offers on, 41–44
 searching for, 37–39, 53
Swaps, 224–225, 270, 287

tax-free, 287
when to make, 287

T

Tax abatements, 292
Tax collector, finding foreclosure proper-
  ties through, 60–61
Tax-exempt financing for senior facilities,
  297
Tax-favored income protections, 284
Tax foreclosure certificates, 297
Tax-free swaps, 287
Tax law changes, 312
Tax strategies, 222–224, 278–279
 steps for keeping taxes low, 225–227
Telephones, installing, 268
Tenant demands, getting free of, 176
Tenants:
 anchor tenants, 211
 upgrading class of, 158
 what makes real estate attractive to,
  294–295
Term, definition of, 16
Third mortgage, 100
Time, as ally, 15–16, 218–219, 257–260
Time pressures, taking advantage of,
  137–138
Timetable, *See* Riches timetable
Title insurance payments, 107
To-do lists, 175
Top-line income:
 building, 145–160
 as area rent expert, 154
 by keeping expenses to minimum,
  155–156
 maintaining zero vacancies, 148
 from rents/services/parking, 146–148
 through collections, 182–183
 through income property, 158–160
 through low-cost marketing methods,
  148–152
 through smart financial controls,
  156–157
Trash disposal companies, getting bids
  from, 155
Trust deed, 5n